The
Oaten
Flute

The
Oaten
Flute

Essays
on
Pastoral Poetry
and the
Pastoral Ideal

Renato Poggioli

Harvard University Press
Cambridge, Massachusetts
1975

Foreword

In a note discussing his writing plans, Renato Poggioli wrote that the book he was working on "tries to reconstruct and reinterpret the bucolic ideal as presented in the idyllic or quasi-idyllic literature of the past. The emphasis lies on the modern bucolic tradition, from the early Renaissance to the seventeenth and eighteenth century neoclassicism and preromanticism, from Sannazaro to Rousseau, but attention is also paid to the great classical precedent, as well as to the conscious or unconscious survivals of the bucolic attitude in the literature of our times. Each chapter or section deals with a separate theme and is centered on the critical analysis of one or more literary texts, typical or representative of that theme." With his death in an automobile accident on May 3, 1963, Poggioli's projected book remained unfinished.

I was asked by Harvard University Press to help determine what material should be included here and how it should be arranged. The author had originally proposed thirty chapters, of which eleven were finished (five had already been published) and three he considered virtually complete. These fourteen chapters constitute this book.

Poggioli's intention was to group his chapters around seminal essays establishing ideal types of pastoral, thus substituting a "thematic outlook," as he put it, for a strictly historial approach. This plan could not be fully realized on the basis of the fourteen chapters. I decided to group the essays as much as possible by types or themes and to arrange the groups in something like chronological order. This solution may not satisfy either those interested in a strictly thematic approach or those who prefer a traditional historical sequence; but in my view such an order responded best to the author's intentions and to the essays that existed in publishable form. Thus, chapters 1 and 2 establish the overall strategy of Poggioli's approach; chapters 3 and 4, which a note in the manuscript said were to follow one another, treat the elegy; chapters 5 and 6 consider Christian pastoral and Dante; chapters 7 through 9 deal with kinds of pastoral communities and the gradual emergence of a solitary figure; and chapters 10 through 14 trace, in various forms, the breakdown of the older pastoral ideals.

New Haven, Connecticut
July 1974

A. Bartlett Giamatti

Acknowledgments

The following essays are reprinted here with the generous permission of the original publishers.

Chapter 1, "The Oaten Flute." From *Harvard Library Bulletin*, XI, no. 2 (spring 1957).

Chapter 6, "Dante 'Poco Tempo Silvano': A Pastoral Oasis in the *Commedia*." From *Eightieth Annual Report of the Dante Society* (1962).

Chapter 8, "The Pastoral of the Self." From *Daedalus*, Journal of the American Academy of Arts and Sciences, Boston, Massachusetts, fall 1959, *Quantity and Quality*.

Chapter 10, "Naboth's Vineyard: The Pastoral View of the Social Order." From *Journal of the History of Ideas*, XXIV, no. 1 (January–March 1963).

Chapter 12, "Gogol's *Old-fashioned Landowners*." From *Indiana Slavic Studies*, III (1963).

Contents

Meanwhile the rural ditties were not mute,
Tempered to th' oaten flute.

Lycidas

1
The
Oaten
Flute

I

The psychological root of the pastoral is a double longing after innocence and happiness, to be recovered not through conversion or regeneration but merely through a retreat. By withdrawing not from the world but from "the world," pastoral man tries to achieve a new life in imitation of the good shepherds of herds, rather than of the Good Shepherd of the Soul. The bucolic ideal stands at the opposite pole from the Christian one, even if it believes with the latter that the lowly will be exalted and that the only bad shepherds are shepherds of men. The bucolic invitation, to be like shepherds, although seemingly easier to follow than the Christian summons to self-sacrifice, has always remained a voice crying in the wilderness. Man has walked farther under the burden of Christ's cross than with the help of the shepherd's rod. Faith moves mountains, while a sentimental or aesthetic illusion is hardly able to force man to cross the short distance that separates town and country, or plowlands from woodlands. Christ kept his promise to his faithful, who found redemption and bliss through renunciation and martyrdom, while the few men who earnestly heeded the pastoral call found in no time that country life is at best a purgatory, and that real shepherds are even less innocent and happy than citydwellers and courtiers.

If the Christian view rests on the cornerstone of creed, the pastoral ideal shifts on the quicksands of wishful thought. Wishful thinking is the weakest of all moral and religious resorts; but it is the stuff dreams, especially daydreams, are made of. Mankind had not to wait for Freud to learn that poetry itself is made of that stuff. The bucolic dream has no other reality than that of imagination and art. This is why it has been so often accused of insincerity by those wondering, with Raleigh, what kind of truth may be found "in every shepherd's tongue." Jacopo Sannazaro did not lie when he named Sincero the hero of his *Arcadia*, the earliest of all modern pastoral romances. Samuel Johnson may have been right in affirming in his *Life of Pope* that pastorals, "not professing to imitate real life, require no experience"; yet his statement must be qualified by saying that they *are* a kind of experience. Although not a "martyr" in the Christian sense, the literary shepherd may still be a "witness," in the ancient meaning of that term. The testimony he bears is simply that it is easier to reach moral truth and peace of mind (in other terms, innocence and happiness) by abandoning the strife of civil and social living and the ordeal of human fellowship for a solitary existence, in communion with nature and with the company of one's musings and thoughts.

The ancient writers of Greece, when dealing with the contrast between town and country, never turned it to the advantage of the latter. All classical Greek poets, on the contrary, including the devotees of the lyric muse in its monodic as well as in its choral forms, expressed and celebrated the city-state, the *polis*, or at least the civic community. This remains true later even for the philosophers, whose peripatetic dialogues took place along the streets of Athens or under the porches of the Academy. Socrates speaks for all Greek culture when he says in the *Phaedrus* that he is looking for knowledge not in the woods and among trees, but within the city walls and among his fellow men. The contrast between town and country is equally alien to the Christian vision. In reply to a question from Charles Martel, Dante affirms (*Par.* viii) that for man on earth it would be worse if he were not civilized ("sarebbe il peggio/per l'omo in terra, se non fosse cive"). The Church itself is an *ecclesia*, or community of the faithful, and the Christian is a citizen of both Rome and the City of God. As Beatrice tells Dante (*Purg.* xxxii), the Earthly Paradise, that Arcadia of the spirit, is but a resting place during the soul's pilgrimage from the worldly to the heavenly city:

> Qui sarai tu poco tempo silvano;
> e sarai meco sanza fine cive
> di quella Roma onde Cristo è romano.

Here you will be for a while a denizen of the woods, and then you will dwell forever with me a citizen in that Rome of which Christ is a Roman.

In brief, the pastoral dispensation and its cultural fruits are neither Christian nor classical in essence. They are not a Hellenic but a Hellenistic product, which Roman literature inherited, and which each neoclassical age has reshaped in its own fashion after the Vergilian pattern or, less frequently, from Theocritus' original model. Theocritus himself was born in a great city, Syracuse, and lived in Alexandria, an even greater one. Thus the birth of the pastoral coincided with the decline of the ancient *polis* or city-state and with the appearance of a quasi-modern metropolis, which, as Rutilius Namatianus later said of imperial Rome, was more an *orbis* than an *urbs*. Yet, perhaps because of its complexity, the new urban center seems to reveal, besides the public and civic, the private and bourgeois side of life. Unlike Vergil's *Eclogues* (Excerpts, in the original sense), not all of Theocritus' *Idylls* (Little Pictures) are bucolic in form and content; several present mimetic scenes, depicting, in the fashion of the comedy of manners or of genre painting, the lives and mores of the little people of the great city. But most are the earliest pastorals we know, establishing for all time the pattern of the bucolic (from βουκόλος, guardian of cattle). They express a genuine love of the countryside, as well as the citydweller's yearning for greener pastures.

Vergil and after him many others have followed Theocritus' example in the pastoral, not only in conformity with the tradition of literary imitation, but also as a means to moral relaxation and emotional release. For pastoral poetry appears whenever the hustle and bustle of metropolitan life grows hard to bear and man tries to evade its pressures at least in thought. As civilization becomes more complex and sophisticated, it tires man's heart, although it sharpens his wit. In the process the artistic and literary mind is made aware of cultural demands and psychological needs hardly felt before. Art and poetry tend to become more realistic and elegant, more ideal and passionate, more subjective and personal. From the very beginning pastoral poets seem to anticipate modern attitudes; to speak in Schillerian terms, they replace the "naive" with the "sentimental," looking with more irony at life and recoiling from the tragic and heroic sides of human experience. (Theocritus' *epyllia* are not miniature epic poems but semifabulous idylls.) Pastoral poets leave the theater and the agora, to cultivate, like Candide, their own garden, where they grow other flowers than those of communal myth and public belief.

II

As with all ways or visions of life, the pastoral implies a new ethos, which, however, is primarily negative. Its code prescribes few virtues, but proscribes many vices. Foremost among the passions that the pastoral opposes and exposes are those related to the misuse, or merely to the possession, of worldly goods. They are the passions of greed: cupidity and avarice, the yearning after property and prosperity, the desire for affluence and opulence, for money and precious things. The bucolic considers the pursuit of wealth—*auri sacra fames*—as an error as well as a crime, since it makes impossible "the pursuit of happiness." An acquisitive society, however, holds those two pursuits to be different aspects of the same virtue and views *enrichissez-vous* as a moral as well as an economic command. Thus the shepherd is the opposite of the *homo oeconomicus* on both ethical and practical grounds. Yet even the pastoral presupposes an economy of its own, which is home economics in the literal sense of the term. Pastoral economy seems to realize the contained self-sufficiency that is the ideal of the tribe, of the clan, of the family. The pastoral community produces all it needs, but nothing more, except for a small margin of security. It equates its desires with its needs; it ignores industry and trade; even its barter with the outside world is more an exchange of gifts than of commodities. Money, credit, and debt have no place in an economy of this kind. By a strange and yet natural miracle, the system seems to avoid any disproportion between production and consumption, despite its lack of planning and foresight. The pastoral family head is never a provider in the bourgeois sense. Thrift is in him an almost mystical trait, even more than a necessary virtue; he never saves for a "rainy day" that supposedly will never come. The shepherd of poetry finds his emblem not in the wise and prudent ant of the fable, who works all year round to be ready to face the challenge of winter, but in the carefree grasshopper, who spends all summer in song and dance.

Such a state of things presupposes a new Garden of Eden, where nature is a fertile mother and generous giver. All shepherds could tell their visitors what Vergil tells Dante when showing him the bounties of the Earthly Paradise (*Purg.* xxvii):

> Vedi l' erbette, i fiori e li arbuscelli,
> che qui la terra sol da sè produce.

Look at the grass, the flowers, and the little trees that earth grows here by itself.

Yet the spontaneous generation of the staples of life does not change the pastoral countryside into a Land of Cockaigne, where sausages hang on the trees and people indulge in a perpetual kermess. Manna does not fall on pastoral soil, and the shepherd neither fasts nor feasts but satisfies his thirst and hunger with earth's simplest gifts, such as fruit and water, or with the milk and cheese he gets from tending his sheep, which provide also the wool for his rustic garments. The shepherd does not need to grow wheat like the farmer, or prey on wildlife like the hunter. He is a vegetarian on moral as well as on utilitarian grounds, choosing to live on a lean diet rather than on the fat of the land. This is why only a few poets, and generally modern ones, describe their favorite pastoral country as a horn of plenty, overflowing with inexhaustible abundance. In his *Fábula de*

Polifemo y Galatea, Góngora evokes fabulous Sicily, the historic breadbasket of the Roman Empire, as "Bacchus' goblet and Pomona's orchard" ("copa es de Baco, huerto de Pomona"). Goethe, in the second part of *Faust,* paints his Arcadia as a land of milk and honey in so literal and exuberant terms as to change it into a wonderland or fairyland (III.9546–49):

> Und mütterlich im stillen Schattenkreise
> Quillt laue Milch bereit für Kind und Lamm;
> Obst ist nicht weit, der Ebnen reife Speise,
> Und Honig trieft vom ausgehöhlten Stamm.

And motherlike, within a quiet circle of shadows, warm milk flows for child and lamb; fruit is at hand, the ripe food of the meadow, and honey drips from the hollowed trunk.

Flowing happily and quietly under the protection of both Ceres and Flora, pastoral life is an economic idyll, made possible not only by nature's generosity but also by its mercy. The shepherd's existence is spared not only thirst and hunger, but also "the penalty of Adam,/ The seasons' difference" (*As You Like It,* II.i): in brief, the inclemency of the weather. Thus all true pastoral lands are blessed with the pleasant mildness of an unchanging climate.

By picking berries and gathering straw the shepherd may fill his bowl and build a roof over his head. This redeems him from the curse of work, which is part of man's estate and the specific lot of the peasant, who earns his daily bread by the sweat of his brow. It is this triumph of the "days" over the "works," rather than the mere replacement of a rural with a pastoral setting, that marks the difference between the bucolic and the georgic. The shepherd enjoys the blessings of idleness even more than the rich man, whose servants hardly lighten his burdens and whose cares never allow him to rest. Thus literary shepherds form an ideal kind of leisure class, free from the compulsions of conspicuous consumption and ostentatious waste. Gratuitous interests, including such leisurely activities as hobbies and pastimes, but excluding such strenuous exercises as sports, are the main endeavor of the pastoral world. "Deus nobis haec otia fecit" (I owe this happy leisure to a god), says Vergil's Tityrus (*Ecl.* i), who

calls divine the donor of his farm for granting him, along with freedom from want, the freedom of his own time, or an exemption from
occupations as well as from preoccupations. While for all other people time is money, the shepherd always has time to waste or to spare;
and this enables him to put fun before duty and pleasure before business; or to follow no other will than his caprice.

This contrasts the shepherd with the merchant, the man who prefers *negotium* to *otium* and whose business is business; and also with
the sailor, who ventures his life for adventure and profit. The shepherd of fiction is likewise neither a pioneer nor a settler but rather a
homesteader or, better, a stay-at-home; he is never a nomad, as real
shepherds are often forced to be. He lives a sedentary life even in the
open, since he prefers to linger in a grove's shade rather than to wander in the woods. He never confronts the true wild, and this is why he
never becomes even a part-time hunter. Venatical attitudes consistently oppose the pastoral: on one side they resemble too closely martial exploits; on the other, they are connected with Diana, the goddess
of chastity, whom shepherds, unlike the hunter Hippolytus, neglect
in favor of Venus. Pastoral life may reserve instead a small place for
the fisherman, if he does not risk his life on the high seas, but throws
his net not too far from shore or sinks his line into a nearby pond or
brook. Such a fisherman is twin brother to the shepherd, and the
congeniality, already discovered by Theocritus, was reasserted by
Sannazaro, the first to write piscatory eclogues in Latin, followed by
Bernardino Rota, who transplanted them into the vulgar tongue. Isaak
Walton's view of amateur fishing as a quasi-pastoral calling is shown
by his description in *The Compleat Angler* of its patient and leisurely
practitioners as "men of mild, and sweet, and peaceable spirits," far
more philosophical and pious than hunters and falconers. Those words
of praise may be applied to the literary shepherd himself, an old
Adam who returns to the Garden of Eden, a stranded traveler who
finds his island on terra firma, to prosper there without labors and
hardships, a happy and indolent Robinson Crusoe.

III

The ideal of the perfect shepherd or, for that matter, of the complete angler is then based, like the Christian one, on the practice of
poverty or, at least, on its praise. Both Christian theologians and pas-

toral poets see in that condition both a sign of humility and a token of grace. The former, however, exalt the pauper's estate because it teaches self-resignation; the latter, because it teaches self-contentment. The first alternative connects poverty with self-mortification and self-abasement; the second, with a self-gratification that finds its check in self-control. In brief, Christian poverty is a quest after innocence; pastoral poverty, after happiness as well. The truth of this may be seen in the very paradox of the main pastoral myth, which calls golden the times when there was no gold. The Golden Age, unlike Eldorado and the Gilded Age, is a dream of happiness without being a dream of wealth.

The logic of renunciation and sacrifice leads the Christian to become an anchorite, and to build the Thebais in the desert. Yet, even when it cloisters itself, a pastoral community cannot choose any hermitage other than the Abbaye de Thélème, where *Fay ce que vouldras* is the golden rule. The shepherd, unlike the saint or the monk, is obsessed by neither temptation nor guilt, and is free from the sense of sin. Being quiet and passive, he is rarely driven to sins of commission; as for sins of omission, he is inclined to treat them as virtues. Poverty teaches him practical rather than mystical lessons, and helps him to avoid the dangers of exaggeration and excess. He easily extends the theory and practice of moderation from the material to the moral field, from the sphere of property to that of power, and rejects ambition as well as greed. If there is a domain where he shows less self-restraint, up to the point of confusing liberty and license, that is only in the realm of sex.

As a conscious or unconscious philosopher, the shepherd is neither a stoic nor a cynic, but rather an epicurean and observes with natural spontaneity the ethics of that school. His eudaemonism is not only spiritual but physical as well, and includes the practice of hedonism. The shepherd, rejecting sybaritc pleasure as spoiled by its extreme refinement and complexity, finds gratification not in the breach but in the observance of his ethos, based on the virtues of sobriety, frugality, and simplicity. Like the aged Leo Tolstoy, the converted shepherd may find sensual delight, as well as moral contentment, by merely satisfying his needs; by discarding the obsessive luxury and the laborious comfort of "high life" for simple living, with its homespun clothes, homely furnishings, and unseasoned meals.

This enlightened hedonism, as well as the fact that vine growing and wine making are hard agricultural tasks, may easily explain why Bacchus, unlike Venus, plays a negligible role in the pastoral world. The drinking habits of shepherds, unlike those of peasants, are exemplary: pastoral mores have no place for intoxication and alcoholism. Only old satyrs, like Silenus, may indulge in that vice. Taking a leaf from the anacreontic, the pastoral allows that weakness as a compensation for the loss of youth, which puts the fruit of love out of man's reach. Age may well take everything away ("Omnia fert aetas"), as Vergil says (*Ecl.* ix), and yet it spares from its heavy toll the consoling oblivion provided, if fleetingly, by strong drink.

IV

Man may linger in the pastoral dreamworld a short while or a whole lifetime. Pastoral poetry makes more poignant and real the dream it wishes to convey when the retreat is not a lasting but a passing experience, acting as a pause in the process of living, as a breathing spell from the fever and anguish of being. Then it fixes the pastoral moment, within the category of space as well as of time, as an interval to be chosen at both the proper hour and the right point. The right point at which to stop and rest from a journey is a secluded spot, appealing to the traveler through the charm of its quiet and shade. Hence the topos of the *locus amoenus*, the "lovely place" or ideal landscape, which, according to E. R. Curtius, medieval Latin literature received from Vergil and bequeathed to vernacular writing.[1] Curtius maintains that the commonplace is directly related to pastoral poetry, although it occurs elsewhere. Its presence in an epic or a chivalric poem, in a romance or a tragicomedy, foretells the unexpected apparition of a bucolic episode, which breaks the main action or pattern, suspending for a while the heroic, romantic, or pathetic mood of the whole. Accordingly the topos itself is but an idyllic prelude to a bucolic interlude, where the characters rest from their adventures or passions. Since the pause normally occurs in an obscure and faraway place, the intermezzo itself should be termed the "pastoral oasis." Such "oases" appear in the *Aeneid*, the *Commedia*, the

Furioso, the *Lusíadas*, *Don Quixote*, and *As You Like It*. One of the most beautiful, and the most typical of them, is in Tasso's *Gerusalemme liberata* (vii). The episode, known as "Erminia's stay among the shepherds," deserves analysis, since it is a complete summary of all the pastoral motifs emphasized up to this point.

The pagan maid Erminia dons the armor of the heroine Clorinda in order to save the wounded Tancredi, a Christian knight whom she loves in secret and without hope. A band of Crusaders pursues her by mistake, and she flees for her life. When night comes, she finds shelter in a wood. At dawn, she is wakened by birdsong, and grieves again about her plight. While weeping, she finds that her refuge is a *locus amoenus*, with lonely pastoral abodes ("alberghi solitarii de' pastori") nearby. Her plaint is suddenly interrupted by a mixed music of human songs ("pastorali accenti") and of rude woodpipes ("boscareccie inculte avene"). She moves forward and suddenly discovers in a shady grove an old man, who sits weaving baskets while watching his herd and listening to the song of three boys. The scene is a vision of perfect pastoral innocence, the more so since women are seemingly absent. The youths are frightened by the maiden's warlike attire, but Erminia takes off her helmet and shows herself to be but a damsel in distress. The situation is symbolic of the pastoral fear of even the signs of might and power. Erminia disclaims any intent to harm or disturb human beings who appear to her the favorites of God and fortune (VII.vii):

> —Seguite,—dice—avventurosa gente
> al Ciel diletta, il bel vostro lavoro:
> ché non portano già guerra quest'armi
> a l'opre vostre, a i vostri dolci carmi.

Continue your lovely work, lucky folk beloved by Heaven; these weapons bring no war to your occupations, nor to your sweet songs.

Erminia then wonders why the security of these people seems not to be threatened by the war raging all over the countryside. The old man explains that they owe the exceptional peace they are enjoying to the obscurity of their dwelling place, to the mercy of the gods, who spare from cruelty and injustice the guiltless and the meek, and, above all, to a poverty that tempts nobody with promises of booty. The old man values highly the condition of poverty, while most men hold it in scorn, as worthless and despicable ("altrui vile e negletta; a me sì cara"); he considers it the pledge of a life untroubled by envy, either given or received. Thus, to its moral advantages, poverty adds practical ones. It guarantees the conservation of life, through a modicum of security. Poverty saves man from the blight of fear: no shepherd will ever think that the spring water he drinks may be poisoned by a rival or an enemy. But, above all, poverty emancipates man from the slavery of desire (VII.ix)—

> Ché poco è il desiderio, e poco è il nostro
> bisogno onde la vita si conservi

Since we desire and need very little to conserve our life—

and relieves man from the burdens of wealth, the chief of which is having charge of a host of servants. The old shepherd is the patriarch but not the master of his clan, and this is why he lives in peace, without the responsibilities and worries of a taskmaster. He is the more conscious of the happy innocence of his way of life, since once he lost it and recovered it only through the ordeal of experience. In his youth he had been tempted into leaving the country for the city, and settled in the center of all splendor and power, the court. Although he served there only as a gardener, he soon realized that he had fallen into a den of iniquity, and returned without regret to his lonely and lovely place.

Erminia addresses the old shepherd with words recalling Vergil's "fortunate senex" (*Ecl.* i), and asks him to grant her hospitality, in the hope that a stay among the shepherds will heal the wounds of her soul. Her sorrowful tale moves the tender heart of the old man, who welcomes and consoles her. He brings her to his wife, who helps her to don a shepherdess's garb. By doing so, Erminia perfectly observes the conventions of the pastoral oasis, which treats the bucolic experience as a temporary retirement to the periphery of life, as an attempt to charm away the cares of the world through the sympathetic magic of a rustic disguise. Yet the episode represents the pastoral ideal not in Erminia's reflected role but in the exemplary images of the old man and his wife "che di conforme cor gli ha data il Cielo" (whom Heaven gave him, endowed with a heart like his).

This means that the natural outcome of the pastoral of innocence is the family situation, or the domestic idyll. As Tasso's episode shows, pastoral poetry prefers generally to present that idyll in terms of old age, rather than of youth. Some modern poets have changed the pattern: so, for instance, Goethe's *Hermann und Dorothea* is a bourgeois pastoral where all promise of domestic happiness is contained in a young couple's troth. Aware of his deviation, Goethe claimed to have followed a Homeric rather than a Vergilian example: to have written an *epyllion* rather than an *eidyllion*. Tasso's episode follows, however, the traditional scheme and portrays its old couple after an ancient and perfect archetype, Ovid's fable of Philemon and Baucis (*Met.* viii). In that fable sexual and parental love play no part and are replaced by the tender affections of the decline of life. It is not only their hospitality but the very purity of their souls that earns for Philemon and Baucis the grace of the gods. Jupiter and Mercury will grant them their wish, which is to die at the same time, and will change them into two trees, with mutually supporting trunks and interwoven branches.

V

If Erminia's stay among the shepherds, or the pastoral oasis of the *Gerusalemme*, mirrors the pastoral of innocence, Tasso's minor masterpiece, the pastoral drama *Aminta*, reflects with equal significance the other side of the picture, or the pastoral of happiness. The bucolic imagination equates happiness with the fulfillment of the passion of love, with the consummation of man's erotic wishes, and identifies unhappiness with the rejection or denial of one's heart's desire, in brief, with unrequited love. The second alternative may recur more frequently than the first, which is why pastoral poetry remodulates constantly in its saddest tunes what one might call after Apollinaire "la chanson du mal aimé." Love, however, may remain unsatisfied even when it is returned: when it is public morality, or the ties of honor and duty, rather than the heart's inconstancy or indifference that prevents the beloved one from heeding the entreaties of her lover. Love was born free, but family and society hold that winged creature in a gilded cage. Often pastoral poetry is but a voice of protest against society's power to replace the fruitions with the frustrations of love. When pastoral man becomes aware of the impossibility of realizing here and now his ideal of an absolute erotic anarchism, his protest has no outlet but the very dream on which his heart feeds. Thus he projects his yearning after free love, his longing for sexual freedom and even license, into a state of nature that exists nowhere, or only in the realm of myth.

The theme of *Aminta's* first chorus is a praise of free love or, rather, of the only time when Eros was really free. That was the Golden Age, which Tasso now lauds for that reason alone. "O bella età de l'oro" (O beauteous Golden Age), exclaims the poet, not for being blessed by the spontaneous fertility of the earth and the everlasting clemency of the weather, nor for being spared the curses of war, trade, and work (I. ii),

> Ma sol perché quel vano
> nome senza soggetto,
> quell'idolo d'errori, idol d'inganno,
> quel che da 'l volgo insano
> Onor poscia fu detto,
> che di nostra natura il feo tiranno,
> non mischiava il suo affanno
> fra le liete dolcezze
> de l'amoroso gregge;
> né fu sua dura legge
> nota a quell'alme in libertate avvezze;
> ma legge aurea e felice
> che Natura scolpì: *S'ei piace, ei lice.*

But only because that vain and hollow name, that idol of error and deceit, which the insane crowd later called honor, thus making it our nature's tyrant, had not yet mixed its worries among the merry delights of the amorous throng; nor was its harsh law known to those souls accustomed to freedom, but rather the happy and golden rule that nature engraved: *What delights, is lawful.*

It is noteworthy that in the closing sentence Tasso uses as a term of praise almost the same words Dante had employed (*Inf.* v) to suggest one of the worst transgressions of the sexual instinct, and to indict that Semiramis who by legalizing incest "libito fé licito in sua legge" (made a law of her pleasure). In Tasso's version, "S'ei piace, ei lice," the formula seems to anticipate the Freudian view, with its acceptance of the libido and the pleasure principle.

The pastoral longing is but the wishful dream of a happiness to be gained without effort, of an erotic bliss made absolute by its own irresponsibility. This, rather than a sense of decency, is the very reason why the pastoral often limits the sexual embrace to mere kissing, so as to escape the danger of parenthood and the nuisance of birth control. (In this connection, nothing is more typical in a pastoral sense than the episode of Rousseau's *Confessions* that goes under the name of "l'idylle des cérises.") Yet in its extreme form pastoral happiness is conceived as an absolute acceptance of the law of instinct, with no sense of guilt or any regard for its consequences. This was well understood by Thomas Mann when he described in *Der Zauberberg* ("Fülle des Wohllauts") the feelings suggested by Debussy's *L'Après-midi d'un faune:*

> Der junge Faun war sehr glücklich auf seiner Sommerwiese. Hier gab es kein "Rechtfertige dich!", keine Verantwortung . . . Hier herrschte das Vergessen selbst, der selige Stillstand, die Unschuld der Zeitlosigkeit: Es war die Liederlichkeit mit bestem Gewissen, die wunschbildhafte Apotheose all und jeder Verneinung des abendländischen Aktivitätskommandos.

> The youthful faun was very happy in his flowery meadow. Here there was no "Justify yourself!", no responsibility . . . Here reigned oblivion itself, the blissful arrest of very motion, the innocence of timelessness. It was licentiousness in quiet conscience, the daydreamlike apotheosis of each and every denial of the Western imperative of action.

All this means that the task of the pastoral imagination is to overcome the conflict between passion and remorse, to reconcile innocence and happiness, to exalt the pleasure principle at the expense of the reality principle. No one prized the pleasure principle more highly than those eighteenth-century representatives of libertine thought whose literary education had been conditioned by pastoral poetry.

Even the greatest among the *philosophes* used the bucolic convention in their protest against authority and conformism in matters of sexual morality. In this field, Diderot was a greater emancipator than even Voltaire or Rousseau. His most extreme affirmation of the legitimacy of free love is the *Supplément au voyage de Bougainville*, which inaugurates the modern attempt to replace the Arcadias of old with the islands of the South Seas, where the white man lives merrily and happily with many female companions, rather than with a single masculine slave or helpmate, as Robinson Crusoe with his man Friday. Diderot stated his message in the subtitle summing up the theme of the *Supplément* as "l'inconvénient d'attacher des idées morales à certaines actions physiques qui n'en comportent pas" (the inconvenience of applying moral standards to certain physical acts for which they have no relevance).

It is the reality principle which, by proving that erotic happiness cannot be fully attained in our civilization, has forced the modern pastoral imagination to find other havens beyond the Western world. Yet the pleasure principle has reasserted itself even within the boundaries of our culture, pushing the moral limits of passion even further than pagan license would have done. Thus many writers of our time have used the pastoral dispensation to justify the claims of homosexual love. André Gide dared to protest the exclusion of that forbidden territory from love's realm in a book that he named after Vergil's Corydon, disregarding the fact that the original Corydon is a half-comic, half-pathetic character, doomed to a hopeless infatuation for a boy. That the dark region of that unnatural passion is still envisaged in pastoral images may be proved by the title *Arcadie* given by a group of Parisian writers to a new little review pleading and preaching the cause of sexual perversion.

The pastoral is aristocratic in temper, yet the operation of the pleasure principle prevents it from falling into the pitfalls of romantic love. A shepherd may love a duchess; but what he loves is the woman in her. Bucolic Eros cares more for *amour-passion* than for *amour-vanité*, for freshness and youth rather than for glamour and charm. Pastoral love is unromantic in the sense that it looks down rather than up, that it prefers a simple and rustic loveliness to the elegant beauty of a fashionable paramour. George Santayana felt this truth when in his *Three Philosophical Poets* he reproached Goethe for having made Helena the queen of Arcadia, during Faust's brief sojourn in that land: "But to live within Arcadia Helen was not needed; any Phyllis would have served." [2] This implies that the pastoral is a private, masculine world, where woman is not a person but a sexual archetype, the eternal Eve.

That world is but a utopian projection of the hedonistic instinct, the demands of which may be stated in Goethe's exhortation in the same Arcadian episode: "Arkadisch frei sei unser Glück!" (Let our bliss be arcadically free!). This obsession with an unrestrained erotic happiness makes a modest pastoral almost impossible. In such a context there is no "cold pastoral" in the Keatsian sense of the term. Yet a "warm pastoral" is equally rare, since the fire of love cannot burn continuously without fuel, and passion's devouring flame is reduced to a flicker under the ashes. It is more human and natural to treat of love in elegiac than in idyllic terms. Hence the most poignant of all pastoral love motifs seem to be, to use the formula by which George Orwell defined Housman's poetry in his essay *Inside the Whale*, nothing more than "hedonism disappointed." When he warns his reader with such words as Vergil's "Nunc scio, quid sit Amor" (Now I know what Love is; *Ecl.* viii), the pastoral poet is about to bare the emptiness, rather than the fullness, of a frustrated heart.

VI

"Hedonism disappointed" is the root of pagan melancholy rather than of Christian sadness. Yet even this has not prevented the literary imagination of the moderns from trying to Christianize the pastoral, or to make Christianity idyllic. Pastoral poetry itself has been one of the main objects or tools in the repeated attempt to reconcile the "two antiquities," the classical and the biblical, in new syncretic forms. Despite the fact that a Christian georgic is far more natural and possible than a Christian bucolic, the pastoral poets of Christendom found in Holy Writ comforting authority for the opposite view. The bucolic, unlike the georgic, exalts the innocent leisure of the shepherd over the peasant's hard task. Thus the Christian pastoral poet will treat as exemplary the story of Cain and Abel, where the latter, who is "a keeper of sheep," is blessed with God's grace, and the former, who is "a tiller of the soil," is cursed by God's wrath; nor will he fail to notice that it was Cain who brought both crime and civilization into this world, first by slaying his shepherd brother and then by becoming the first builder of cities. Dante himself is one of the many who pointed out another Christian-pastoral parallel, the one between the Golden Age and the Garden of Eden. When he reaches the top of the mountain of Purgatory, he claims through Matelda that the pagan poets of old had already prefigured the Earthly Paradise in the myth of the Golden Age (*Purg.* xxviii):

> Quelli ch'anticamente poetaro
> l'età de l'oro e suo stato felice,
> forse in Parnaso esto loco sognaro.

Those who anciently sang of the Golden Age and its happy state dreamed perhaps in Parnassus of this place.

Even in modern times sacred history has been interpreted in pastoral terms. Nietzsche (*Jenseits von Gut und Böse*) saw in the Gospels a rather prosaic idyll, in contrast with the sublime magnificence of the Old Testament, while Renan (*Vie de Jésus*, iii) saw instead a charming pastoral ("une délicieuse pastorale") in Jesus' early life and in primitive Christianity itself.

Christian popular imagination had already given a pastoral turn to the legend of Christ's birth, following in this Luke's lead. While Matthew (ii.1–12) had told the story of the three wise men, of the three eastern kings who had followed the comet to bear tribute to a humble child born in a stable like a lamb, it was Luke (ii.6–20) who claimed that the angels had first revealed His birth to the "poor in spirit," to "shepherds abiding in the field, keeping watch over their flock by night." Thus the shepherds had been the first to learn the newborn would bring "on earth peace, good will toward men." Yet the Christian literary imagination, all too steeped in classical lore, did not content itself with so simple a fable as this, and chose to rewrite these two evangelical texts after the pattern of one of the most famous bucolic poems of classical antiquity.

This poem is Vergil's Fourth Eclogue, which medieval humanism read as if it were a supplement to the Holy Writ. Vergil himself was aware that his poem hardly agreed with the pastoral canon: and in the opening lines he warned the muses who had inspired his other eclogues that he would sing now of a more exalted theme ("paulo maiora canamus"); that for once he would change the woodlands so much as to make them worthy of a consul ("silvae sint consule dignae"). As for the eclogue itself, he turned it into a statement as mysterious and prophetic as an oracle. Following the so-called Sibylline Books, Vergil announced that mankind had just reached a turning point, that "magnus ab integro saeclorum nascitur ordo" (a great order is being born from the fullness of time).

Vergil envisaged the advent of this new order as a restoration of the Golden Age, which once unfolded under the rule of Saturn. This second coming of the Golden Age was made manifest by the return of Astraea, the virgin goddess of justice; and the instrument of this palingenesis would be a child not yet born, sent to us by the gods:

> Iam redit et Virgo, redeunt Saturnia regna;
> iam nova progenies caelo demittitur alto.

The Virgin and Saturn's rule are now coming back; a new offspring is now being sent from high heaven.

Vergil wrote the Fourth Eclogue in his early maturity, one or two generations before the coming of Christ, to celebrate the expected birth of a child to the consul to whom he refers at the beginning of the poem. That consul, whom scholarship has failed to identify, is certainly a historical figure. Yet Christians read the poem as a miraculous announcement of the Nativity, seeing in Astraea an allegory of the Virgin and interpreting the new Golden Age to come not as the worldly order of the *pax romana*, but as the metaphysical order of the *pax christiana*, to be reestablished through the new covenant between man and God. This interpretation was possible because the pagan poet and his Christian commentators shared in different form the same archaic belief in a humble redeemer or wonder child born into this world to save mankind from ruin and to lead it back on the path of righteousness. While for the pagan poet the salvation of mankind meant conjuring away the curse of war, for his Christian readers it meant instead the redemption of the human race from original sin.

Yet later Christian poets chose to restate that belief at least in part in Vergilian terms, within a context that was not only classical but pagan as well.

This could occur because Vergil had already paradoxically reinterpreted the most important of all pastoral myths. While the whole of antiquity, as Renan says (*Vie de Jésus*, i), had relegated the dream of mankind's happy state to the beginning of time ("avait placé le paradis à l'origine"), Vergil here projected that dream into the age to come. Christianity would do the same, following in this the example of Israel, which had always placed the Golden Age in the future ("mettait l'âge d'or dans l'avenir"). Christianity saw the new Golden Age not only in the distant promise of Christ's second coming but also in his everlasting presence in men's hearts. Thus many Christian poets were to rewrite the Fourth Eclogue in a celebratory rather than in a prophetic mood—as a recurring apotheosis or anniversary poem, in the mysticopastoral form of a nativity hymn.

Despite this, the critical mind can only treat as failures all attempts to Christianize the pastoral, or to translate Christianity into pastoral terms. If Milton's definition of *On the Morning of Christ's Nativity* as a "humble ode" sounds like a contradiction in terms, San Juan de la Cruz's reduction of the virgin saints of the Christian calendar to the status of "nymphs" appears an absurdity. Christian imagination, as a matter of fact, was able to use consistently the pastoral convention only as an allegorical travesty and satirical mask. The allegorical pastoral, starting with Battista Mantovano's Latin eclogues, is primarily a polemical tool: the religious mind uses that form to indict the bad shepherds or the wolves in sheep's clothing who mislead and destroy the Christian flock. In Catholic hands, the allegorical pastoral was the instrument of a moral and spiritual protest against a temporal and secular Church, which had betrayed the poverty and simplicity of primitive Christianity for worldly power and pagan pomp. Milton made of it also an instrument for glorification of the puritan ministry, and introduced both the negative and the positive version of the allegorical pastoral in *Lycidas* itself. Johnson (*Life of Milton*) rightly condemned this contamination on religious as well as on literary grounds: "The shepherd likewise is now a feeder of sheep, and afterwards an ecclesiastical pastor, a superintendent of a Christian flock. Such equivocations are always unskilful; but here they are indecent, and at least approach to impiety."

VII

If, instead of being a biblical character, Abel the shepherd had been a pastoral one, he could have spoken the same words by which Cain answered the Lord: "Am I my brother's keeper?" The shepherd is not his brother's keeper, nor the keeper of his friend, although the pagan or neopagan vision of life, which excludes the pastoral of brotherhood, still reserves a place of honor for the pastoral of friendship. The bucolic imagination conceives of friendship in lyrical rather than in epic or dramatic terms; it treats friendship as a state of grace or spiritual communion, which the stress of life never puts to the test of loyalty or sacrifice. Pastoral friendship means a common devotion to the bucolic callings, which are poetry and music. "Who would not sing for Lycidas?" asks Milton: "He knew himself to sing, and build the lofty rhyme." The ideal formula for this is Vergil's "Arcades ambo" (*Ecl.* vii), which implies that pastoral friendship is enhanced, rather than denied, by artistic competition and rivalry. Yet the bond is such that it can be broken only by death. Therefore the pastoral of friendship finds its highest expression in the funeral elegy, which is but a shepherd's lament for a friend "dead ere his prime."

The function of the funeral elegy is not merely to convey the individual grief of the survivor, but also man's recurrent sense of the everlasting presence of death. The task of that poetic form is to remind the pastoral mind that nature is not only a provider but also a destroyer: that it generates from its womb not only life but also death. Vergil sums up this feeling in the image of the snake hidden in the grass: "Latet anguis in herba" (*Ecl.* iii). Still the pagan funeral elegy accepts death as a law of nature, and weeps over it the tear of a private and personal rather than of a cosmic or metaphysical grief. This feeling is perfectly expressed in Poussin's famous painting, which represents a group of mournful shepherds gathered about a tomb bearing the epigraph *Et in Arcadia ego.* In this context the words are those of the deceased, and have been taken to mean: "I too lived once in Arcadia." In an earlier painting by Guercino, however, the same inscription had appeared on a sepulchre covered by a skull, as if the words were uttered by death itself, thus saying: "Even in Arcadia am I." As Erwin Panofsky finally demonstrated, this and no other is the first and correct meaning of the words.[3] Accordingly, at least in its original sense, the formula states an antipagan and antipastoral view, a Christian and baroque obsession with death. Yet one could still say that the funeral elegy tends to express the same obsessive feeling: our all too human awareness that death stalks us even in Arcadia, although it tries to hide the horror of that realization under a mask of pagan piety. In reality the Christian pastoral of death conflicts with the pagan one even more when the former replaces the sense of awe before the death of the body with the hope of an afterlife for the soul. There is no better example of this conflict than Milton's *Lycidas*, where the dead shepherd does not remain in his watery grave, but ascends to heaven and returns to the Kingdom of God. No pastoral poet ever believes in man's return or ascent from the realm of the dead: the apotheosis closing a funeral elegy is always merely conventional and literary. The pastoral looks earthward, not heavenward; with his mystical invocation, "Look homeward, Angel," Milton breaks the pattern of both the funeral elegy and the pastoral of friendship.

VIII

The pastoral of friendship may take sometimes the form of the idyll, thus becoming a variant of the pastoral of mirth. The funeral elegy, however, is the most extreme manifestation of the pastoral of melancholy. Despite the fact that in both of them the poet turns his loving attention to a fellow shepherd, either living or dead, they are but different versions of the pastoral of the self. In either case, pastoral poetry seems to transcend the motifs of innocence and happiness: or to reduce them to mere mirrors or mirages of the poet's soul. The pastorals of melancholy and mirth achieve this by bringing to a degree of extreme tension or purity the lyrical quality of the bucolic mood. In its simplest expression, the pastoral of innocence views the human condition from the standpoint of the family, and speaks in plural form. The straightforward pastoral of happiness, which reduces all human intercourse to an everlasting tête-à-tête, conveys its message, at least apparently, in a dual mode. But the pastoral of the self sings solo, and speaks in singular terms. Its root is the pastoral of solitude, which in turn may be also conceived as an elegy or an idyll, after the pattern of either *L'Allegro* or *Il Penseroso*. The second alternative is by far the more frequent of the two. Shakespeare, for instance, identified the pastoral of solitude with the pastoral of melancholy, and saw in both the opposite of the pastoral of happiness and love. He clearly stated this antithesis in the exchange closing the debate between two characters in *As You Like It* (III.ii):

> *Jaques.* I'll tarry no longer with you. Farewell, good Signior Love.
> *Orlando.* I am glad of your departure. Adieu, good Monsieur Melancholy.

In his poem *The Garden*, Andrew Marvell pushed even further the opposition between the pastoral of love and the pastoral of the self. He deprived the latter of melancholy's bittersweet taste, but seasoned it with a mirthful and witty misogyny:

> Such was that happy Garden-state,
> While man there walk'd without a mate . . .
> Two paradises 'twere in one
> To live in Paradise alone.

By doing so Marvell proved that the pastoral remains a masculine dreamworld even when it abandons the realm of sex. As the pastoral poet replaces the labors and troubles of love with an exclusive concern for the self, he changes into a new Narcissus, contemplating with passionate interest not his body but his soul. At this point, he deals only, in Whitman's words, with "the single, solitary soul," and the pastoral becomes the poetic vehicle of solipsism. The most important document of this transformation is Rousseau's *Rêveries d'un promeneur solitaire*, where the ego idly and indifferently enjoys "le sentiment de l'existence . . . sans prendre la peine de penser" (the feeling of existing without bothering to think). What Rousseau terms "rêverie" is a state of passive introspection, by which the pastoral psyche reflects its shadow in nature's mirror, fondly and blissfully losing its being within the image of itself. Here sensibility and selfhood merge, and man ceases to distinguish between conscience and consciousness, wish and will. The individual seems to achieve perfection through the sense of a happiness untouched by doubt, of an innocence unblemished by sin. It was by bringing back both melancholy and remorse that the romantics finally destroyed this extreme version of the pastoral of selfhood. Tempted by pride, and yet aware of their guilt, they restored the idea of the soul to that Christian tradition which they could not deny precisely because they were of the devil's party, and knew it.

IX

Before dissolving itself within this apotheosis of the self, pastoral poetry had been primarily the exaltation of a particular conception of private life, as well as the spiritual autobiography of the man of letters cultivating it. The idea of pastoral leisure is after all but an imaginative projection of the classical and humanistic antinomy of mechanical and liberal arts. The former are the natural activities of the slave, the latter, of the freeborn. By this very definition, the shepherd becomes the symbol of the scholar and the humanist in his moments of leisure and ease—when he is no longer a learned man, but rather a sage, reaching not for knowledge but for beauty and wisdom. The shepherd then represents man neither as *homo sapiens* nor as *homo faber*, but only as *homo artifex* or, more simply, as a musician and a poet. Vergil considers music and poetry as a pastoral monopoly (*Ecl.* x): "Soli cantare periti/Arcades" (Arcadians are the only ones who know how to sing); and one could say that one of the main tasks of pastoral poetry is to portray either artist as man or man as artist.

If the artist or the poet dons so often a pastoral disguise, it is only because he wishes to emphasize his personality in private rather than in public terms. That emphasis is but a symbolic protest, and acts as a romantic and nostalgic denial of those cultural or material circumstances that condition his social status and make him at the same time a public figure or a civil servant. In neoclassical ages the poet or the artist does not flourish on nature's soil, but in the grove of Academe or in the hothouse of the court. When the poet is unable to escape into Arcadia, pastoral strategy requires that he retreat at least into an orchard or a park. Sometimes all the court follows him into that retreat, and the poet celebrates the event with a courtly pastoral. The courtly pastoral is but a costumed garden party, where even the great personages of the world play for a while, if only in emblematic fashion, the conventional role of shepherds and shepherdesses. They do so to imitate the poet, or rather to prove that they feel the charms of intimacy and privacy as strongly as he does, that they are endowed with a soul as delicate and sensitive as his. The poet repays the compliment by revealing all the glamour and grandeur hardly hidden under the pastoral disguise that his betters had chosen to wear. And the great of the world profit by the occasion to indulge more freely than usual in the game of love, looking for the *pays du tendre* in nearby Versailles and finding nests of pastoral dalliance in a Petit Trianon.

The real aim of the courtly pastoral is flattery, and precisely the flattery of simplicity, which enhances the splendor of its object under the mask of humility. The artfulness of this kind of flattery reaches its peak when the poet uses the pastoral convention to spread the veil of beauty not only over the dazzling light of glory, but also over the sudden darkening of that light. When the revolutions of fortune force a public figure to a permanent or temporary withdrawal into private life, the bucolic poet may describe the fall of his patron from grace as a voluntary retreat into pastoral obscurity. While accompanying his protector to his country house, the courtly poet soothes with the balm of song the wounds of pride. Here pastoral poetry becomes a catharsis of worldly failure, and sublimates that failure into a triumph of the spirit. Its flattering courtliness remains unchanged in the process: instead of lowering himself to his new, and simpler surroundings, the retired man of power ennobles them with his presence. It is by such subtle craft, to quote Boileau's echo of Vergil in *L'Art poétique* (ii), that the eclogue sometimes "makes the country and the woods worthy of a consul" ("rend dignes d'un consul la campagne et les bois").

X

A French or Italian neoclassical garden is not a product of nature but of convention and artifice. Yet, even when they offer us the broader vistas of open and uncultivated lands, pastoral landscapes are but "nature methodis'd." All bucolic poets remind us that the god of Arcadia was Pan, and yet there is no panic or cosmic feeling in pastoral poetry, as is shown by the fact that it survived even beyond the mysterious announcement that the great Pan was dead. At any rate even in the ancient pastoral Pan does not really play the role of a god: he is merely a *genius loci* or patron saint, whom everybody worships but nobody hears or sees. "Pan curat ovis oviumque magistros" (Pan cares for the sheep and the masters of the sheep), says Vergil (*Ecl.* ii), and stops at that. This means that Arcadia, Sicily, and all other bucolic lands are rather unfavorable soil for the growth of a fabulous vision of life, of a mythological world view. This remains true even though pastoral poets populate those lands not only with shepherds but also with satyrs and nymphs. Those divine beings, however, have only a literary reality. Thus, when Milton conjured away from the idyllic locale of his hymn in *On the Morning of Christ's Nativity* the lovely pagan deities of nature along with the barbaric monsters and oriental idols dethroned by the God of the Bible, he exorcised in the latter ghosts that had never haunted any pastoral landscape and, in the former, spirits who did not live in Arcadia any more.

If Pan, except as an icon or a name, was already dead even for the pastoral poets of classical antiquity, nymphs and satyrs survived in bucolic poetry as vague shadows or decorative images. "Quis caneret Nymphas?" (Who would sing the nymphs?), asks Vergil (*Ecl.* ix), with a question that is wholly rhetorical. With the progress of time, "nymph" becomes more and more a synonym for rural lassie or country maid, or an elegant symbol for the "eternal feminine"; while the satyr's shape and Silenus' figure are finally reduced to transparent disguises for *l'homme moyen sensuel*, for the aged or middle-aged male, with his ungratified sexual longings, with his yearning to drink from the fountain of beauty and youth. Mallarmé understood this very well in his *L'Après-midi d'un faune*, where, in contrast with Debussy's musical version of the same "églogue," there is no sexual consummation except in the realm of thought. The poem itself evokes not the panic hour of noon, which is the culmination of nature and time, but the afternoon of life, with its regrets and daydreams. Hence Mallarmé's faun becomes a kind of Narcissus among his peers, but one in love with a beauty and youth no longer his own, whom a natural rather than a mythological metamorphosis transforms into a "thinking reed."

That in the bucolic the satyr is hardly more than a trope is proved by the treatment of another and less beastlike mythological figure: Polyphemus, the one-eyed giant living in the volcanic island of Sicily. It was a native of that island, Theocritus of Syracuse, who introduced this Homeric monster into pastoral poetry, reducing him, as he did so, to human proportions. By relating the sad tale of the Cyclops' unrequited love for the nymph Galatea, a story that so many poets were to retell after him, Theocritus changed forever Homer's Polyphemus into one of the stock figures of the pastoral: into the type of the rustic swain, misshapen and uncouth, destined to reap no reward for the love he feels in his all too sensitive heart. If the pastoral treats even such mythological creatures as satyrs and Cyclopes as mere reflections of the human condition or, more precisely, of the masculine plight in the affairs of the heart, then we know how to answer the question that Goethe asks in the second part of *Faust*, when we see for the first time the happy dwellers of his Arcadia: "Wir staunen . . . ob's Götter, ob es Menschen sind." There is really no reason to "wonder whether they are men or gods." We know that pastoral characters are not immortal but mortal, and that Arcadia is inhabited by human beings only a little better and happier than we are.

XI

The pastoral concern with private life, and with its two external manifestations, which are love and friendship, means that bucolic poetry is largely indifferent to the lot of man in collective terms. Occasionally, however, it goes beyond the pastoral of the self, and dreams of the human condition in terms of a universal brotherhood. The pastoral poet's yearning after innocence and happiness helps him sometimes to see how rarely that ideal may be achieved by his fellow men. While praising the life of the poor and the meek for being free from internal troubles, he may complain about those external disorders that prevent even such beings from enjoying the happiness that should be the reward for their purity. What threatens most of the equilibrium of a pastoral community is the violence of those who are neither humble nor poor. The realization by the community that their peace, and even their very existence, may be destroyed by willful deeds, as well as by "acts of God," produces a sense both of insecurity and of injustice. To restore at least ideally its own moral balance, the pastoral turns back to the myth of the Golden Age and claims that in prehistoric times there existed a state of perfect equality and absolute justice, which lasted as long as the goddess Astraea graced the earth with her presence. The notion implied in this claim is that in the Silver, Bronze, and Iron Ages justice is no longer an actuality but merely a vision, which can be made real only intermittently, at the price of struggle and strife. Shepherds, however, are passive and resigned beings and leave to others the duty of defending their rights. Sir Philip Sidney seemed willing to assign this protective function to pastoral poetry itself, since one of its purposes, he maintains in his *Defence of Poetry,* is to "show the misery of people under hard lords or ravening soldiers." This assertion of the right of the poor and the weak to be protected, and of the duty of the rich and the strong to protect them, is for Sidney one of the chief tasks of the pastoral, second only to its general aim, which is to prove "what blessedness is derived to them that lie lowest from the goodness of them that sit highest." This simply means that those that *lie* lowest are at the mercy of those that *sit* highest (how significant the choice of these two verbs!), and that they owe their subsistence, and their very existence, to the generosity and clemency of those in power. But generosity and clemency can fail, and justice may yield to injustice. When this happens, the pastoral world has no recourse but to the weapons of pity, while the upholding of justice requires bearing the arms of war and using them against justice's enemies. Don Quixote felt that peace could be restored among men only by the sword of the knight, which he considered almost as holy as the cross of the saint. He stated this view to that group of ignorant herdsmen whom he met at the beginning of his adventures, telling them of the Golden Age of yore, when all men were shepherds and lived as innocent and happy as gods. But the Golden Age had disappeared long ago, and this is why chivalry had come into being, to chastise evildoers, to redress wrongs, and to save damsels in distress.

Don Quixote's and Sir Philip Sidney's are but different versions of the aristocratic view of pastoral justice, which, like all aristocratic views, is a retrospective utopia, a backward-looking dream. It was up to democratic thought to bring in prospective utopias and forward-looking dreams. At first the modern mind unfolded them within the pastoral's framework. This was done by Montaigne and by Shake-

speare, who conceived a pastoral utopia in both economic and political
terms, as is shown by Gonzalo's speech in *The Tempest* (II.i):

> All things in common nature should produce
> Without sweat or endeavour. Treason, felony,
> Sword, pike, knife, gun, or need of any engine,
> Would I not have; but nature should bring forth,
> Of it own kind, all foison, all abundance,
> To feed my innocent people.

This was done likewise by Rousseau, whose literary and sentimental
education had been formed by Tasso's *Aminta* and d'Urfés *L'Astrée*,
and who, in his *Discours sur l'inégalité*, presented his versions of both
the old and the new dream. The beginning of the *Discours* reevokes
the primitive "state of nature" at once in Hobbesian and in pastoral
terms. Based on man's natural equality, that state enjoyed a wild
freedom and provided a stern justice of its own. Primitive man was
not cursed by the vice of social organization, which through the institution of property would later legalize injustice itself. The final
effect of the social contract, by which the individual exchanged freedom for security, was to establish social and economic inequality. Man
should correct this unnatural injustice not by returning to the state
of nature but by reproducing in the near future a situation similar to
that occurring immediately after the compact between the individual
and the group, when freedom and equality were still possible. Here
Rousseau merged the pastoral vision with the theory of natural law,
with the belief that society should restore to man the rights God had
granted him. If man's reason can grasp the idea of his natural rights,
then man's will should embody that idea in a new society, as well as
in an eternal code of laws. This postulate was bound to produce within
modern political thought all the variants of the agrarian dream, from
Jefferson to Thoreau, from New Harmony to Russian populism.

Rousseau's vision was equally affected by the opposite ideals of regress and progress. But when the latter triumphs over the former, man
rejects all backward-looking dreams and projects his wishes into the
fair vistas of a new hope. At this stage the utopia suddenly emerges,
independent and full-fledged, from the pastoral ideal. Utopia, after all,

is but the idyll of the future. Recognition of this truth is to be found in the early nineteenth-century manifesto, *De la réorganisation de la société européenne*, written jointly by Saint-Simon and Augustin Thierry:

> L'imagination des poètes a placé l'âge d'or au berceau de l'espèce humaine parmi l'ignorance et la grossièreté des premiers temps: c'était bien plutôt l'âge de fer qu'il fallait y reléguer. L'âge d'or du genre humain n'est point derrière nous, il est au-devant, il est dans la perfection de l'ordre social; nos pères ne l'ont point vu, nos enfants y arriveront un jour: c'est à nous de leur en frayer la route.

> The imagination of the poets placed the Golden Age at the dawn of the human race, amidst the ignorance and rudeness of primitive times. It is rather the Iron Age that should be banished there. The Golden Age of mankind is not behind, but before us; and it lies in the perfection of the social order; our fathers have not seen it, our children will one day reach it: it is for us to prepare their way.

The manifesto translates the idea of progress into a messianic creed, into the belief that man may help, but not hinder, the realization of the pastoral visions of old. But when the ideal yields to doubt, when man fears that the forces of the past or reaction will prevent the automatic fulfillment of his heart's desire, then he becomes a radical and a rebel. Since involution seems to prevail over evolution, he recurs to revolution itself. When the hour strikes, the pastoral rebel will declare, in Chamfort's words, "war to the manors, peace to the huts" ("guerre aux châteaux, paix aux chaumières!"). Yet when he does so he shatters the pastoral dream. The shepherd of pastoral poetry does not care for property, whether public or private, and recoils from direct action, refusing to expropriate even the expropriators of his small plot.

Thus William Empson is right when he claims that we may have pastorals with artisans or working men instead of shepherds, but he is wrong when he maintains that proletarian fiction is an offshoot of the pastoral.[4] Proletarian novels idealize the urban masses without idealizing their way of life; while exalting the moral virtues of the common man, they protest against the social vices that condition his lot. The pastoral, however, treats that lot not as a curse to be dispelled but as a blessing to be restored. This means that normally there is no political pastoral but of the conservative Right, and this is why Marx used contemptuously the epithet idyllic to define the social relations of feudalism. A pastoral of the Left is conceivable only in terms of a nonviolent resistance against an authority enforcing not so much conservatism and conformity as displacement and change, and it expresses almost always, as in the case of Tolstoy, the temper of a passive and ethical anarchism.

Goethe understood this, and understood equally well that the nonviolent resistance of the pastoral mind can end only in defeat. He also knew that the instrument of that defeat is the force variously called "history," "evolution," or "social change." This is why in *Faust* (pt. II, act V) he rewrote, in a tragic version, Ovid's famous idyll. Philemon and Baucis refuse to exchange their poor plot for the rich farm that Faust offers them when he wants to remove the old couple from the marshland he plans to reclaim for his own sake as well as for the benefit of the human race, and they die together in the fire of their hut, the victims of Faust's will to power, when his henchmen try to evict them forcibly from the wretched place where they had spent all their life. Here the pastoral oasis is destroyed by the attempt to change the surrounding desert into the land of a new promise.

In general, whether of the Left or of the Right, the political pastoral is not a plea for a better society but a protest against society itself. In this it joins hands with the pastoral of love, which protests against the moral order on which society rests. This double protest springs from a utopian longing or hope that, in *Die Zukunft einer Illusion*, Freud defined in the following terms:

> Man sollte meinen, es müsste eine Neuregelung der menschlichen Beziehungen möglich sein, welche die Quellen der Unzufriedenheit mit der Kultur versagen macht, indem sie auf den Zwang und die Triebunterdrückung verzichtet. . . . Das wäre das goldene Zeitalter, allein es fragt sich, ob ein solcher Zustand zu verwirklichen ist. Es scheint vielmehr, dass sich jede Kultur auf Zwang und Triebverzicht aufbauen muss.

> One might suppose the possibility of reorganizing human relations in such a way that by rejecting coercion and the repression

of the instincts one could remove the causes of man's discontent with civilization. . . . This would be the Golden Age, but it is doubtful whether such a condition can ever become a reality. It is far more probable that each civilization must be built on coercion and the renunciation of our instincts.

The function of pastoral poetry is to translate to the plane of imagination man's sentimental reaction against compulsory labor, social obligations, and ethical bonds; yet, while doing so, it acts as the catharsis of its own inner pathos, and sublimates the instinctual impulses to which it gives outlet. It therefore performs with especial intensity the role that Freud assigns to art in general: that of acting as a vicarious compensation for the renunciations imposed by the social order on its individual members, and of reconciling men to the sacrifices they have made in civilization's behalf.

XII

While creating quasi-pastoral utopias, the modern world destroyed the conventional and traditional pastoral through four cultural trends that arose together and partly coincided. These were the humanitarian outlook, the idea of material progress, the scientific spirit, and artistic realism. The humanitarian view inspired George Crabbe's *The Village*, one of the earliest country poems to pay attention to the physical and moral ugliness, rather than to the ideal and sentimental charms, of the peasant's estate. Crabbe was aware of the novelty of his task, which was to convey "what form the real picture of the poor." Real herdsmen no longer praise "their country's beauty or their nymphs," yet poets still sing of the unreal passions of shepherds who never existed. The muses never knew the country people and their real pains. The latter have other grievances than those of love, "the only pains, alas! they never feel." Thus, instead of uttering "idle praises" of a poverty cursed by hardship rather than blessed with leisure, instead of describing fictitious beings and an imaginary way of life, Crabbe chooses to depict "the poor laborious natives of the place," and to sing, like Gray in his *Elegy*, "the short and simple annals of the poor."

The idea of an indefinite material progress, the enthusiastic acceptance of the development of industry and commerce, with its attendant increases in comfort and luxury, inspires a famous poem by Voltaire, significantly entitled "Le Mondain." Its main point is the denial of the

Rousseauian exaltation of the state of nature, or, in pastoral terms, of the Golden Age. The poet leaves that nostalgia to all those who would like to walk again on all fours, as he said once of Rousseau:

> Regrettera qui veut le bon vieux temps,
> Et l'âge d'or, et le règne d'Astrée.

Let those who wish to do so long for the good old times, for the Golden Age, and for Astraea's rule.

No Golden Age, state of nature, or Garden of Eden will do for Voltaire, who states his unqualified preference for the secular and civilized living of the present time ("ce temps profane est fait pour mes moeurs"). Prosperity is better than poverty; new desires are welcome because they produce new needs as well as new delights. "How good is this Iron Age!" ("O le bon temps que ce siècle de fer!"), exclaims the poet after comparing his own epoch with the Golden Age of the past, and concludes that the supposed virtue of primitive man was only ignorance.

The scientific attitude is but one of the many aspects of the new spirit of "truth" that inspired modern Western culture even in the artistic field. The coming of romanticism introduced a novel imagination, equally hostile to the conventional and the fanciful. That imagination expanded nature into a boundless realm, which replaced the meadows and groves, as well as the orchards and gardens, of traditional poetry. Through its "call to the wilderness" romanticism served, almost as effectively as realism, the cause of the "true," although it preferred to call the "true" by other names, such as the "real" or the "natural." Both romanticism and realism saw poetry and literature as a "song of experience" rather than as a "song of innocence." But this, to use Rimbaud's words, means "the end of the idyll" ("la fin de l'idylle"). Yeats stated the same view at the beginning of the early poem originally called *Song of the Last Arcadian*, later placed by him at the head of all his poems:

> The woods of Arcady are dead,
> And over is their antique joy;
> Of old the world on dreaming fed;
> Grey Truth is now her painted toy.

Thus pastoral poetry finally died, and disappeared from sight. Yet the pastoral ideal survived, although devitalized and unrecognizable. As such it is still able to inspire a few modern versions of the pastoral, which go under many names and disguises. The most obvious form for such survivals is "the back to nature" movement or, more generally, the cult of the primitive, which is also the most recent variant of the myth of the noble savage. In modern culture the noble savage is often found near home, and is part not so much of anthropology as of folklore. For this reason the modern pastoral often replaces the reed pipe of ancient poetry with the more prosaic bagpipe. In brief, the bucolic imagination of our time, as William Empson observed, follows the example of the Newgate pastorals, where plebeians and urban outcasts fill the role once played by countrymen and villagers.[5] Modern pastorals, however, oppose the traditional ones also in other ways than this. They are almost always written in prose, and break all traditional patterns and attitudes. Many of them, paradoxically, are "indoor" or "winter" pastorals, as well as "urban" ones. Sometimes they transplant the pastoral yearning for a solitary independence, for the self-sufficiency of a purely private life, from the open spaces of the countryside to a secluded corner or cell-like enclosure designated by Virginia Woolf "a room of one's own." In many cases the roles of the pastoral actors are played not by shepherds or peasants but by animals or children. Sometimes this contemplation of the bucolic vision through a childish or animal perspective achieves a magic of its own, as shown by such different tales as Alain Fournier's *Le Grand Meaulnes*, Richard Hughes's *A High Wind in Jamaica*, Tolstoy's *Kholstomer* (*Yardstick*, the story of a horse), and D. H. Lawrence's *The Fox*. Such a conversion of the pastoral into a modern fable or fairy tale signifies, in Baudelaire's words, the sublime puerility of all idyllic dreaming ("tout ce que l'Idylle a de plus enfantin"), as well as its charming *bêtise*. The pastoral ideal seems to survive in varied metamorphoses, even in our mores, where the old-fashioned retreat to a farm or a villa is replaced by a flight to suburbia and the elegant *bergeries* of our ancestors become roadside outings, with their picnics or barbecues.

When self-conscious, the modern pastoral is, however, ironic and ambiguous, since it begins as imitation and ends as parody. In brief, it is an inverted pastoral, presenting a bucolic aspiration only to deny it. Russian literature offers us two perfect examples of this inversion of the pastoral dream. The first is Gogol's tale *Old-fashioned Landowners,* which describes the existence of an old couple apparently patterned after Ovid's Philemon and Baucis, in order to show, even more than the triumph of death, the triumph of lifelessness. The other is Tolstoy's *Domestic Happiness,* which begins as a pure and absolute love idyll, as a triumph of beauty and youth, later destroyed by the hard realities of family and marriage. While Gogol's is an inverted pastoral of innocence, Tolstoy's is an inverted pastoral of happiness.

XIII

The pastoral ideal is rooted not only in a vision of life but also in a view of art and literature. The pastoral has its poetic, as well as its ideology. That poetic was fully developed in the neoclassical age, and found its most typical exponent in Boileau. Boileau compares the pastoral to a young shepherdess not in ordinary dress but in festive attire, wearing on her blond hair a garland of wild flowers, far more becoming than a crown of jewels. Its beauty should not be bare, or clouded by ostentatious luxury; its elegance should consist in unassuming grace. Boileau concludes his simile with the following precept (*L'Art poétique,* ii):

> Telle, aimable en son air, mais humble dans son style,
> Doit éclater sans pompe une élégante idylle.

Such, lovely in its appearance, but humble in its style, an elegant idyll should shine without pomp.

Thus for Boileau pastoral poetry must strike a middle note between the high and the low. Sometimes it may follow the Vergilian exhortation, "paulo maiora canamus," without, however, raising its humble strains to the heroic mode, since the sound of the war bugle will frighten Pan and the nymphs away from the woods. Yet, along with this ambition of hovering in the sky, the pastoral must also avoid the temptation of sinking down to the level of the earth, to the level of what we moderns call "realism." Boileau wishes the pastoral to be "natural" in a literary sense. He does not want unadulterated reality and unvarnished truth, but rather, like Pope, "nature to advantage dress'd." This is why he condemns as both bad taste and bad manners the tendency on the part of some poets to do what a modern realistic writer would do, that is, to make lowly characters discourse in rustic speech:

> ... Cet autre, abject en son langage,
> Fait parler ses bergers comme on parle au village

another one, abject in his diction, makes his shepherds speak as one speaks in the country

and to call guardians of herds not by fictitious names, but by real ones:

> Et changer, sans respect de l'oreille et du son,
> Lycidas en Pierrot, et Philis en Toinon.

and to change, without regard for ear and sound, Lycidas into Pierrot, and Phyllis into Toinon.

Boileau's statement is exemplary; and yet we learn more from less friendly critics, such as Samuel Johnson, who indicted the pastoral not because it conflicted with the prose of life but because it denied the demands of decorum and common sense and failed to voice the natural feeling that poetry should strive to express. It was Johnson who before the modern revulsion from arcadian affectation made the strongest accusation against the insincerity of the form. Speaking of *Lycidas* in his *Life of Milton*, he said: "Passion plucks no berries from the myrtle and ivy, nor calls upon Arethuse and Mincius, nor tells of rough *satyrs* and *fauns with cloven heel*. Where there is leisure for fiction there is little grief."

Even more is to be learned about the pastoral from those great poets who practiced the form in their spare time, Cervantes and Shakespeare. Unlike Boileau and Johnson, Cervantes looks at the pastoral with mixed feelings, with a sympathy not devoid of ambiguity. Thus Don Quixote, we recall, claims that chivalry came into being to compensate for the passing of the Golden Age; yet, after his first return home (I.vi) when the hidalgo's friends are burning most of his library, his niece asks them to throw his pastoral books on the bonfire also, fearing they might otherwise seduce her uncle into becoming a shepherd after his failure as a knight. And her fear is well founded, for on his last homecoming (II.lxxiii) Don Quixote declares his intention of taking up a shepherd's life. In sum, the pastoral dream may in its turn replace the chivalric ideal. Here Cervantes speaks through his hero, and refers in fictional form to the central decision of his life, which was to turn from a warrior into a poet or, as he would have said, to abandon the career of *las armas* for that of *las letras*. In this he follows the Renaissance tendency to identify the pastoral calling with the literary profession. In his case the identification is not invalidated by the existence of but a single bucolic work from his pen, the *egloga* or pastoral romance *Galatea;* or by his mockery, in the *Coloquio de los perros,* a dialogue in Lucian's vein, of the pastoral as conventional and false. For the mocker is after all a dog: his condemnation of the genre as unreal implies a cynical denial of literature itself. By so doing the dog ranges himself with Sancho Panza, and rejects all of poetry as a deluding lie.

Yet art is never a rejection of life, and fancy may enhance the emotion rather than weaken it. Nurture is as necessary as nature, and is nature's offspring. Shakespeare made this point in *The Winter's Tale* (IV.iv), when Polixenes calls on Perdita and visits her "rustic garden." Perdita apologizes for the absence from among her plants of those "carnations and streak'd gillyflowers/Which some call Nature's bastards," since they may grow only by graft, or by an artifice added to the natural process. Polixenes admits that "this is an art/Which does mend nature, change it rather," but objects that "the art itself is Nature," and begs Perdita not to call "bastards" flowers produced by graft. The pastoral may be one of such grafted flowers, an artificial breed, one of poetry's "bastards." Yet even here nature does not deny nurture, since it works not against nature's laws but according to them. Convention may become invention, thus creating reality anew.

XIV

Shakespeare's definition of the function of pastoral fancy with regard to art and reality is to be seen in his romantic comedy *As You Like It.* The life of the exiled Duke and his companions is described in terms of both tradition and folklore (I.i): "They say he is already in the forest of Arden, and a many merry men with him; and there they live like the old Robin Hood of England. They say many young gentlemen flock to him every day, and fleet the time carelessly, as they did in the golden world." Here the "golden world" stands for nurture, and Robin Hood's green world stands for nature. Yet the whole work is based on the interplay of more complex assumptions than those implied in this contrast. The play moves at once on three different levels, with a different set of characters corresponding to each. The first level includes the exiled Duke, his retinue, Orlando, Celia, and Rosalind; the second, the shepherds Corin, Silvius, and Phebe; the third, two peasants, Audrey and William. All other characters are outsiders, like the two villains, the usurping Duke and Oliver, Orlando's wicked brother, who act merely as the cogs of the plot; or like the clown Touchstone, who comments mockingly on men's follies and the whims of fate. The characters of the first level enter the rude Arcadia of Arden not as free agents but as persecuted people, forced to abandon their land and home. Theirs is a flight, not a retreat: by accepting their quasi-pastoral lot, they make a virtue out of necessity. They look at their refuge with neither illusion nor pretense, and this saves them from the delusion that pastoral life is heaven on earth. This disenchantment is symbolized by the fact that their new habitat is not blessed by a perennial spring but cursed by cold spells and icy winds, causing physical discomfort and dispelling all leisure and ease. This unexpected deviation from the pastoral scheme is a happy paradox, inspiring the lovely songs of the play, which are at once charming pastorals of winter and lively idylls of the north.

The Duke and his courtiers are equally aware that the forest of Arden is a place where man must earn his bread with the sweat of his brow. Since a nobleman cannot till without becoming a *villano,* in the sense still preserved by that Italian word, each of them turns hunter, although still grieving for those "native burghers of this desert city" (II.i), whether birds or beasts, that are now fair game for his bow. This leads the melancholy Jaques to maintain that the violence committed by the intruders against the wild creatures of the forest is more of a usurpation than that practiced against the exiles by the wicked Duke in the human world of the city and the court.

The second set of characters are actual shepherds but also, as their names show, literary ones, thus representing bucolic life both from without and within. The elderly Corin becomes the natural spokes-

man for the pastoral of innocence, which he praises for its moral rewards, while complaining of the toil and hardship it entails (III.ii):
"Sir, I am a true labourer. I earn that I eat, get that I wear, owe no man
hate, envy no man's happiness, glad of other men's good, content with
my harm, and the greatest of my pride is to see my ewes graze and my
lambs suck." Corin's independence is a moral rather than a material
circumstance, since the flock he tends and calls his own belongs not to
him but to his master. This is true also of his abode, and this is why
he is unable to practice the pastoral virtue of hospitality. The scene
where he fails to heed the request of Rosalind, who is in masculine
disguise, that he shelter under his roof her and her companion, the
fair maid Celia, "with travel much oppressed" (II.iv), is unique in the
whole bucolic tradition. This episode shows that there are Arcadias
where man may be as churlish as the wind.

Churlish in a rustic way are the characters of the third set, William,
the country lad, and Audrey, the country wench. They play a minor
and yet significant role, within the play's world, since their lowly
peasant status, indicated by their everyday names, prevents their
idealization and introduces a humorous earthiness into the play's
sophisticated atmosphere. The poet achieves an antipastoral effect by
placing this down-to-earth view of country life beside its ideal image.
If the play's noble characters live in the higher sphere of glamour and
romance, the two rustic swains move at the low level of comic realism, while Corin and the other shepherds occupy a middle ground between these two extremes. Thus noblemen, shepherds, and peasants
stand respectively for poetry, literature, and reality, and the third
group is set against the other two.

The chief point is that the bucolic category taken least seriously by
the poet is the pastoral of love. The directness with which Audrey and
William exchange their vows gives an air of unreality to the conventional fidelity of Silvius and to the equally conventional inconstancy
of Phebe. Silvius' foolish wooing and Phebe's capricious coyness are
harshly condemned by Rosalind, who begins by liking the pastoral
casuistry of love ("this shepherd's passion is much upon my fashion",
II.iv) but ends by disliking it. The poet shares her final view, and
consequently closes the play with no less than three marriages. This
multiple and hardly pastoral happy ending suggests that pastoral love,

or the pastoral experience in general, is but a brief holiday or vacation from the business of life. The play ends with a "rustic revelry" precisely because the pastoral interlude is now over. The Duke is restored to his duchy, and goes back with his family and friends to the city and the court. If Jaques, who stands here for the pastoral of the self as well as of melancholy and solitude, disapproves of their return as he did of their withdrawal, Orlando is happy to see the end of the indolence that, in his eyes, led the Duke and his lords to "lose and neglect the creeping hours of time" (II.vii).

This denial of bucolic idleness puts in doubt even the pastoral of happiness. The play's obvious message is that shepherd's existence is neither worse nor better than other states: that, like all ways of life, it has its good sides but also its bad ones. Touchstone makes this clear in his talk with Corin (III.ii): "Truly, shepherd, in respect of itself, it is a good life; but in respect that it is a shepherd's life, it is naught. In respect that it is solitary, I like it very well; but in respect that it is private, it is a very vile life. Now, in respect it is in the fields, it pleaseth me well; but in respect it is not in the court, it is tedious. As it is a spare life, look you, it fits my humour well; but as there is no more plenty in it, it goes much against my stomach." Through the apparent nonsense of his witty clown Shakespeare seems to reply to three important questions. The first is whether he values or scorns the pastoral ideal. The second is whether this comedy is a pastoral play. The third is whether it reaffirms or denies the traditional poetics of the pastoral. The equivocal answer that the clown gives to all three on behalf of the poet amounts to an echo of the comedy's title: as you like it.

XV

The poetic of the pastoral fully reveals that all its subgenres must be reduced to the common denominator of the lyrical mode. The *epyllion* is not epic; the pastoral romance is not narrative; pastoral drama is not dramatic; tragicomedy is neither comic nor tragic. Nothing is more significant than the fact that Molière failed to bring to completion both a *Pastorale héroïque* and a *Pastorale comique*. The pastoral is not merely lyrical in the modern or general sense; it is also melic in the special and traditional meaning of the latter term. This is the reason why, as both Nietzsche and De Sanctis realized, pastoral inspiration was bound to transcend the domain of literature and invade the newly found lands of the opera and the ballet. The dancing master of Molière's *Bourgeois Gentilhomme* already knew the reason for this:

> Lorsqu'on a des personnes à faire parler en musique, il faut bien que, pour la vraisemblance, on donne dans la bergerie. Le chant a été de tout temps affecté aux bergers; et il n'est guère naturel en dialogue que des princes ou des bourgeois chantent leurs passions.

> When characters must speak in music, they are required by verisimilitude to fall into the pastoral. Singing has been from all time the shepherd's prerogative; and in dialogue it would hardly be natural for princes or burghers to sing their passions.

As for the pastoral poets themselves, they speak almost always of poetry and music as if they were one and the same thing. Often they treat poetry and music not as conscious cultural activities but as spontaneous sentimental manifestations, as something akin to what we call self-expression; and, even more frequently, as outlets for the feelings and emotions. Poetry and music then become avenues of escape from disappointment and sorrow. Hence the pastoral implies a view of the psychological function of art that could be summed up in the proverb *qui chante son mal enchante* (who sings, charms his ill). This *mal*, to continue the same word play, is disenchantment and, primarily, disenchantment in the affairs of the heart. It is to charm away this disenchantment that Mallarmé's faun plays on his pipe, which, by turning toward itself the tears of the player ("détournant à soi le trouble de la joue"), ends by becoming a vehicle of escape ("instrument des fuites"). Its ascending and sublimating melody, made almost perceptible to our eye by the sorcery of art ("le visible et serein souffle artificiel de l'inspiration, qui régagne le ciel"), transforms into abstract visions our nightmares and daydreams, and purifies into lucid images our ungratified yearnings ("trop d'hymen souhaité de qui cherche le *la*").

This is another way of saying that the poetry of the pastoral embraces both longing and wish fulfillment. As a consequence, the definition of poetry that Bacon gives in *The Advancement of Learning*

(II.iv) is particularly well suited to the pastoral, since this poetic form succeeds even better than others in "submitting the shows of things to the desires of the mind." The definition itself acts as a kind of justification of the pastoral fallacy, which appears no less potent than the pathetic one, and may well be a variant of it. The pastoral fallacy and its equivalents are deeply rooted in human nature; this explains the recurrence or permanence of their manifestations and the survival of pastoral make-believe even in such an Iron Age as ours. One could say that there is a pastoral cluster in any form of poetry; and so we find pastoral oases even in nonpastoral writing. In a certain sense, and in its purest form, the pastoral represents ideally the Golden Age of poetry. Poetry, however, is not only the child of fancy, but also the daughter of memory; and this makes her the sister of history. It is when she tries to forget her sister, and yearns after a dreamland outside of time, that poetry becomes idyllic, if not in form at least in spirit.

2
Pastoral
Love

I

If the episode in Tasso's *Gerusalemme* about Erminia's stay among the shepherds sums up, better than any other example, the bucolic aspiration toward a life of perfect innocence, the first chorus in his drama *Aminta* presents, with more poignancy than any similar text, the other side of the pastoral, the aspiration toward a life of blissful happiness. As we already know, happiness means in pastoral terms always one and the same thing: the fulfillment of the passion of love, the consummation of man's erotic wishes, as much as unhappiness means exactly the opposite, the rejection or denial of his heart's desire. The most obvious form of such unhappiness is unrequited love. Yet very often love remains unsatisfied not because it is not returned but because public morality prevents the beloved one from responding to the lover's entreaties. Although love was born free, the institutions of the family and society try to confine that winged creature in an iron, or a gilded, cage. But Cupid is a god, and cannot be enslaved. So men have no other resort but to imprison instead his devotees, now secluding them with physical barriers, within walls or behind gates; now binding them with the moral chains of fidelity oaths or virginity vows. Wives and fiancées must remain faithful, and daughters and sisters chaste: and often, at least formally, similar obligations are imposed on men too. The pastoral protests against this situation and accuses society of being responsible for this state of things. But with all their vehemence, the protest and the accusation remain, so to speak, platonic and ineffectual. Thus, being aware of the impossibility of realizing here and now its own ideal of an absolute erotic anarchism, the pastoral is left no outlet except the very dreams it feeds on. So it projects its yearning after free love, its eagerness for sexual freedom and even sexual license, its longing for a passion with no master except its own caprice or whim, into a state of nature that exists nowhere, or only in the realm of myth.

Since the theme of Tasso's chorus is the exaltation of free love, the poet had no other alternative but to praise the only time in which one supposes that love was really free: the Golden Age. The first stanza is entirely taken up with the statement that all the usual reasons for praising the Golden Age are not the important ones. By making use of the rhetorical figure called preterition, the poet lists all the merits normally attributed to the Golden Age, only to deny that they are relevant. All the natural properties of that age, such as the spontaneous fertility of the soil and the everlasting clemency of the climate, now mean very little; and even its ways of life, uncontaminated by manual labor, trade, or warfare, are mentioned with the intent of proving that per se they are of little account (I.ii):

> O bella età de l'oro,
> non già perché di latte
> se 'n corse il fiume e stillò mele il bosco:
> non perché i frutti loro
> dier da l'aratro intatte

le terre e gli angui errâr senz'ira o tosco:
non perché nuvol fosco
non spiegò allor suo velo,
ma in primavera eterna,
ch'ora s'accende e verna,
rise di luce e di sereno il cielo;
né portò peregrino
o guerra o merce a gli altrui lidi il pino.

O beautous Golden Age!
Yet not for this—that flowed
With milk the stream, the bough with honey dripped;
Or this—that blushing wage
Of fruits the earth bestowed,
Untilled; while meek the unscathing serpent slipped;
Or this—that cloudless tripped,
Dimmed with no misty veil,
A gentle Spring eternal,
Like this that, mild and vernal,
Now gleams; and smiled the heavens with azure pale;
While yet, from shore to shore,
Nor war nor gear the sordid galley bore.[1]

What is indeed of great account, and does fully justify all the praises
of the Golden Age, must be seen in the failure or refusal of that
happy-go-lucky time to acknowledge one of the most harmful taboos
or fetishes of civilized life. That taboo is adored by human society
under the name of Honor: a name which is both proud and vain, since
beneath the word there is no real substance but only hollow deceit. Yet
the idolatry and credulity of the foolish crowd make of that fictitious
deity the cruel tyrant of our life. The blessed ignorance of our earliest
ancestors prevented that false value from troubling their minds, from
poisoning their joys, from ruling over their good, healthy, and natural
instincts. The only law governing mankind in the state of nature was
the law of nature, according to which any pleasure is permissible, nay
legitimate: "S'ei piace, ei lice" (What delights, is lawful).

The second stanza of Tasso's chorus describes the thoughtless hap-

piness of primitive humanity, with couples of lovers sporting harm-
lessly in the open air, under the indulgent eye of Cupids without those
bows and torches they need in our tainted times. If the scene were not,
as it is, hedonistic in the most simple and direct sense; if it did not
ignore, as it does, any metaphysical pretense; if it were less indifferent
than it is to any panic or cosmic view, one could perhaps consider it as
an announcement of those visions of D. H. Lawrence, where man and
woman join their bodies and souls under the open sky, in communion
with the world of nature and with the entire universe. So, if this were
not equally anachronistic, one could say that Tasso's shepherds are
practicing already, like some peculiar nature lovers of our times, what
goes now under the name of nudism.

> Allor tra fiori e linfe
> traean dolci carole
> gli Amoretti senz'archi e senza faci;
> sedean pastori e ninfe
> meschiando a le parole
> vezzi e susurri ed a i susurri i baci
> strettamente tenaci;
> la verginella ignude
> scopria sue fresche rose
> ch'or tien ne 'l velo ascose,
> e le poma de 'l seno acerbe e crude;
> e spesso in fonte o in lago
> scherzar si vide con l'amata il vago.

> O then, 'mid streams and flowers,
> Tuning their liquid throats,
> The shaftless, torchless Loves taught innocent graces
> Whileas, in glades and bowers,
> Shepherds and nymphs blent notes
> Of fluting joy with whispers and embraces
> Of fondling arms and faces.
> The veilless virgin bloomed
> With all the guileless roses
> That no more discloses

Her living loveliness, to eyes entombed;
And oft the river's edge
Saw simple lovers sport in wave and sedge.

It was Honor that destroyed man's primitive happiness, by generating shame, teaching modesty, and enforcing the use of clothing; yet in spite of so many constraints, our instincts were restrained but not tamed. So they tried to satisfy their needs and gratify their wishes in secret and by stealth, using the weapons of lie and deceit. Love, once freely granted and freely received as a friendly gift, can thus now be acquired only through theft. What the law of nature considered a normal and innocent act was changed by the law of man into a transgression, into what society calls crime, and religion, sin. Thus fair was made foul, and foul, fair:

> Tu prima, Onor, velasti
> la fonte de i diletti,
> negando l'onde a l'amorosa sete:
> tu a' begli occhi insegnasti
> di starne in sé ristretti,
> e tener lor bellezze altrui secrete:
> tu raccogliesti in rete
> le chiome a l'aura sparte:
> tu i dolci atti lascivi
> festi ritrosi e schivi,
> a i detti il fren ponesti, a i passi l'arte;
> opra è tua sola, o Onore,
> che furto sia quel che fu don d'Amore.

> Thou first, proud Shame, didst screen
> The fountains of delight,
> To longing love's clear sinless glance denied—
> That so no more were seen
> Eyes innocently bright,
> Taught to withhold and all their yearnings hide;
> Glad golden locks, uptied,
> No more the breezes blew;

Hearts wonted to exchange
Their sweets, thou didst estrange;
And lips and feet thy leaden fetters knew,
And thy cold, niggard creed
Made theft the bliss Love made the lover's meed.

The last stanza opens with an ironic praise of Honor, who may be proud of having wreaked so much havoc and brought so much grief among men. But since the simplest and humblest human beings seem to be unable to appreciate her greatness, Honor should leave them in peace and go among the famous and powerful, who respect her even though she troubles their sleep. As for ourselves, let us love and be loved, says the poet, closing the chorus with an envoi which is but a splendid replica of the usual commonplace about the caducity of life— our day is brief, while the night of death will last forever:

E son tuoi fatti egregi
le pene e i pianti nostri.
Ma tu, d'Amore e di Natura donno,
tu domator de' regi,
che fai tra questi chiostri
che la grandezza tua capir non ponno?
Vattene e turba il sonno
a gl'illustri e potenti:
noi qui negletta e bassa
turba, senza te lassa
viver ne l'uso de l'antiche genti.
Amian, ché non ha tregua
con gli anni umana vita e si dilegua.

Aniam, ché 'l Sol si muore e poi rinasce:
a noi sua breve luce
s'asconde, e 'l sonno eterna notte adduce.

This, this thy sceptre brings:
The pang and fruitless tear!
But thou, Love's lord and Nature's tyrant grown,

Fit ruler over kings—
What mak'st, what mak'st thou here,
Where none thy state confess, thy lordship own?
Hence, hence!—and build thy throne
In gilded bowers and halls!
To these thyself betake;
Us, lowly folk, forsake,
And let us live, as erst, kind Nature's thralls;
And let us love—since hearts
No truce of time may know,
And youth departs!

Ay! let us love: sun sinks, but sink to soar.
On us, our brief day o'er,
Night falls and sleep descends forevermore!

II

Tasso's chorus shows us that Eros reigns in any Arcadian land; and
that his sovereignty is *ex lege*, without and beyond the law. This freedom from any norm does not mean that pastoral love is devoid of a
code of its own. Its code is in reality a set of conventions, the most
common of which being that love is the business of youth and beauty.
The rule is easily extended to the masculine partner, but it applies universally only to the feminine one. While in a pastoral amorous tie the
woman must be always endowed without exception with beauty as
well as youth, the man may be safely deprived of either or even both.
Certainly masculine ugliness must not be so excessive as to become
deformity, which prevents the reciprocation of love—as proved by
the story of Polyphemus, whom pastoral poetry from Theocritus on
has always treated in pathetic terms, with some sympathy for the
grief of the one-eyed giant. The desperate passion of the Cyclops for
the nymph Galatea did thus become the most typical representation
of the plight of the lovelorn, a plight which is perhaps adumbrated
also in the universal folk theme of the Beauty and the Beast.

The very fact that the pastoral imagination had to recur to a monster to typify the man whom no woman will ever love confirms our
claim that the two amorous standards of beauty and youth are not

equally binding on the two sexes. Thus a genuine liaison between a fresh maiden and an older man is conceded as valid and accepted as possible; on the other hand, the code rejects as unworthy even of consideration a love affair with the woman as the older partner. In the bucolic view, a woman no longer young is by definition no longer beautiful, but even ugly. One of the roles the pastoral normally attributes to such a woman is to work for other people's happiness, and to help along a young couple's love match. But when she is directly affected by the pangs of love, she wants them to be cured by a man much too young for her, thus becoming ridiculous and making a fool of herself. On some occasions, she plays the deadly role of the scorned woman, who has no recourse but to perfidy, even sorcery (an old wench is always called a witch), in order to secure by foul means what she cannot get by fair. Such is, for instance, the case of the scheming and intriguing Corisca in Guarini's pastoral drama *Il Pastor fido*.

The erotic hedonism of the pastoral is always, at least almost always, elegiac; and the bittersweet taste of an unripe fruit acquires even greater flavor and delight with the very thought that its freshness and loveliness are the miracle of a moment, and soon will pass. Feminine beauty is a short-lived flower, which is at its best under the dew of the morning and in its earliest bloom; all its attractiveness lies in our awareness of this fact, in our somber knowledge that it is fated to be corrupted by a swift withering and a precocious death. From this knowledge derives the commonplace comparison between love, beauty, youth, and the ephemeral queen of all flowers, that rose which lasts *l'espace d'un matin*. Even more frequent than the simile of the rose is that of spring, and its very frequency suggests that the pastoral ideal of feminine beauty is but a reflection of the rustic charms of the early season of the year, when earth seems to grow young again among the new flowers and the fresh grass. Youth is the spring of life, as spring is the youth of the year. Dante must have felt this when he conceived the figure of Matelda, the mysterious being who watches over the forests and meadows of the Earthly Paradise, and suggested her loveliness in terms of flowers and spring. This emphasis on precocity and freshness may easily explain why the immortal beauty of Venus, working wonders on gods, men, and beasts, and seducing so easily even the immature and wayward adolescence of the all too handsome and not too masculine Adonis (who, by the way, is not a shepherd but a hunter), forms a kind of alien pattern, which does not partake of the conventions of pastoral myth.

The willingness to admit the possibility for a man with neither beauty nor youth to love and be loved, while denying the same chance or right to a woman equally devoid of these attributes, brings new evidence to the view of the pastoral as a man's world, built on the masculine pretense of mirroring oneself into the fountain of youth, while drinking intermittently and wistfully from the rejuvenating water of that fabulous spring. Yet the very idea that a plant of ivy, new and green, may willingly embrace the gray and knotty trunk of an oak tree, is based on something more than mere masculine self-indulgence. How literal such a symbol can be is seen in Tolstoy's *War and Peace*, where the mature and widowed Prince Andrey decides to abandon himself to his love for the youthful Natasha when, passing again through the forest, he sees surrounded by the greenery of spring the same old oak that shortly before he had seen bare and alone in the desolation of winter; and he finds that in his heart there is place for a new love and a second youth. A love of this kind may plant its roots in the need for lasting affection and security so often felt by a girl with no experience of life and even fearful of it, as well as in the irresistible attraction which the purity of a youthful heart and the naive innocence of a youthful mind may have for a wise and saddened old man. In cases like this, the maidenhood of the loving and beloved girl is but a token of the virginity of her soul. The best theoretical statement of the psychological validity of a situation of this kind is given by Stendahl in *De l'amour:*

> Le premier amour d'un jeune homme qui entre dans le monde est ordinairement un amour ambitieux. Il se déclare rarement pour une jeune fille douce, aimable, innocente. . . . C'est au déclin de la vie qu'on en revient tristement à aimer le simple et l'innocent, désespérant du sublime.

> The first love of a young man entering the world is usually an ambitious love. He is seldom attracted by a gentle, charming and innocent girl. . . . It is in the decline of life that a man sadly arrives at loving simplicity and innocence, despairing of the sublime.[2]

In the field of poetry, this situation found its highest expression in the biblical story of the rich and old Boaz and the poor maiden Ruth, which in modern times inspired one of most beautiful idylls of literature, Victor Hugo's *Booz endormi*.

The situation remains, however, a difficult one: it is hard to keep it well balanced between the opposite poles of ethos and pathos; it must be held in check in order to avoid the obvious pitfalls and to prevent it from going beyond limits it cannot safely trespass. What those pitfalls are, and where those limits must be traced, may be easily shown by comparing the tale of Boaz and Ruth with another biblical episode which acts like its opposite, where senile love appears not as a wonder but as a scandal. I am thinking of the scene where the two old men (the fact that there are two is highly significant) watch in hiding, with wicked desires and impure thoughts, the splendid beauty of Susanna taking her bath in the pool. *Omnia munda mundis:* so the obscenity of the situation lies only in the leering eyes and the filthy minds of the two old voyeurs. Yet the sinfulness of the occasion is to be seen also in the fact that Susanna is a married woman, surprised by the two intruders in the privacy of her house. If the garden pool were to be replaced by a lake amid the woods, and the splendid beauty of Susanna by the unveiled charms of a rustic girl, the casual watching of her nudity would produce on beholders, as well as on the reader, a sense of innocence rather than of impiety.

In the first part of Tolstoy's *Domestic Happiness*, which describes the betrothal of the middle-aged country squire, Sergey Mikhaylych, to his neighbor, the youthful orphan Masha, the man tells the girl one of those commonplaces which mankind, in similar cases, has heard and repeated innumerable times. "You have youth and beauty," he says, as if he were aware that those two, and no others, are the paramount virtues for romantic as well as for pastoral love. The acknowledgment, and the situation dictating it, seem also to suggest that youth and beauty are relevant only in their feminine form, but negligible, or at least secondary, in masculine shape or dress. Even more significantly, the observation contains the implicit statement that the pertinence of beauty and youth, as far as romantic and pastoral love are concerned, lies not in their separate entities but in their joint manifestation, in the alliance of their qualities as well as in the fusion of their differences. This is the reason why the beauty of a country lass or a rural nymph may easily descend to the level of simple loveliness or mere comeliness without destroying or even endangering itself. The perfect, extreme, and mature beauty of a woman of the world, of a glamorous mistress or paramour, of that kind of woman who in the rhetoric of love is sometimes called a siren (a Venus or Cleopatra, an Angela Pietragwa or an Anna Karenina) is out of place in the eclogue. One recalls Santayana's comment on Goethe's having made Helena the queen of Arcadia: "But to live within Arcadia Helen was not needed; any Phyllis would have served." [3]

Pride, however, makes man less willing to admit that, for the nymph he admires, any passionate shepherd would do as well as or even better than himself; yet pastoral poetry reminds us all too often that it is the most obscure of her swains who wins a shepherdess's heart, as, with almost equal frequency, it is the most undistinguished suitor, the least pretentious of her pretenders, who conquers a girl's hand. If feminine love is blind even to the powerful attractions of beauty and youth, it must be even blinder to those advantages that the pastoral does not recognize as such; these include not only the external and material endowments of power, money, and success, but the far more genuine and inner values of character, valor, and talent. If Mistral's Mirèio rejects the prosperous shepherd Alari for the humble basket weaver who becomes her fiancé, Ariosto's Angelica refuses the love of all the paladins, and even of Roland, the noblest hero of Christendom, to give herself to the stupid and coarse Medoro who, however, is both handsome and young. This does not mean that worldly glitter is always devoid of any attraction and charm; literature abounds in incidents about the naive country maiden who loses her head to a courtier or a "city slicker": think of the scene in Molière's Dom Juan where the peasant Charlotte is willing to elope with the great philanderer just before her marriage to poor Pierrot.

Cases like this, when the seduction succeeds, and when they transcend the common themes of the inconstancy and unpredictability of love, are at the margin of the eclogue, and imply a betrayal of all pastoral values. Those values are not denied but reaffirmed when the attraction joining two individuals of different sex, one belonging to the bucolic world and the other not, creates a genuine, if not a lasting, bond. Such a situation is generally looked at from within, according to the viewpoint of the insider, who of the two members of the partnership is the one representing the pastoral view. So it is up to the other partner to accept as his or her own the customs and conventions of the pastoral commonwealth. Situations of this kind appear rather frequently in romantic poetry, for instance in Byron's verse tales and in Pushkin's *The Gypsies*, where, however, the civilized man who has joined the primitive life of the gypsy tribe proves that his conversion has been skin-deep by letting himself be mastered by the passion of jealousy, which brings him to murder his wife instead of recognizing her right to choose a new lover among the young men of the clan. So the gypsies repudiate him as a traitor, and banish him as an outcast. But more frequently, especially when the pastoral hero plays the role of the outsider, his love adventures and experiences in an alien society aim at teaching the old-fashioned lesson that love knows no barriers and that it especially ignores the distinctions of class and wealth. No one preached this sermon with greater enthusiasm than Rousseau, especially in his story of the idyll, both sensual and platonic, between Saint-Preux the commoner and Héloïse the blue blood. Here we have a restatement of the eternal masculine wish to love shepherdesses as if they were duchesses, and duchesses as if they were shepherdesses: even in love man wants to make the world his province and to extend his Arcadian privileges, his right to enjoy woman's beauty and charms, to all estates as well as to all lands.

III

The pastoral hero treats woman as an object, even if a free and willing one. This passivity of the pastoral heroine emphasizes again that her dominant traits must be the naive candor and the charming immaturity of youth. It is perhaps the premium which the pastoral Eros puts on the immaturity and freshness of the love fruit that makes kissing, rather than embracing, the great idyllic pastime, the bucolic activity par excellence. This is especially true of the pastoral of the Italian Renaissance: no reader of Tasso's *Aminta* will forget the famous episode in which the lovelorn protagonist pretends to be stung by a bee, and is cured (or better, made even sicker for love) by the charming Silvia, who, out of pity and naively unaware of her power over him, heals his swollen lip by applying repeated kisses: a treatment, and a treat, which Aminta himself relates to another shepherd in a musical fugue of about seventy lines, with notes as suggestive and languorous as the occasion demands. In other poets and texts, this obsession with kissing, innocent and indecent at the same time, falls all too easily into the ridiculous, and reduces human passion to a kind of "lovey-dovey." To be sure, very often the imagery of kissing is but an impudic, and impudent, veil which a vicarious hypocrisy, rather than a genuine feeling of shame, lays over the realities of physical love: or a frivolous and libertine metaphor, enhancing into a kind of glamorous elegance the crudities of the sexual act. We must still observe, however, that the pastoral insists on the preliminaries of love rather than on its final consummation; and often reduces passion to the level of *galanterie* and courtship, or even of mere flirtation. *Post coitum animal triste:* and the pastoral, although so often elegiac, prefers not to dwell upon that kind of sadness, with its implied awareness that love is willed by nature even against man's will. It is perhaps significant that it was in a madrigal by a pastoral poet, Guarini, that the verb "to die" took on for the first time the added meaning of experiencing sexual orgasm: a double entendre which remained without echo in Italian literature, but which was to obtain widespread acceptance in the poetic language of Elizabethan England.

From the viewpoint of its psychological significance, the imagery of kissing may reveal to us realities of greater range and depth: it may for instance symbolize man's wistful desire to enjoy the pleasures of the flesh without being threatened by the wages of sin. The kiss symbol may well represent what was once called the neo-Malthusian position, by which the sexual urge is gratified without fear of parenthood. Birth control, or the prevention of conception, need not be exercised, exactly because it is not even contemplated in the pastoral. There is therefore no need to take into account the burden of a future family and the duty of raising the children to come. Like Eve before the fall, all the shepherdesses and nymphs of the pastoral seem to ignore the curse, as well as the blessing, of motherhood, and to be unaffected by woman's destiny or fate, which is to bring children, with great suffering and joy, into the world. This is another way of saying that the pastoral view of life dreams of a love free from the natural and social responsibility of its very acts. Man's private interest reacts in this way against what Schopenhauer calls nature's deceit: the illusion it fosters in man that his impulses are the active servants of his personal pleasures, while they are instead the passive instruments of the cosmic will.

It is exactly because of this unwillingness to accept fully the realities of the sexual condition of man that family life and conjugal love appear so rarely within the framework of the pastoral. Thus, after writing in a bucolic key the greater part of *Domestic Happiness*, the part describing the betrothal of the two protagonists and the romantic pathos of the girl, Tolstoy writes in an antipastoral key the second part, which describes the girl's disenchantment with marriage and her gradual realization that domestic happiness lies not in the "wild ecstasy" of sentiment but in the habit of duty and in the ethos of service and sacrifice. Tolstoy later went so far as to preach, if not to practice, the doctrine of sexual asceticism, and deny the moral validity even of marriage, in which he saw, as in extramarital love, what, talking with Gorki, he once called "the tragedy of the bedroom." [4]

Yet, in the first part of *Domestic Happiness* (which, at least formally, is entirely written from the viewpoint of the girl), Tolstoy understood very well the bucolic view of passion, with its refusal to accept love's subordination to duty, or the denial of love in name of a higher ideal. It is for this reason that the pastoral imagination treats marriage itself as something unreal and abstract. Bucolic poetry may show us quite often a wedding ceremony, as a kind of alluring vision or a charming festivity; but it never dwells at length on the life of a young married couple, on the intimate joys or the secret pains of their days and nights. This is only natural, because in the pastoral married love and wedded bliss are almost contradictions in terms. No pastoral poet, at least when keeping his inspiration within the bounds of the genre, has felt any inclination to raise his humble eclogue to the level of a solemn epithalamium, or to drown the quiet music of his idyll under the noise of wedding bells. This in spite of the fact that so many pastorals end with a marriage which in the course of the story was more hoped for than expected; and which is postponed as late as possible (as for instance in d'Urfés *L'Astrée*, the marriage between the protagonist and her Céladon), in order to permit all possible digressions and divagations about subtler or more attractive forms of love.

When, for example, as in Goethe's *Hermann und Dorothea,* the entire story leads to no other consummation than that of the marriage feast and the nuptial bed (with the expectation that several cradles will soon be added to the bridal room), we may safely assert that we have before us not a real pastoral but a bourgeois idyll.

In another quasi-pastoral work, Mistral's *Mirèio,* where the love theme is treated in a more romantic vein, the poet avoids the fatal transformation of his idyllic heroine into a buxom spouse or a prosaic housewife by changing the eclogue into an elegy, and by creating a chain of events leading the maiden to an early death. After all, no real pastoral likes to end with the traditional clause, "and they lived happily ever after." The pastoral does not like happy endings as such precisely because it does not like happiness to end. Exactly because its blissfulness may be only a dream, it prefers to project it on the screen of the present, to arrest for a while the most fleeting instants of human life, which are those we call "good times." Even when conjugal love is considered, it is generally contemplated statically, in an eternal present, or represented in a typical moment, often taking place a long time after the marriage itself. In such a case, the poet evokes not so much the flames of Eros' fire as its ashes: in other words, the tie of affection still binding together a man and a woman is only as a remembrance of things past, the romance of their beauty and youth. Since the pastoral celebrates conjugal love preferably within the perspective of old age, it is evident that its representation partakes more of the motif of innocence than that of happiness.

This conception finds its highest and most durable expression in the tale of Philemon and Baucis (perhaps the most famous of all old couples in literature) as told by Ovid in his *Metamorphoses* (viii). Philemon and Baucis are living peacefully and contentedly one of the many days of a long and serene life, when they welcome under their poor roof two unknown visitors to whom their neighbors had refused to open their doors. Philemon and Baucis are the only ones to fulfill one of the highest pastoral duties: the duty of hospitality. They offer the newcomers all they have, when suddenly their obscure guests reveal themselves for the great gods they are: Jupiter and Mercury. Jupiter shows his power by several acts of wonder, finally changing the shabby hut into a splendid temple. He then requests the old couple to tell him what they wish as a token of the gods' gratitude, and Philemon and Baucis ask to be made the guardians of the temple, to live their last days together and when the hour comes to die at the same time. All their wishes are granted, and after death they are transformed into an oak and a linden tree, shading the temple under their entwined branches.

Strangely enough, even in the pastoral of innocence the Philemons and the Baucises are never surrounded by grown-up sons and daughters, since they never had any offspring. But even among shepherds the young grow old; even in Arcadia a new generation must be rising as the other is about to decline. So there must be children somewhere; yet we rarely get a glimpse of them. The pastoral ignores openly the infant and his mode of life; it closes its eyes not only to the realities of childbearing but even of child raising. We should not pay too much attention to Rousseau's polemic against the use of hired wet nurses, and to his eloquent plea that rich mothers feed their children from their breasts. Here Rousseau's ideology runs counter to his deeper nature: Rousseau the man, who abandoned his newborn children to the foundling hospital, is more in agreement with the pastoral ideal than Rouseau the *philosophe* or the polemical writer. On the other hand, nothing proves more eloquently that Tolstoy's *War and Peace* is more than a mere idyll of the ancient way of life among the Russian landed gentry than the fact that the slender and glamorous Natasha changes at the end into a prosaic and prosperous mother, busy with her children's swaddling clothes and even with their diapers. The pastoral cannot afford to ignore older children as it does infants. Yet it treats them as if they were mere extras rather than small actors, or even bit players, on the bucolic stage. This is quite significant in the light of the fact that the urge toward the authentic and primitive so often leads modern literature toward the pastoral of childhood (and, in a few extreme cases, toward the pastoral of animal life). Shepherds and shepherdesses are ready to play their bucolic role only when they have reached the age of puberty; only then do they become full-fledged characters and rightful members of the pastoral community. After all, adolescence and early adulthood are the only important pastoral ages, since they coincide with the mating seasons of human life.

As we have already stated, it is only when it emphasizes the theme of innocence that the pastoral may look at the human condition from the standpoint of the family. This institution, however, is not conceived in the modern manner as a small circle of children with the parents at the center, but in the traditional way, as a patriarchal community, representing three or more generations, formed by many members including distant relatives and domestic retainers: all this is organized in a clanlike structure shaped like a pyramid. Thus, one can say that the pastoral of innocence tends to express itself in collective, or plural, terms. The pastoral of happiness, which subordinates all sorts of human intercourse to a lover's tête-à-tête, prefers instead to convey its message in dual form. But sometimes innocence and happiness, blended and merged together, seem to be attained by the individual in the most personal and direct way, without the cooperation of one's fellow shepherds or brethren, without the help or even presence of a single mate. Such a situation, as well as the varied modes and moods it may assume, is more properly represented in singular terms, in order to emphasize its uniqueness. When something like this takes place, we have the pastoral of solitude, where the retreat into Arcadia is in reality a retreat into the soul, with no company except the self. While the erotic pastoral complains of loneliness, this other kind of idyll or eclogue considers solitude as a sort of golden age of individual life and as man's only happy state. English poetry has developed so fully the pastoral of innocence that it has neglected the pastoral of love and happiness; and it was perhaps an excessive dependence upon purely English examples that prevented William Empson, who understood so well even the least obvious implications of bucolic poetry and who recognized all its modern derivations and variants, from realizing the overall importance of Eros and of lovemaking in all Arcadian lands.[5]

IV

Almost all kinds of bucolic culminate in the love idyll. This is particularly true of the eclogue of the Renaissance, as developed by the peculiar temper of the Italian genius. It was in Italy that the ancient pastoral found a soil and climate more favorable for transplantation. This happened at a time when the ascetic ideal of the Middle Ages was on the wane, and in the temples of both life and culture the *amor sacro* was triumphantly replaced by the *amor profano*. Thus, the reemergence of the genre was made possible not only by the revival of learning and the literary practice of formal imitation after the models of the ancients, but also by the new sentimental and psychological atmosphere created by Renaissance culture. But it was at the threshold of the baroque age, when the Renaissance world view was being superseded by the moral and religious reaction of the Counter Reformation, that Italy, which claimed to be both the most classical and the most catholic country of the West, became the Arcadian land par excellence. A century later, as a matter of fact, Italian culture annexed all of Arcadia to itself, enclosing it within the walls of a Roman villa and making an academy of what was once an open land. What one might call the reduction of the poetry and art of Italy to the common denominator of the pastoral took place in the age of transition, during which a less free and less sincere form of *amor sacro* tried to replace in its turn *amor profano* not only on the altars of the cult, but also in the minds of men.

At the very time that the Church veiled the nudities of the saints in its pictures and murals, and enforced everywhere a stricter morality in matters of sex, often leading souls not on the thorny path of conversion and redemption but on the easier and wider road of hypocrisy, or even of outright duplicity, the still untamed and unbridled sexual imagination of the Italians found a better outlet in a kind of pervasive and obsessive pastoral dream, invading all forms of literary creation and overflowing into the newly found land of secular music. The pastoral of simplicity and innocence seemed to recede and leave an open field to the pastoral of love and happiness, which flourishes all the more luxuriantly when the sexual instincts are at the same time excited and frustrated, and so are forced to express themselves more in dreams than in deeds. Where such a situation occurs, the souls of men are torn by the conflict between the totalitarian dictatorship of social authority and the libertarian anarchism of their instincts. The forbidden fruits and delights denied by the law are secretly and vicariously enjoyed by the imagination, the most difficult to control among the faculties of man.

This means that the pastoral declines and disappears when the authority of society in matters of sex becomes more lenient and indulgent, and the sanctions against transgression elapse or relax. This happened in the eighteenth century, when the *philosophes* and the encyclopedists protested against tradition and authority even in the field of sexual morality. In this field, Diderot was a far greater emancipator than Voltaire or Rousseau. Diderot's most important statement on free love took the form of a fictitious commentary on a famous travel book of the time, and was therefore entitled *Supplément au voyage de Bougainville*. The commentary is developed in the shape of a dialogue, whose interlocutors discuss at length two documents, which Diderot claims were unpublished, although they were part of Bougainville's memoirs. The message of the entire work is fully contained in the subtitle, by which Diderot explains what the dialogue is about: "l'inconvénient d'attacher des idées morales à certains actions physiques qui n'en comportent pas." In other terms, the uninhibited erotic mores of the inhabitants of one of the most beautiful islands of Polynesia are considered by Diderot as both legitimate and exemplary; and he suggests that we learn from them the lesson of nature and practice an absolute erotic freedom. Diderot's Tahiti seems thus to inaugurate the modern myth of the blessed islands of the South Seas.

Our Arcadia is Bali even more than the Tahiti of Diderot and Gauguin: that is, there are somewhere a few places where Western man may lead the thoughtless life of a beachcomber, enjoying without doubt or scruples the privileges of polygamy and promiscuity. Man's eternal dream of erotic and primitive happiness is no longer conceived in terms of retreat, but of flight and escape; still the destination of such flight or escape is a local habitation, not a mere name. Arcadia was a region of Greece; yet it scarcely existed except on the literary map. Our Arcadias seem instead to exist in reality, even if only in the most remote corners of our world. Significantly enough, they are placed not far from the equator, near the torrid zone, in tropical or at least subtropical lands. They are never placed on the mainland or in the older continents of our world: they are always faraway islands, and the vastness of the ocean surrounding them seems to symbolize how alien they are to us.

This physical barrier is also a moral one; yet the very fact that we know, or believe, that such islands and such a way of life really do exist implies a moral change even in the temperate regions of our mind and earth, and may well explain the decline of the pastoral in the culture of the modern world. The real reason is of course the one mentioned previously: the process of sexual emancipation which Western civilization has been undergoing in the last century or two. Yet when the progress seems to lag, when individuals or groups wish to extend the benefits of the new sexual dispensation to certain neglected spheres of human experience or to certain human groups previously excluded from the privileges of free love, pastoral inspiration reappears once more. So, for instance, when George Sand took upon herself to preach the cause of the sexual emancipation of woman, she chose quite naturally a quasi-pastoral framework to convey her feminist message and to point out her sex's inequality with man even in the field of love. Even Rousseau before her, raised as he was in an age neither chaste nor chastised, and all too easily inclined to give an extreme libertine interpretation to the gospel of the liberty of love, had no recourse but to express in bucolic terms his deep feelings of reaction against some of the social pressures limiting the freedom of love, such as the class prejudices preventing marriage or even liaison between commoner and nobleman.

The pastoral message of *La Nouvelle Héloïse* is that there is no *mésalliance* between two loving souls. Yet both convention and sentiment prevent Saint-Preux and Héloïse from betraying the trust of the noble Wolmar, so that their love survives only in platonic form. This solution implies a failure, and the ending of *La Nouvelle Héloïse* seems to show Rousseau's awareness that the erotic ideal of the pastoral is no less utopian than its economic or political one. As a matter of fact, the economic and political utopia of the pastoral was to be the more easily realized of the two, even if this happened willy-nilly. The Rousseau of the *Contrat social* was a better prophet than the Rousseau of *Héloïse;* this truth may be stated also by saying that Marx has shown himself a better doctor than Freud.

Yet Freud himself has a great place in our story—exactly because he proved that yearnings similar to those expressed by so many poets and artists in pastoral form lie unveiled and repressed in the soul of Everyman. But, expressed or repressed, gratified or not, those yearnings represent only what one might call the normal erotic impulses. There is nothing more antipastoral than so-called decadent literature, not only because it exalts any form of sexual deviation but because the deviation is enjoyed as such, as a violation of the social code or a transgression of the ethical norm: in other words, as a conscious will to sin. The pastoral Eros stops short of perversion; it exalts a kind of love that may be in conflict with the law of society but that is in agreement with the law of nature. Its modern master is Rousseau, not the Marquis de Sade. At any rate, it rejects the obscene and the wicked, especially when man is led to them by a taste for blasphemy and iconoclasm. Thus, even Vergil, in a time when homosexuality was more easily condoned, deals with the theme with such discretion and tact as to describe the shepherd Corydon in a slightly comical vein and to attenuate the scandal of his vice by leaving unrequited his love for a boy. In some of the pastorals of the Counter Reformation there often appear morbid intimations of vicarious sexual pleasures without, however, bridging the gap dividing natural and unnatural love. Even in the Renaissance, the paganism of both the culture and the mores was still so permeated with the ethos of Christianity as to prevent, in spite of the slavish imitation of the ancients, any characterization patterned after Vergil's Corydon.

This means that the pastoral operates at its best when there is some prudery left, when it still partakes of the inhibitions against which it raises its protest or dissent. When the normal restraints are relaxed, the voice of the pastoral is no longer heard. It needs the spur of a new prohibition at the frontier of love to rise again from oblivion and silence. Modern life has pushed that frontier very far, but it has still not reached the strange dark land of homosexual love. In *Corydon* Gide asks society to look with understanding and sympathy on his hero's vice or, better, his plight. But Gide's work is a treatise or a pamphlet, a plea rather than a song. It was his contemporary, Proust, who at least once reevoked in terms of the pastoral imagination the troubled joys of that least innocent and least happy of all loves. I think of the perverted, libertine, and yet idyllic scene in which Albertine sports on the grass with a peasant girl. The languorous cry of one of the two lesbians, "Tu me mets aux anges," seems to partake of the imagery with which the pastoral poets of old suggested some of the joys of love. The two French writers placed their Arcadias in "the cities of the plain": Gide in Sodom and Proust in Gomorrah. This may seem to contradict the statement that pastoral love is a man's world, but it does not, because Proust's transference is understood in another sense: as a disguise in feminine dress for his own homosexual experiences. What gives poignancy to his passion is the desperate jealousy tormenting him, even in his memory, in *Albertine disparue:* and it matters very little that in real life Albertine was a man. Without attempting further indiscretion, we wish to end with this allusion to the love which dares not to tell its name our survey of the erotic casuistics of the pastoral.

3
The
Funeral
Elegy

I

Even in the land of innocence and happiness, blessed by nature's bounty and by an everlasting spring, there lurk evil and ill. Yet the bucolic imagination tends to banish evil without its borders, as if it were a prerogative of the outer world. When forced to admit evil within its Arcadias, it limits its presence to such harmless manifestations as rustic superstitions or love charms. As for ill, it simply pretends it does not exist. Arcadians know of no ailment or illness: among shepherds there is room for artisans and craftsmen, artists and poets, even for priests, but there is no place for doctors, as there is none for lawyers, because their way of life is based, no less than on natural justice, on natural health. Pastoral clans or rustic tribes may sometimes need a wonder-worker; but even then they would better profit by the services of a rainmaker than by those of a medicine man. The only ailment the idyllic imagination avows is the most natural and universal of all illnesses: old age, at which, however, it looks with indulgent contempt, as if it were more of a disgrace than a disease.

Yet even the bucolic mind realizes that nature is not only a provider but also a destroyer, generating from its womb forces hindering life as well as fostering it. Death, the fatal illness of all living beings, can hardly be ignored: thus it is only *sub specie mortis* that pastoral poetry contemplates all the mysterious powers imperiling our frail human frame, which Vergil symbolizes in the image of the snake hidden in the grass (*Ecl.* iii). To most pastoral poets Eros and Thanatos appear to be twins: or, in Freudian terms, they seem to know that the pleasure principle is related to the death principle. Thus, while dealing with the first of these two principles in many different manners, the main ones being the love idyll and the elegy of love, pastoral poetry deals with the second almost exclusively in a single lyrical genre, brought forth for this purpose, the so-called funeral elegy.

The bucolic tradition of classical antiquity, within which this genre was created, has bequeathed to posterity four pastoral poems that may be viewed as funeral elegies: *Thyrsis,* or Theocritus' First Idyll; Bion's *Lament for Adonis; Lament for Bion,* or Moschus' Third Idyll; *Daphnis,* or Vergil's Fifth Eclogue. In the first and last of these poems the elegiac song does not coincide with the whole composition, even though it occupies most of it. In the first the funeral elegy is made to appear as a poem within a poem; it is presented within the framework of a dialogue between two shepherds, in the shape of a quoted song chanted by one of them. This is not fully true in the case of *Daphnis*— there Vergil twice interrupts the dialogue of his two rustics in order to offer two songs, for each singer wishes to celebrate the same deceased friend. This doubling has a special significance, since it involves something more than a mere repetition of motif. As will be suggested later, it represents Vergil's most original contribution to the conventional pattern and traditional inspiration of the funeral elegy. All this notwithstanding, it is clear that Vergil forged the Fifth Eclogue, at least as much as on any other model, on Theocritus' *Thyrsis:* a truth confirmed by his calling the shepherd mourned in his eclogue Daphnis, the name Theocritus gave to the shepherd mourned in his idyll.

Bion's *Lament for Adonis* and Moschus' *Lament for Bion* share the opposite trait: instead of being made to appear as complaints sung by the characters, they are presented as direct utterances of the poets themselves. Yet, except for this, Moschus' *Lament for Bion* belongs with Theocritus' *Thyrsis* and Vergil's *Daphnis*, whereas Bion's *Lament for Adonis* stands apart, as something different and even unique. This distinction is not simply due to the fact that Bion's Adonis is a mythological being whereas Moschus' Bion is a historical one—the pastoral is full of historical and mythological persons who are handled as fictional figures, no less literary than the Daphnis of both Theocritus and Vergil. The real distinction is that Theocritus, Moschus, and Vergil each lament the death of a shepherd whom either author or characters treat as a personal friend sadly lost. Bion, on the contrary, takes his mythological personage both seriously and literally, since he weeps over the death of a god or demigod who in his human life had befriended neither man nor beast, and had loved not a mortal but a goddess. There is reason to believe that Bion's *Lament* was written to be recited in the Adonis festivals, for ritual and religious purposes. Yet there is no need to consider this to realize that the poem transcends the pastoral canon; that it is not really a funeral elegy is made evident by its stance, which is that of love rather than of friendship.

In many a funeral elegy love appears as the very cause that led the lamented shepherd to his death. This is particularly true of Theocritus' idyll, in which Aphrodite appears in person to witness her own triumph, since poor Daphnis is dying of the very passion he had once held in contempt. But even in such cases the ethos of the funeral elegy is that of friendship: its pathos is that of grieving over a friend's death. In contrast, Bion's complaint on Adonis' untimely and violent end is made on Aphrodite's behalf; the pity the poet conveys is directed more to the bereaved mistress than to the dead youth. Nothing proves this more eloquently than the lovely passage in which Aphrodite's sacred island repeats in all its recesses nature's complaint for the goddess who has lost her lover:

... ἁ δὲ Κυθήρα
πάντας ἀνὰ κναμώς, ἀνὰ πᾶν νάπος οἰκτρὸν ἀείδει
'αἰαῖ τὰν Κυθέρειαν, ἀπώλετο καλὸς Ἄδωνις.'
'Αχὼ δ' ἀντεβόασεν 'ἀπώλετο καλὸς Ἄδωνις.'

And Cythera over every foothill, every glen piteously sings:
Alas for Cythera, Adonis fair is dead. And to the cry Echo
responds: *Adonis fair is dead.*

In these lines the second part of the refrain acts as an echo of the
first, so as to imply that the grief for Adonis' death follows only in
the wake of the grief for Aphrodite's loss. That the poem's main
concern is with the pains of a passion which can no longer be assuaged or consoled is confirmed by the successive line, closing the
passage with the rhetorical question: Κύπριδος αἰνὸν ἔρωτα τίς οὐκ
ἔκλαυσεν ἄν αἰαῖ; (Who would not weep over the sorry tale of Cypris'
love?).

The stance of friendship, as distinguished from that of love, is
already present in Theocritus' *Thyrsis*, but with less prominent a display than in any other funeral elegy. The shepherd after whom the
poem takes its title and the unnamed goatherd who at noontime meet
together in the fields are two friendly companions, gently kind to
each other, as shown by their mutual compliments. They behave as
fellow craftsmen, rather than as rivals, in the art of song. Sicilian
as they are, one could say of them "Arcades ambo" (both of them
are Arcadians), in the sense these words take on the lips of Meliboeus, when praising both Corydon and Thyrsis just before their
singing match, in a Vergilian eclogue (vii). And there is no doubt
that when Theocritus' Thyrsis finally accepts the invitation of his
companion to sing for him "The Affliction of Daphnis" (an invitation made more tempting by the promised gift of a richly engraved
cup, which the goatherd describes in detail), both singer and listener
act as if the song were a true story and the lamented Daphnis a real
person, nay, a friend who once had been dear to them both.

Yet one should admit after granting this point that otherwise the
poem differs considerably from what was to become the typical pattern of the funeral elegy. The stance of friendship is but one of its

many attitudes, and by itself it fails to determine the whole. Thyrsis' song, beginning with a refrain that is an appeal to the Muses of pastoral poetry: Ἄρχετε βουκολικᾶς Μοῖσαι φίλαι ἄρχετ' ἀοιδᾶς (Raise, O dear Muses, raise a country song), evokes in a detailed sequence all that happened in the hour of Daphnis' death. Except for Pan, still lingering in Arcadia's hills, and the nymphs, still haunting the dales of Greece: πᾷ ποκ' ἄρ' ἦσθ', ὄκα Δάφνις ἐτάκετο, πᾷ ποκα Νύμφαι; (Where were you, nymphs, when Daphnis pined away? Where were you, nymphs?) all his human and divine friends came to the Sicilian fields where the poor youth was lying. Hermes and Priapus mingled with his fellow herdsmen and asked Daphnis what was ailing him. The dying man refused to answer such questions, but when Aphrodite came and gently chided him for having once mocked the passion now causing his ruin, he replied to the goddess with angry wrath. It was thus made clear what everybody suspected: Daphnis was willfully dying, refusing to heal the wounds of love in his heart. After venting his spleen on Aphrodite, Daphnis uttered his last wish, or rather curse: that after his death all things would go askew, so that figs would grow on pine trees and owls' screeches would conquer nightingales' trills.

The joining of the two themes of love's despair and love's spite indicates that the inspiration of Thyrsis' song is partly comic. The frequence of direct speech, the dramatic structure of the scene reevoked in song, the vividness of the opening and closing dialogues: all this supports the hypothesis that the poem was written not as a lyrical composition but as a mime. There is no doubt that what we witness in the central scene is not a mortal agon, but the tragicomedy of love; and it is worth remarking that when the goatherd invites Thyrsis to sing of Daphnis, he cites the song's subject or title as being Daphnis' "affliction" rather than his "death." This explains why, though imitated in many points by Vergil and other pastoral poets, Theocritus' *Thyrsis* cannot be considered as the original archetype or universal model of the funeral elegy as such.

II

The genuine archetype or model of the funeral elegy should rather be seen in Moschus' Third Idyll, better known as the *Lament for Bion*, in which the stance of friendship is dominant and the mood is that of the elegiac, if not tragic, pathos of death. What makes this poem particularly moving is that here the funeral elegy is not a part but the whole; that the lament is a direct, rather than quoted, pastoral song; and finally that the character whose death is lamented, even though fully transfigured by the poet's imagination, is not a literary creation but a real person. Yet it is not only for all these reasons, cogent as they are, that Moschus' *Lament* was destined to become such an admired and influential model: it is also for the consummate artistry and the dazzling beauty of the work. The great Italian poet Leopardi, who penned a lovely translation of this poem, did not hesitate to call it "un capo d'opera nel genere lugubre pastorale" (a masterpiece in the funeral-pastoral genre),[1] and we may certainly say that in the whole history of the form only Milton's *Lycidas* deserves comparison with it.

Moschus does not merely emphasize that the man of whose death he complains had been a dear friend; he emphasizes equally that he had been a fellow poet—nay, his teacher, as well as the great master of pastoral poetry or, as Moschus says, of "Dorian song." This reference to the poetic or musical calling as being the highest mark of distinction of the dead person will become one of the most important traits of the funeral elegy. Such a trait was not wholly new: Theocritis had not failed to mention that Daphnis was a man dear to the Muses as well as to the nymphs. Even more significantly he had made Daphnis turn, just before dying, to the absent Pan, wishing to hand his own pipe not to a human rival but to the patron god of the shepherds and of pastoral song.[2]

Yet, even though he makes far more of Bion's poetic calling than Theocritus does of Daphnis', Moschus refuses to handle one of the themes that seem to be required by the writing of a poet's epitaph in Hellenistic as well as humanistic terms. What indeed makes Moschus' poem so moving is the conspicuous absence of a motif which in similar circumstances no Alexandrian or Renaissance author would fail to develop. Such a motif is the belief in the survival of Bion as a poet if not as a man: in brief, his apotheosis in the temple of memory, his deification in the pantheon of the mind. Moschus does not seek a consolation of this kind, as if he were aware that the afterlife of fame is but illusion and deceit. The immortality of one's name is immortality only in name, and one modern poet is right when depicting historical glory in these terms:

> Maigre immortalité noire et dorée,
> Consolatrice affreusement laurée.[3]

Lean immortality, golden and black, O you awfully laureled consoler.

Moschus' indifference to poetic renown is not denied by his parallel of Bion with Homer or by the list of cities that will mourn him, as they mourned the greatest of all poets: the parallel and the list merely tend to emphasize that the world of man will grieve over Bion's death no less than the world of nature. There is no doubt that for Moschus a crown of laurel is no compensation for Bion's death, nor a consolation to his friends for their loss.[4] And this explains why, although knowing that he will himself give new luster to the pastoral genre in which Bion excelled, Moschus still claims that "Dorian song" is dead with his master.[5]

It has already been hinted that while being utterly different in inspiration, Moschus' *Lament for Bion* is still shaped after Theocritus' *Thyrsis*. Such a parallelism, which also implies a divergence, is particularly apparent in the relation between the two poems' refrains. Whereas Moschus' is rigidly fixed, Theocritus' refrain is not uniform and appears in three slight variations of the initial model: "Raise, O dear Muses, raise a country song." There is no doubt that this line is the direct precedent of Moschus' ἄρχετε Σικελικαὶ τῶ πένθεος ἄρχετε Μοῖσαι (Raise, O Sicilian Muses, raise the dirge). The change is slight, yet its significance is very great. Theocritus' refrain defines generically the song he introduces as being a pastoral one but fails to indicate whether it is going to be merry or sad. Moschus' refrain instead informs us once and for all that the poem of which it is a part is specifically a funeral lament.

Since Moschus' refrain appears for the first time after the poem's prelude, from which we already know that the lamented man was a poet ("the beautiful musician is dead"), then this call to the Muses, far from being a conventional request for their help, is a moving appeal for their participation in the mourning of all things and beings over Bion's death. Such things and beings are more numerous and varied than in the case of Theocritus' Daphnis, who was pitied only by wild and domestic animals. It is no less true that Daphnis' death was attended by men and gods: yet it seems that they came not to mourn but to watch, the deities as inquirers and the shepherds as onlookers. This cannot be said of all the creatures and elements that Moschus summons to share his sorrow: the dales, ponds, rivers, and woods of the Sicilian landscape; then plants, flowers, and birds. These are followed by the domestic animals that Bion the herdsman had tended, cows and sheep. After them such nature gods as fauns and nymphs join the lay. At the end, as if to give an eloquent sign of their mute sorrow, sheep cease to give milk, trees to bear fruit. The literary if not the poetic climax of the *Lament* is the long mythological passage in which Moschus lists all the human creatures once subjected to an animal or vegetable metamorphosis, only to claim that their wailings cannot diminish the present universal plaint over Bion's death.

This death seems to have come not from natural causes but from enemy hands. By alluding, as he does toward the end, to the poison which supposedly cut short his friend's life, Moschus introduces for the first time in the funeral elegy the "dead ere his prime" motif, or the theme of the cruel, violent, or untimely end. Yet the poet does not insist on this fact. He curses, without mentioning their names, the guilty ones, while glossing over, so to speak, the crime itself. The only evil that concerns him is death itself, which he views as our common destiny, whether or not it has been hastened by human hands. There is no unnatural death, since the end of life is always due to natural causes; this is why the sorrow for Bion's passing is a sorrow for the mortality of all men. This is shown in the passage in which Moschus contrasts our destiny with that of the herbs in a garden: they fade at the end of a year to reflower at the beginning of the next, but we, unlike them, never awaken from the sleep of death. Such a sleep, as Socrates says in the *Apologia*, is not only without awakening but also without dreams. Yet even the pagan imagination seeks to project beyond that sleep the dream of a life after death. Such a vision, however, being not a religious but a poetic illusion, is denied the assent of hope and the sanction of belief. Whereas the

Christian imagination, which bases its vision of the soul's immortality on faith and revelation, glorifies that immortality as a triumph over both life and death, as an eternal existence transcending in splendor or grandeur the joys and pains of earth, the pagan imagination depicts the afterlife as a far paler reflection, a far lesser replica, of our existence in this world. Hence pagan Hades (within which it matters little whether one dwells in an Elysium-Paradise or in an Erebus-Hell) is but a shadowy and degraded image of human life and of the natural world. There the dead seemingly survive, but as larvae of their previous selves. It is in full accordance with these contrasting sets of images that Moschus represents death both as an absolute denial of life and as its debasement to a lower level of being. This is why he first conveys the sense of Bion's death by emphasizing his absence, by complaining that he is no longer with us, that he can never do again what he once used to do for the delight of himself and all his human and nonhuman friends:

κεῖνος ὁ ταῖς ἀγέλαισιν ἐράσ μιος οὐκέτι μέλπει,
οὐκέτ' ἐρημαίαισιν ὑπὸ δρυσὶν ἥμενος ᾄδει.

Alas, the man who dear was to the herds sings no more in their midst; he sits no more, he sings no more under the lonely oaks.

Yet immediately after this the poet suggests the very opposite, imagining that his friend is now doing as an underworld ghost, in a mood of gentle sadness, what he had been doing so joyfully on earth: ἀλλὰ παρὰ Πλουτῆϊ μέλος Ληθαῖον ἀείδει (but sings in Pluto's house the song of Lethe). Which means that even when we sing the song of memory for them, the dead themselves can only sing the song of their own oblivion.

III

Vergil's *Daphnis* opens, like Theocritus' *Thyrsis*, with a lively scene. Two shepherds meet and Menalcas, who is the elder, suggests that they sit together to sing and play under the elms. The younger, who is named Mopsus, formally accepts the suggestion as if it were a command; yet he gently hints that a nearby cave might be a better resting place than the one his senior has proposed. While walking there together, Menalcas, thinking to flatter Mopsus, states that in all the region Amyntas is the only singer who might compete with him: a compliment his companion resents, since he believes he has no rivals worth the name in their land. As soon as they reach the cave, Mopsus begins his song and Menalcas makes handsome amend for his tactless remark, praising Mopsus to the skies for his art. He calls him a divine poet; describes in three lovely lines the delight produced by the charming song; and declares to the youth that from now on he will be the worthy successor of his great master: "Fortunate puer, tu nunc eris alter ab illo" (Happy lad: from now on you are his peer).

Mopsus had been the disciple of Daphnis, the very man whose death he has just sung. It is from Menalcas' comments, rather than from Mopsus' song, that we learn that the dead man had been a poet, like Theocritus' Daphnis or Moschus' Bion. It is again from Menalcas, from what he says when announcing his own song, that we learn that his and Mopsus' lays on Daphnis are, as in Theocritus' and Moschus' funeral elegies, the complaints of friends for a friend. Menalcas makes more humanly moving this allusion to the ties of friendship by emphasizing not his own and Mopsus' affection for Daphnis, but Daphnis' affection for them—not only for his disciple but for Menalcas himself "Amavit nos quoque Daphnis" (Daphnis did love me as well).

Mopsus' song, the first of the two, opens by evoking the nymphs who weep, sharing the despair of Daphnis' mother, who embraces the body of her son. She calls cruel the gods and the stars, blaming them for Daphnis' death, called cruel by the singer himself. Yet his main intent is to mourn, or rather to describe the mournful effects of Daphnis' passing on nature and all of its creatures: no herdsman brings his cattle to drink; wild beasts howl from afar; Pales and Apollo desert the fields. The singer concludes by conveying to his fellow shepherds Daphnis' last request: that they raise him a mound among strewn leaves and shaded springs, and carve this epitaph on its top:

> Daphnis ego in silvis, hinc usque ad sidera notus,
> formosi pecoris custos, formosior ipse.

Daphnis am I among these woods, from here up to the stars renowned, and even fairer than my fair shepherd's flock.

It is now the turn of Menalcas, who will sing of Daphnis' triumph, not of his death. This triumph is the dead man's elevation to the heavens, which Menalcas announces beforehand as if it were the work of his song: "Daphnimque tuum tollemus ad astra" (And we will raise your Daphnis to the stars). Now we see why the introduction of a second song must be viewed as Vergil's unique contribution to the structure and ethos of the funeral elegy: this second song acts as if it were a palinode of the first, since it conveys the jubilation of the pastoral world for the elevation of one of its own to the rank of a tutelar deity. By setting a song of rejoicing beside a song of grieving Vergil follows the pattern of the Adonis festivals, or of the joint ritual celebration of the death and resurrection of a vegetarian god.[6] But Daphnis had been born and had died a man: what we witness is his apotheosis, not his rebirth, a novelty so unique within the pastoral canon as to induce many interpreters to believe that it was determined by an exceptional historical accident. For most of them this accident must have been the recent murder of Caesar, which, like Daphnis', had certainly been a cruel death. There is some external and internal evidence to support the hypothesis that the poem should be read as an allegory, veiling under the apotheosis of Daphnis the tender of sheep the apotheosis of Caesar the shepherd of men. The argument may even be strengthened by a literary parallel: by the fact that Vergil broke pastoral precedents in another celebrated eclogue, his Fourth. In a sense, both the Fifth and the Fourth might be viewed as topical or occasional poems, the occasion being in the case of the Fourth the expected birth of a noble child which the poet takes as a pretext for projecting the vision of the Golden Age from a prehistorical past into a future to be immediately engendered by the historical present. Yet, even if we could find political as well as literary analogies between the obvious allegory of the Fourth Eclogue and the not so obvious one of the Fifth, it is evident that the poetry of the latter does not lie in its allegorical spirit, but in the letter of its pastoral vision, based on the peculiar *pietas* of a natural religion, of a rustic cult.

Menalcas begins his song by evoking the radiant Daphnis as he stands on the threshhold of heaven, watching the stars and clouds below. Down on earth Pan, the Dryads, and the shepherds are rejoicing for his apotheosis, which reconciles hunters and hunted, wolves and sheep.[7] This is how it should be, because Daphnis stands for peace: a peace to be understood not as the wise rule of a stable civil order, but as an inner and outer serenity, as that secure and careless leisure which only Mother Nature can give. What Menalcas says of Daphnis in such a context—"Amat bonus otia Daphnis" (for the good Daphnis loves idling in peace)—could hardly be meant literally for the great leader who had turned Rome into an empire. The joy of the creatures at Daphnis' apotheosis is shared by the landscape, and dumb nature breaks into speech to avow that Daphnis is now a divine being. The mountains, the rocks, and the groves proclaim to the singer, "Deus, deus ille, Menalca!" (He is a god, Menalcas, a god).

The rest of the poem takes the form of a prayer that the singer addresses to Daphnis on behalf of all who once were his friends and are now his faithful. The prayer opens with a propitiation, "Sis bonus o felixque tuis!" (Be generous and propitious to thine own), and unfolds with the promise that the shepherds will render the new god the tributes of his cult. They will raise to Daphnis two altars, as to Apollo; they will offer him libations of milk, oil, and wine; they will celebrate his festivals twice a year, in winter and summer, with plenty of drinking and merrymaking. "Haec tibi semper erunt" (These rites will be forever yours), says Menalcas, and concludes by assuring Daphnis that his fame and name will endure. At the end of the song, Mopsus praises his friend, and the poem ends with an exchange of gifts. The young singer is rewarded with the pipe of Menalcas, while the latter gets a handsome shepherd's crook, which suits the older man very well.

The Fifth Eclogue cannot be fully understood without contrasting and comparing its two funeral songs. The first appears to be a genuine dirge, yet there flows less grief than in Moschus' Lament. The formal praise of the dead plays in Daphnis a role at least as important as mourning itself. It is indeed Mopsus who first pays tribute to the many virtues of the deceased, attributing to him the merit of having taught his companions how to celebrate the rites of the Dionysian cult. As for Menalcas, the tone of his song is consistently encomiastic; it is in a more sustained and substantial strain that he repeats or restates what Mopsus has already declared in his apostrophe to Daphnis: "Tu decus omne tuis" (You alone give ornament to your people). Thus, if we take the two songs together, we must conclude that the mode of the dirge yields to the mode of the panegyric;[8] and this takes the sting out of the grief for Daphnis' death. By turning the panegyric into a literal apotheosis, Vergil also turns Menalcas' song from a lament into a hymn. The term is apt, since that song is to pastoral poetry what the so-called Homeric Hymns[9] are to the epic tradition. The difference is that Vergil's Menalcas celebrates not an old and major deity but a new and minor god, whom only shepherds may now call their own.

It is evident that the Fifth Eclogue is open to varying interpretation, according to whether we identify the funeral elegy it contains with one of its two songs or with both of them. If we believe that in *Daphnis* the evocation of the sense of human mortality rests on the *concordia discors* of Mopsus' dirge and Menalcas' apotheosis, then we must conclude that Vergil's poem represents the pagan vision of death in its most serene, exalted, and spiritual mood. This would certainly explain the appeal which the Fifth Eclogue held for all the later poets who tried to merge into a single strain the contrasting accords of the pastoral and of the Christian conception of death. The foremost of these poets will be John Milton, who in his celebrated funeral elegy plays at once the roles of Mopsus and Menalcas, first weeping over the death of his Lycidas and then rejoicing at his ascent among the blessed, thus joining together the dirge and the apotheosis in the same song.

IV

The reference just made to Milton's *Lycidas* suggests that the apotheosis introduced by Vergil was bound to appeal more to his Christian than to his pagan imitators; but this novelty would not by itself break the norm of the classical funeral elegy. That norm may be summed up with the rule that of its components the one which is both necessary and sufficient is the dirge, and the dirge alone. If this is true, then there is no room within the canon of the funeral elegy for *Gallus*, Vergil's Tenth Eclogue, despite the fact that, even more than the Fifth, it is faithfully patterned after the scene of Daphnis'

death in Theocritus' First Idyll. But in the Tenth Eclogue there is no
real dirge or, rather, the dirge is unreal: Gallus seems about to die,
like Daphnis, and for the same cause, but he survives in the end. The
main reason for this change of ending is undoubtedly an external and
objective one. As stated in the opening lines, the only ones directly
alluding to the theme of friendship, Vergil has composed this poem
for his fellow poet Gallus, to be read by him and by his lovely and
flighty mistress, Lycoris. Nothing of what Gallus wrote is left—a
great loss for posterity, since Vergil is but one of the many ancient
authors holding Gallus' work in high esteem. Yet, at the time of the
composition of this poem, which is the last of the *Eclogues*, Gallus
was already famous for the elegies evoking his love for the woman he
called Lycoris. Political and military ambition, however, had already
been tempting him away from the pursuit of a literary career; he was
soon to seek garlands of palm and oak, or the rewards of civic virtue
and martial valor, rather than the crown of laurel, the prize of poetic
merit.[10]

It is evident then that Gallus could die only metaphorically in the
eclogue dedicated to him. Yet in giving a different ending to a scene
almost identical to Theocritus' mime, Vergil was certainly also guided
by more subjective considerations, thus serving an inner design or
another poetic purpose. By so doing he showed a profound understanding of its model, which is far less mournful than any other funeral elegy, since it gives expression to the pains of both death and
love. The parallelism of the general situation and of the specific details could not be more striking. So, for instance, like Theocritus or,
rather, like Thyrsis, Vergil begins by noticing that, whereas the
nymphs are missing, all other creatures, beasts, and plants, men and
gods, are attending Gallus' apparent agony. Such gods as Apollo and
Pan, as well as humble shepherds, address him, as in Daphnis' case,
with the usual question: " 'Unde amor iste' rogant 'tibi?' " ("Whence
does it come," they ask, "this love of yours?") By imitating the situation while reversing the outcome, Vergil proves that his model is virtually an elegy of love within the framework of an elegy of death:
and his imitation actually turns the latter into the former.[11] Yet the
main reason that makes Vergil's Tenth Eclogue worthy of comment

in the present context is that just before uttering his regret for never having led the life of a shepherd:

> Atque utinam ex vobis unus vestrique fuissem
> aut custos gregis aut maturae vinitor uvae

Would to God that I had been one among you, tending your ripened grapes and your flocks

Gallus projects his own death from today to a distant tomorrow, thus depriving the idea of mortality of both pathos and self-pity.[12] This is important precisely because the novelty of this eclogue lies in the fact that the death the speaker evokes is not a friend's but his own. What Gallus conveys in his apostrophe to those watching his present sufferings is but a subjective premonition of death:

> ... O mihi tum quam molliter ossa quiescant,
> vestra meos olim si fistula dicat amores

And how my bones may then sweetly repose if once more your pipes will sing of my love.

In brief, whereas in all genuine funeral elegies death is present, so to speak, in the dimension of the past, here it is present in the dimension of the future. By placing the Tenth Eclogue beside the Fifth, or beside Moschus' *Lament*, we realize that even in them there is a hidden concern for the death of the mourner, as well as for the death of the mourned one. The funeral elegy laments mortality not only in individual or personal terms but also in subjective ones. By evoking death as a distant shadow rather than as a threatening presence, Gallus' words help us to understand the real function of the pagan funeral elegy, which is to sublimate one's coming death through compassion for the recent death of a dear one. This compassion is made sweeter by the dream that the dead will rest in peace in the bosom of nature, and survive for a while in the hearts of those who loved them. This explains why the pastoral of death must also be, as most frequently it is, a pastoral of friendship: it is only by grieving over a dead friend that a bucolic poet may safely hint that the death principle rules both world and self.

V

Such is the typical pastoral version of the pagan conception of death. Very few of the poets and artists who were genuinely Christian in their inspiration were able to share this view of human mortality; the most they could do was to accept it merely as a first and passing phase in the sorrow of a bereaved soul. On the other hand, most modern pastoral writers, hardly Christian in temper, have been tending to turn to the pagan, or simply all too human, view in their contemplation of death. Even so they may look in two slightly different moods at the most inexorable of all the necessities of the human condition: either broodingly or musingly, with a resigned but poignant sadness, or with so quiet a melancholy as to seem serene. This means that their inspiration respectively resembles that of Moschus in the Third Idyll and that of Vergil in the Fifth Eclogue. In the second case, they choose to follow primarily the example set by the first of the two songs, since their view of the funeral elegy conforms better to Mopsus' dirge than to Menalcas' apotheosis. This is another way of saying that for them Vergil's *Daphnis* is a more suitable model than Moschus' *Bion*.

The passage that most strikes all the readers of Moschus is the one which contrasts the world of the living, forever deserted by Bion and no longer reechoing his merry songs, with the world of the dead, where the ghost of the dead poet sings sad tunes to the nether gods. In that passage Moschus conveys the sense of death through the negative image of absence, since Bion's survival in the underworld is but a shadow of the mind, cast by the fear of nonbeing. But in Vergil's poem there are a few lines, just at the end of Mopsus' dirge, in which the dead man speaks in the first person to hint the very opposite or to suggest his own spiritual survival in the forests that once were his abode: "Daphnis ego in silvis." One should not forget that the silent voice speaking here is not that of Daphnis but of the friends who will engrave those words as an epitaph on his grave, so as to claim his enduring presence in both nature and their hearts. This lovely poetic figure, with its implied psychological turn (which is to transfer to the dead man the task of proclaiming his survival in the loving memory of his friends), seems to sum up, fully and concisely, the ethos and pathos of the classical funeral elegy.[13]

This is the reason that Vergil's *Daphnis* reminds us of Poussin's painting *Et in Arcadia ego*.[14] Its affinity with the poem is made more evident by the use of an epitaph wherein a dead man, a shepherd who remains nameless, also speaks on his own behalf. The painting shows mournful shepherds gathered around a tomb inscribed *Et in Arcadia ego*. The words, which are obviously those of the deceased, have been interpreted: "I too lived once in Arcadia." But in an earlier painting by Guercino,[15] the same inscription appears on a sepulchre covered by a skull, as if the words were uttered by death itself: "Even in Arcadia am I." As many people guessed, and as Erwin Panofsky fully showed,[16] this is the correct meaning of the words. Yet the similarity between the Vergilian epitaph and the one Poussin made his own is so great that there are reasons to believe that *Et in Arcadia ego* was originally coined as a deliberate imitation of *Daphnis ego in silvis*. It now seems probable that the caption was originally fashioned by a high Roman prelate, who may also have suggested or commissioned Guercino's painting by the same title;[17] this would tend to prove that the famous motto had been indeed created after the pattern of Vergil's epitaph, but to affirm a contrary view. Therefore, rather than as a new version of *Daphnis ego in silvis*, *Et in Arcadia ego* would have been meant as its palinode, an utter denial of the pagan and pastoral conception of death. Yet, if Poussin interpreted the motto in the way he did, it was not only because of the aesthetic and sentimental demands of his classical outlook, but also because of the attraction he felt for the pastoral vision, as expressed in both poetry and painting. Panofsky suggests that the painter was familiar with the pictorial device of the "speaking tomb," and that he was well acquainted with the *Arcadia* of Sannazaro, in which pastoral graves with suitable inscriptions abound.

In any case, no bucolic grave or epitaph has impressed the modern idyllic imagination as much as *Et in Arcadia ego*, and it is quite significant that even when it was read out of context that motto was almost universally construed to mean what it signifies in Poussin's painting. Many who took the motto in isolation, and misread it accordingly, tended even to forget that in the two paintings in which they first appeared those words had served as two different epitaphs. In brief, the motto was usually deprived of its original reference and connotation, which were respectively the image of the tomb and the idea of death. In such cases the celebrated and often misquoted phrase was used to suggest that the speaking "I" was not someone who had lived and died in Arcadia, but someone still living who simply had once stayed or visited there. The peculiar function of this particular misinterpretation was to reassert the view that the pastoral experience is a necessary but passing experience in human life: a time of rest or, to reemploy terms that have already done good service elsewhere, a "pause" or an "oasis" that restores the human spirit, wearied by the fever of living. Goethe employed the motto in a different sense when he placed it at the head of his *Italienische Reise*, thus suggesting that its author had visited another sacred and ideal land, Italy, or the Arcadia of beauty and art, rather than of innocence and happiness or of friendship and love. Even such metaphorical and willful misuses are eloquent proof not only of the popularity of the motto, but also of the survival of the bucolic ideal in the eighteenth century, during the very age that by affirming the primacy of the critical spirit was preparing its ultimate death.

Yet it is evident that the most poetic and significant of all these misreadings is Poussin's, the earliest one, precisely because it preserves its connection with the idea of mortality while destroying the link of that idea with the Christian view. In Guercino's painting we witness a baroque version of the medieval triumph of death. Its message is that death triumphs even in Arcadia, the illusory land of innocence and happiness, of leisure and sport: and that its triumph is as merciless as it is inexorable. But in Poussin's we witness instead a modern version of the classical belief that the pathos of death is assuaged by the ethos of friendship, or at least of human fellowship.[18] What counts even more is that in his painting Poussin severs the ties binding the funeral elegy of antiquity and the Renaissance elegy of love.[19] Yet, like Vergil in the Tenth Eclogue, Poussin expresses the pathos of death also in subjective terms: the survivors surrounding the grave contemplate their own mortality through the revelation of the fraternity of the grave.

In brief, whereas Guercino's painting is a denial, Poussin's is a reaffirmation of the pastoral ideal. If and when understood in this way the four words *Et in Arcadia ego* seem indeed to capture in lapidary style the dominant spirit of the pagan or, at least, of the classical funeral elegy. Such an elegy accepts death as a law of nature, over which it sheds the regrets of a private and personal mourning, rather than the laments of a cosmic or metaphysical grief. Its function is to express our awareness that even in Arcadia death stalks us, while soothing the wound which that truth leaves in all human souls with the balm of a "melodious tear."

4
Milton's
Lycidas

In the brief prose statement that follows
the title for the sake of relating the sad
event dictating the poem, Milton calls *Lycidas* a monody.[1] The use of this term may
imply, as will be shown later, something
more specific than the poet's awareness
that his composition is a single, direct, and
whole utterance,[2] like Moschus' *Lament*,
and unlike Vergil's *Daphnis*, with its double song within a dialogue frame. The first
section acts as a prelude, and the opening
lines take the form of an apostrophe to the
plants the singer intends to pluck by writing the poem. This ideal gesture prefigures
the poetic act he is about to perform as
well as its purpose. The first three lines are
an elaborate rephrasing of the simple line
by which Corydon addresses two of the
same plants in Vergil's Second Eclogue:

"Et vos, o lauri, carpam et te, proxima myrte" (I will pluck also you, laurels, and you, myrtles that lie nearby). Yet, whereas the plants that Corydon wants to pluck are real and literal,[3] those to which the author or singer of *Lycidas* turns with the same apparent intent are but symbols or figures. Milton's laurels and myrtles stand respectively for poetry and death: more precisely, for the glory that poetry seeks and for the mourning that death requires. To these two plants Milton adds on his own account a third one, the ivy, which as an evergreen stands for fidelity and loyalty: hence its negative attribute, "never sere," which, like the natural mournful color of the myrtles, as suggested by their epithet "brown," is just as suitable from the botanical as from the emblematical standpoint.

By such a threefold symbolic vehicle the poet first announces that his poem is, as it should be, both a funeral elegy and a pastoral of friendship; and then he implies, deviating in this from the pastoral norm, that by singing the death of his friend he will serve the demands of the mind, longing for fame, as well as those of his grieving heart. Let us not forget, however, that the plant the poet has chosen to call "never sere" is not the laurel of fame but the ivy of friendship. Nor should we fail to notice that in order to prove that the desire for glory is but the lesser of his motivations, the poet hastens to state that, had not his friend suddenly died, he would have postponed writing eclogues to better times, and to more mature years. Hence the significant declaration that the actual poem is as *immature* as the death forcing its dictation had been *premature*. His friend Edward King had indeed just died in the flower of his age: and the poet defines this event, with an oxymoron, as the "sad occasion dear" compelling him to write before his powers are ready. The paradox suggested here is that of the timely writing, upon a premature death, of an immature poem. This is what Milton means when, by rephrasing Vergil's rhetorical question, "Neget quis carmina Gallo?" (Who would deny songs to Gallus; *Ecl.* x), he states that no one could refuse to pay the tribute of musical song to someone who, like Moschus' Bion and the Daphnis of both Theocritius and Vergil, had been a poet himself.[4] It would not be fair to deny to Lycidas' body, still tossed about by the waves of his shipwreck, the consolation of friendly mourning, or, as the poet says with a phrase that reads like a concise definition of the very end of the funeral elegy, "the meed of some melodious tear." The complexity, even the intricacy, of all the motifs woven together in the prelude is indeed striking, as proved by the reading of the whole opening section:[5]

> Yet once more, O ye laurels, and once more,
> Ye myrtles brown, with ivy never sere,
> I come to pluck your berries harsh and crude,
> And with forced fingers rude
> Shatter your leaves before the mellowing year.
> Bitter constraint and sad occasion dear
> Compels me to disturb your season due;
> For Lycidas is dead, dead ere his prime,
> Young Lycidas, and hath not left his peer.
> Who would not sing for Lycidas? he knew
> Himself to sing, and build the lofty rhyme.
> He must not float upon his watery bier
> Unwept, and welter to the parching wind,
> Without the meed of some melodious tear.

What makes this prelude deeply moving is the climactic announcement of Lycidas' death, with the triple emphasis on death itself *(dead . . . dead);* on its untimeliness *(ere his prime . . . young Lycidas);* and on the rare qualities of the dead man as a poet *(hath not left his peer . . . he knew himself to sing, and build the lofty rhyme).* Yet with the dual purpose of relaxing the tension and of imitating suitable literary precedents, the poet changes tone and mood, and turns the second section into an invocation to the muses. The poet's request for their help is the more fitting in view of the immaturity he has just avowed; yet, with a highly original turn, after alluding to the hesitation he had felt for a moment before writing the poem required by that "sad occasion," he takes his decision to do so as a guarantee that, should he himself suddenly die, a fellow poet would not deny a similar tribute to him. This means that, as many other pastoral poets had done before, Milton projects the vision of his death, through and beyond the commemoration of the recent passing of a shepherd who had been his friend. This proves again that the funeral elegy both hides and reveals a subjective concern with death, which Milton, like most of his predecessors, conveys with the greatest discretion in a mood of serene melancholy, with self-compassion but without self-commiseration. The lines in which he does this are among the loveliest of the poem:

> So may some gentle Muse
> With lucky words favour my destined urn,
> And as he passes turn,
> And bid fair peace be to my sable shroud!

Such a vision can be but a fleeting one, and this is why the following lines, closing the second section, are a forceful restatement of the dominant theme, which is the bond of personal as well as of pastoral fellowship:

> For we were nursed upon the self-same hill,
> Fed the same flock, by fountain, shade, and rill.

The third section is the work of memory: or a remembrance of the life the two friends used to live together. What the poem recollects is a typical day, with its common tasks and customary activities. Such activities would include little labor (it is no work for two shepherds to drive and pasture from morn to night their flocks in the fields), but plenty of leisure, a leisure primarily filled with music and song. Whereas the present tune of the survivor is a song of mourning, those they once used to sing together were tunes of mirth, and this is why they would attract, and for the same purpose, some of the same creatures which Silenus' chant attracts in Vergil's Sixth Eclogue: "Tum vero in numerum Faunosque feras videres/ludere" (You might indeed have seen fauns and wild beasts dance to its cadence).

It is perhaps significant that in the case of Lycidas and his friend such creatures included satyrs, who differ but little from fauns, but failed to include wild beasts. Since the absence of the latter may well reveal the intention of making this scene more human and less pagan, we may find even more significant the poet's refusal to do what most

other pastoral poets would have certainly done in his stead: to replace the missing wild beasts with nymphs. That the poet's aim was
to assuage the mythological and naturistic quality by which Vergil
had marked the original scene is proved by the fact that in the end
the "rural ditties" and the "oaten flute" of Lycidas and his friend
would attract another human being, an older shepherd, seemingly
hiding under the bucolic name attributed to him, a beloved Cambridge
teacher who had probably encouraged the first literary efforts of both
Milton and King:

> Meanwhile the rural ditties were not mute,
> Tempered to th' oaten flute;
> Rough Satyrs danced, and Fauns with cloven heel
> From the glad sound would not be absent long;
> And old Damoetas loved to hear our song.

The fourth section contrasts the joyful past with the melancholy
present: the "glad sound" of an earlier time becomes now a sad one.
The "oaten flute" of the poet is now playing other tunes: not an idyll
of friendship but an elegy of death. The complaint over Lycidas unfolds as an emphatic comment upon his everlasting absence, an absence regretted, according to the usual pattern of the funeral elegy,
even more than by his fellow men, by Mother Nature and all her
creatures, especially the vegetal ones:

> But, oh! the heavy change, now thou art gone,
> Now thou art gone, and never must return!
> Thee, Shepherd, thee the woods, and desert caves,
> With wild thyme and the gadding vine o'ergrown,
> And all their echoes, mourn.

As in Moschus' *Lament for Bion*, these and other plants miss Lycidas
not only as a man but as a poet: hence the image of the willows
and hazels no longer waving their branches to the sound of his
song. His human friends miss Lycidas for this reason as well, as the
poet states in the long, threefold simile comparing what his death

means to his peers to the death frost brings to all flowers, or to the damage that two conquering worms make to the health of calf and lamb, or to the life of a rose. The phrase closing this simile is also the line sealing the section: "Such, Lycidas, thy loss to shepherd's ear."

Milton opens the fifth section with the questioning appeal which both Theocritus in his *Thyrsis* and Vergil in his *Daphnis* address to the absent nymphs. As in Vergil's case, Milton's are more properly Naiads, or water nymphs, and this makes even more paradoxical their absence at the moment of Lycidas' death, since that death occurred in the liquid element. In the prose statement preceding the poem, the poet has already informed the reader that Edward King lost his life in a shipwreck; and in the prelude he alludes to Lycidas' "watery bier." But it is only now that he begins to deal in earnest with his friend's "death by water." Even here, however, Milton fails to touch one of the commonplaces of pastoral poetry: the device whereby the secure and happy existence of the land dweller is praised through an invidious comparison with the precarious way of life of the seafarer, whether he crosses the waters as a sailor, a merchant, or a traveler.

Nonetheless, the traditional motif of the nymphs' absence from the scene of death offers many other opportunities to the poet: foremost among them, the nymphs themselves can be absolved of all blame. One can hardly expect that they would abide in such a northern and barbaric site as the Irish Seas; or that they would sport near "the remorseless deep" in which Lycidas drowned:

> For neither were ye playing on the steep,
> Where your old bards, the famous Druids, lie.

Yet in this passage the poet uses that highly effective rhetorical figure, preterition, evoking against his apparent intention the almost romantic seascape where Lycidas lost his life. That the nymphs cannot be blamed for his death is made clear by the rhetorical question: "Had ye been there, . . . for what could that have done?" to which the poet replies that they could have done nothing, just as the great-

est of all Muses, Calliope, could do nothing to save her son when the
Baccantes tore his body to pieces and threw his remains into the river
that was to carry them to the Aegean Sea, or, in Milton's words:
"Down the swift Hebrus to the Lesbian shore."

The pertinence of this mythological allusion lies in the implication
that Lycidas was in life and death another Orpheus; and this explains
why in the following section the author refers to Lycidas' poetic
calling, wondering whether all the time and labor that in his too short
life he spent on that calling had been worthwhile. Quite properly and
conventionally, Milton identifies the poetic vocation with the pastoral
state; yet, in a manner that may seem both untraditional and unsuitable, he describes the pursuits of that vocation in terms of constant, rigorous, and painful exertion, rather than of careless ease and
amusing leisure:

> Alas! what boots it with incessant care
> To tend the homely, slighted, shepherd's trade,
> And strictly meditate the thankless Muse?

Such a muse hardly looks pastoral, precisely because she does not
seem to offer the normal reward of bucolic poetry, which is the fleeting joy of singing for the song's sake. If Milton calls the muse thankless, it is because the strenuous effort of poetic creation all too often
fails to earn the only prize worth the price. It is for this reason that
the poet wonders whether it would not have been more natural and
profitable, especially for Lycidas but also for himself, to follow the
example of those who choose to devote themselves to the thoughtless
enjoyment and mirthful celebration of the game of love:

> Were it not better done, as others use,
> To sport with Amaryllis in the shade,
> Or with the tangles of Neaera's hair?

It is a commonplace in the poem's exegesis that in the three lines
just quoted the puritan Milton is alluding to the light and libertine
verse of Suckling and other Cavalier poets. This is undoubtedly true,

but the passage is significant beyond its topical allusion or the moral and literary polemics it so obviously implies. Let us not forget that the Cavalier poets, who were not always idyllic in temper, are here described as fellow shepherds or, more precisely, as bucolic poets of a different kind. What these lines suggest is thus a generic denial of the pastoral of love,[6] or at least its specific rejection from the canon of the funeral elegy. Like Moschus, but unlike Theocritus and Vergil, Milton seems to be saying that the idyll, or the love elegy, cannot mix well with the death elegy. This may explain why in the passage describing the effect of Lycidas and his own "rural ditties" the nymphs fail to join the fauns in dancing at their "soft lays." It was not only the puritan but also the humanist in him that led Milton to reject the pastoral conception of poetry as the effortless product of joyful leisure: he viewed poetry as a difficult craft and as an arduous task, requiring not only inspiration but also knowledge,[7] and thus earning the deserved admiration of mankind for its practitioners. Then, if Milton calls the muse "thankless," he does so only rhetorically; this explains the initial apostrophe to the laurels, as well as the long statement about fame which occupies the remainder of this section.

This statement begins as an oblique reply to the previous question, by which, if only rhetorically, the poet had seemed to doubt whether Lycidas' devotion to the muse was worth the sacrifice it required. The reply is oblique because Milton is at first tempted to give a contradictory answer to affirm two opposite principles at the same time—that such devotion and sacrifice are both worthless and worthwhile. They are worthwhile for being inspired by that yearning for renown which is at once an unsound illusion and a lofty ideal:

> Fame is the spur that the clear spirit doth raise
> (That last infirmity of noble mind)
> To scorn delights, and live laborious days.

Yet that devotion and sacrifice are also worthless since, as happened in Lycidas' case, sudden death may make the poet's efforts vain and deny him the reward he seeks, which is the survival of his own name. The author conveys this thought in the first person plural, as if to show that he speaks here for both his friend and himself, thus revealing his own doubts and fears:

> But the fair guerdon when we hope to find,
> And think to burst out into sudden blaze,
> Comes the blind Fury with th' abhorred shears,
> And slits the thin-spun life. . . .

If Milton represents here human mortality under a fabulous mask, it is not merely for the sake of imitation or for literary effect. The mask by which he invokes the fatality of death is the last of the three Parcae, the one cutting the thread of life, and it is perhaps significant that he willfully confuses her with one of the Furies, even though the Parcae and Furies are different mythical beings. The mythological veil serves an expressive rather than a decorative purpose, precisely because here Milton, if only for a while, is looking at death in pagan terms, as inexorable fate.

But the author of *Lycidas* is a Christian as well as a neoclassical poet, and with one of those paradoxes to which Dante had already accustomed his readers, he now calls in a pagan deity, Phoebus-Apollo, to resolve the antinomies between human fame and divine grace, and between everlasting death and everlasting life. Phoebus suddenly speaks to interrupt the words of the poet, or rather to correct them, and to give a final and total answer reconciling the contradictions implied in the poet's doubting and tentative reply. The poet makes Phoebus break his own utterance in such a way as to prevent himself from finishing the sentence describing the Parca who comes to do her fatal work:

> And slits the thin-spun life. "But not the praise,"
> Phoebus replied, and touched my trembling ears.

The effect of Phoebus' answer, which has the quality of repartee, is to transform worldly glory into its opposite, heavenly glory, thus anticipating the metamorphosis of the complaint over Lycidas' death into his spiritual apotheosis. Yet Phoebus' speech (especially in its use of the term "fame") is a little equivocal: there is undoubtedly a deliberate obscurity, or a significant ambiguity, in what he says. In Phoebus' words we detect some confusion between the immortality aspired to by a "clear spirit" and that aspired to by a pure soul; he seems to imply that the "all-judging Jove," or the Christian God, will reward Lycidas for having died not only in His own grace, but also in that of the Muses: or even in the grace of Phoebus himself, who after all is the holy patron of the arts. This at least is how we read Phoebus' speech:

> Fame is no plant that grows on mortal soil,
> Nor in the glistening foil
> Set off to the world, nor in broad rumour lies,
> But lives and spreads aloft by those pure eyes
> And perfect witness of all-judging Jove;
> As he pronounces lastly on each deed,
> Of so much fame in heaven expect thy meed.

The reader cannot avoid suspecting that, for Milton, the God who judges everything will judge poetry as well, and will reward in Heaven the deeds of both the mind and the heart. It is not improper to imagine that for Milton Christian poets should be reserved a place in Paradise, just as the poets of the pagan world are reserved a place in Dante's Limbo, the Hell of the just.

After Phoebus' unexpected intervention, exalted in diction as well as in thought, the author returns to the normal level and mode of his poetic discourse: hence his apostrophe to the fountain Arethusa and the river Mincius, by which he means that he becomes again a pastoral poet, a disciple of Theocritus and Vergil. The tone is lowered, as the poet indirectly acknowledges when he states that the previous tune (Phoebus' speech) had been a loftier harmony:

> O fountain Arethuse, and thou honoured flood,
> Smooth-sliding Mincius, crowned with vocal reeds,
> That strain I heard was of a higher mood.[8]

The author is evidently aware that Phoebus' speech had transcended the formal and thematic limits of the pastoral genre, and feels that his poem should now revert to the simple content and humble style which are that genre's norms. Such is certainly the sense of the following line: "But now my oat proceeds." Yet despite these words, the poet's "oat" in fact fails to proceed: in this central part of the poem, it moves only by stops and starts. More frequently than not, the poet's instrument remains utterly silent; it only "listens," as the poet says, to other voices than its own. Such voices are those of four apparitions, which now enter the scene, one after the other. The first two are mythological beings: the third an allegorical figure; the fourth St. Peter in person.

The first of the two fabulous figures is the "Herald of the Sea," or Triton, who "came in Neptune's plea," to ask the waves and the winds: "What hard mishap hath doomed this gentle swain?" The other one is "sage Hippotades," or Aeolus, who replies to Triton's inquiry. The answer of the god of the winds is that at the time of the shipwreck no breath troubled the still air, no wave stirred the calm sea; the peace of the element was so great that the Naiads were mirthfully playing on the quiet waters. Then it was only the "fatal and perfidious bark" that caused Lycidas' ruin or, as the poet says in an apostrophe to his friend: "That sunk so low that sacred head of thine." It is by laying the responsibility for Lycidas' death on his accursed vessel that Milton sounds one of the few bucolic notes in this part of the poem. Still one may recognize a vague bucolic quality also in the following apparition, that of the river Cam, personified in the revered old man Camus, whom the poet describes in his attire, including headgear bearing on its edge as signs of mourning a dim figure and a somber color which are, as the poet says: "Like to that sanguine flower inscribed with woe." [9] Camus indeed departs after grieving over the death of his "dearest pledge," to be immediately followed by St. Peter. The poet fails to mention the name of the saint, and chooses to refer to him by way of periphrasis, which perhaps has also the function of preserving the water imagery that dominates this and other passages of the poem:

> Last came, and last did go,
> The Pilot of the Galilean Lake.

Yet, so as to avoid any misunderstanding concerning the identity of this personage, Milton hastens to supply him with the miter and the two keys which are the unmistakable attributes of the gatekeeper of Paradise. Thus the setting is ready for St. Peter's speech, which takes nineteen lines, a considerable amount of the central part of the poem.

This long utterance finds its justification, and its biographical or ideological pretext, in the fact that both King and Milton had thought of entering the priesthood. But Milton failed to heed the call because of the repulsion he felt, as he says in the prose statement at the head of the poem, for "our corrupted Clergy, then in their height." Yet the poet must have felt that the speech also had an inner justification: that in adopting the letter and the spirit of the allegorical pastoral, it was a fitting interpolation within a bucolic poem. It is evident that Milton did act on such a presumption, which is not without precedent, but the presumption itself is questionable. Such questioning, however, cannot be made until the poem's analysis is completed and the essence and function of the allegorical pastoral is clarified.

The allegorical pastoral is a serious travesty, rather than a burlesque. Its inspiration is at best that of a satire; at worst, that of an invective. Its use of the conventions of the eclogue is a literary pretext, serving a nonliterary, or at least a nonimaginative, purpose. For this special and minor genre the pastoral vision is but machinery or, at its simplest, a device, based on no other motivation than the verbal identity, or metaphorical parallelism, between shepherds of sheep and shepherds of souls. It is obviously by something more than a mere coincidence that the Catholic priest or the Protestant minister came to be called a *pastor:* the origins of this name go back as far as the evangelical parable of the lost sheep, or at least as the early Christian symbol of the good shepherd. The negative aspect of such an analogy was bound to tempt all the critics of the worldly and temporal aims of the religious and ecclesiastical polity: all those who blamed the Church for harboring too many bad shepherds among the tenders of its flocks, and even of raising to its highest seat a wolf in sheep's clothing. In brief, the allegorical pastoral turns the praise of pastoral life into an indictment of the bad shepherds of the Church; and if it evokes an ideal of bucolic purity and idyllic innocence, it is only to make more severe its condemnation of the pastors who betray it.

Whereas poets like Dante and Spenser are content with suggesting this invidious comparison only in passing, within or without a pastoral framework, but never trespassing the limits of an extended metaphor, such authors as Petrarch and Mantuan develop the negative analogy out of all proportion, turning it into a genre of its own, which they cultivate in Latin eclogues written with that single explicit polemical intent. The use of such a genre is in Milton's poem unique, since there the allegorical pastoral becomes exceptionally a partial component, or at least an important ingredient, of a literal and lyrical one. In *Lycidas* the former acts within the latter as a poem within a poem, and the question is whether it adds to or detracts from the harmony of the whole. What makes the interpolation moving, if not convincing, is the passionate and burning eloquence of its accents; otherwise Milton is only rephrasing in his own way the typical commonplaces of the genre. Some of these are written in such a manner as to reecho similar passages in Dante and Spenser, as for instance the detailed description of the bad shepherds filling their bellies while:

> The hungry sheep look up, and are not fed,
> But, swoln with wind. . . .

St. Peter's speech unfolds with similar images; culminates in the representation of the Church as a devouring wolf that is not even in sheep's clothing; and ends with the prophecy of its doom.

This allegorical interpolation serves, so to speak, as the coda of the central part of the poem, but acts as its climax as well. The length, violence, and even incongruity of the passage compel the poet to relax the tension and, as soon as that tension is over, to resume the humble bucolic tone, to strike again the sad chords of the funeral elegy. This is why he calls back the Muse of pastoral poetry, which here he evokes only in Theocritean terms, through Sicily and the river Alpheus:

> Return, Alpheus, the dread voice is past
> That shrunk thy streams; return, Sicilian Muse.

The Sicilian Muse is not only called back but is also asked to exact from nature the tribute of flowers due Lycidas' bier:

> And call the vales, and bid them hither cast
> Theirs bells and flowrets of a thousand hues.

As if to make this request more pressing and direct, the poet repeats it to the valleys themselves, naming one after the other the suitable flowers which nature should offer: "To strew the laureate hearse where Lycid lies." That the intended effect of this passage is to relax the tension produced by St. Peter's speech is proved by the very length of the flowers catalogue,[10] which occupies sixteen lines, as well as by the statement closing the catalogue:

> For so, to interpose a little ease,
> Let our frail thoughts dally with false surmise.

By these lines the poet avows that the floral offering he has just described was but a wishful fantasy, meant to assuage the grief over a death the more cruel for having occurred far from land, thus depriving its victim of the due honors men render to those who die in their midst, who return to the earth and sleep in peace there. The avowal that death by water has prevented Lycidas from receiving the tribute of tears to which he is entitled provokes a poignant realization of the injury done to his remains, which are now tossed about in the vast expanses or in the awful depths of the sea. The lines conveying this cosmic and tragic vision have great poetic power:

> Ay me! whilst thee the shores and sounding seas
> Wash far away, where'er your bones are hurled;
> Whether beyond the stormy Hebrides,
> Where thou perhaps under the whelming tide
> Visit'st the bottom of the monstrous world.

The poet, however, cannot end such a vision on a note of despair. Since Lycidas is refused the considerations of burial and the grave, consisting of the tears which the friends of the dead shed on their urns, Milton grants him instead the sublime reward of the companionship of a spirit incommensurably higher than any human soul. Such a spirit is St. Michael, who according to the legend mounts guard on Europe's Land End, Cape Finisterre in Spain, from which the Archangel watches the ocean surrounding the continent. The poet invokes St. Michael, and prays that he turn his gaze toward the seas of England and grieve over the youth who died not too far from his native land: "Look homeward, Angel, now, and melt with ruth." This Christian appeal is immediately followed by a mythological one: the poet now addresses his words to those gentle sea creatures who saved the drowning Arion, asking that this time they bring back to shore the body of Lycidas, who can sing no longer for man or beast: "And, O ye dolphins, waft the hapless youth." [11]

The invocation to St. Michael foreshadows Lycidas' apotheosis, which occupies in full the twenty-one lines that follow and, to all purposes, close the song. Whereas in the previous part the poet had played the role of the grieving Mopsus, here he plays the role of the exulting Menalcas. Yet he unfolds Lycidas' apotheosis in a highly original manner, even though he may follow, along with the Vergil of *Daphnis*, many a modern imitator of the Fifth Eclogue. The author introduces the apotheosis of his dead friend as if it were a last and final return to the pastoral inspiration of the poem. As he had done in each previous case, he announces such a return by means of a fitting apostrophe, which this time sounds far more moving and direct for being addressed not to such abstract beings as the Muses, or to such symbolic entities as the river Mincius or the fountain Arethusa, but to Lycidas' own brethren. Whereas it was proper to expect that even the creatures of nature should share the grief over his death, no participation in the rejoicing for his resurrection can be required from others than his fellow shepherds. Only beings endowed with an immortal soul may be consoled by the knowledge that Lycidas has found eternal consolation in Heaven. This is why the poet bids them shed no more tears:

> Weep no more, woeful shepherds, weep no more,
> For Lycidas, your sorrow, is not dead,
> Sunk though he be beneath the wat'ry floor:

So sinks the day-star in the ocean bed
And yet anon repairs his drooping head,
And tricks his beams, and with new-spangled ore
Flames in the forehead of the morning sky:
So Lycidas sunk low, but mounted high,
Through the dear might of Him that walked the waves;
Where, other groves and other streams along,
With nectar pure his oozy locks he laves,
And hears the unexpressive nuptial song,
In the blest kingdoms meek of joy and love.
There entertain him all the Saints above,
In solemn troops, and sweet societies,
That sing, and singing in their glory move,
And wipe the tears for ever from his eyes.

In these splendid lines the Christian and the pastoral vision merge in perfect harmony, here the poet gives mystical significance to any detail connected with Lycidas' life and death. He contrasts the physical fate of his body, submerged to the very depths of the sea, with the spiritual destiny of his soul, ascending now toward Heaven, thus teaching the bucolic and evangelical lesson that the lowly and the humble will be exalted. And he compares the death and resurrection of Lycidas to the alternate phases of sunset and sunrise to reconfirm our ultimate faith in the victory of everlasting life over everlasting death. If he names Jesus, the savior of Lycidas and of the human soul, with the periphrasis of "Him that walked the waves," it is because only Jesus could have helped the spirit of Lycidas to rise from the deep. Finally, just when both Lycidas and his mourners have ceased to weep, he turns to the dead man to make of him, in both Christian and pagan terms, the sacred patron of the place where he had drowned, the holy protector of all those who will again risk their lives on its waters:

Now, Lycidas, the shepherds weep no more;
Henceforth thou art the Genius of the shore
In thy large recompense, and shalt be good
To all that wander in that perilous flood.

The most significant and suggestive of all the traits of this apotheosis is, however, the evocation of Lycidas' new abode as that of a pastoral commonwealth against the background of a bucolic landscape. Here Heaven turns into a garden, lovlier than Eden; here Paradise becomes, so to speak, an eternal Arcadia of the soul. Such a vision finds its sanction, beyond the pastoral framework of this poem, in the very limits of our mind, which often cannot conceive of heavenly bliss except in the simplest and earthiest terms of our experience of the natural world. This is the reason why the biblical and the Christian imagination were bound to accept that vision, at least on the plane of "the letter" if not of "the spirit." Dante was one of the poets who chose to represent Heaven as a realm of magnificence, rather than merely as a kingdom "meek of joy and love"; hence his refusal to extend to the Heavenly Paradise the pastoral attributes with which he had so beautifully endowed the terrestrial one.[12]

But many other Italian poets, especially Boccaccio and Sannazaro, chose instead to depict heavenly bliss in pastoral figures, as a higher version of the innocent happiness of bucolic life. Boccaccio did so in one of his Latin eclogues, the Fourteenth, which is entitled *Olympia* because it describes, in the manner indicated, the Christian Empyrean. Sannazaro did the same in the Fifth Eclogue of his *Arcadia*, which for about three centuries was destined to remain an exemplary and familiar text in European literature. What makes it worth discussing in the present context is that the poem in question is also a funeral elegy.

The Fifth Eclogue of Sannazaro's *Arcadia* is the farewell song which Ergasto sings on the tomb of the shepherd Androgeo, and this is why it is also called *Sovra la sepoltura*. The preceding prose account reads like a literal translation of that passage in Vergil's Fifth Eclogue in which Menalcas lists in detail all the rites the shepherds promise to render henceforth to the dead friend who has just become their tutelar god. It is this account, and this account alone, that makes the reader realize that the poet had meant to write that song as an imitation of the Vergilian *Daphnis*, and especially of its second part. But when read by itself this song hardly sounds pagan, and its Christian inspiration becomes even more apparent when we see that in this dirge the apotheosis precedes, rather than follows, the complaint, and that it alone determines the tone and mood of the poem. Nothing proves this point better than the opening apostrophe, addressing the spirit of the dead Androgeo with epithets and metaphors that befit only the Christian conception of the soul:

> Alma beata e bella,
> che da' legami sciolta
> nuda salisti nei superni chiostri.

O fair and blissful soul, which, all your ties unbound, rose naked to the cloisters most aloft.

Yet, despite the image of cloisters, of Paradise, Sannazaro proceeds to represent Heaven as a pastoral abode:

> E fra pure fontane e sacri mirti
> pasci celesti greggi,
> e i tuoi cari pastor quindi correggi.

And amidst fountains pure and holy myrtles you drive celestial flocks and teach your fellow shepherds.

In brief, the only difference between our earthly Arcadia and that of Heaven is that the latter is lovelier, fresher, and purer than the former:

> Altri monti, altri piani,
> altri boschetti e rivi
> vedi nel cielo, e più novelli fiori.

Other mountains, other plains, other groves and rivers in heaven now you see, and newer flowers.

Milton's phrase "other groves and other streams along" proves that he had read these lines. There is no doubt that he knew the whole poem, and we may surmise that the author of *Lycidas* patterned his own apotheosis on this eclogue, or that he learned from this song, as contrasted with the related prose, how to turn a pagan pastoral into a Christian one.[13] Lovely as his model was, Milton was certainly far more successful than his master in making Paradise the "pastoral oasis" par excellence: certainly the most spiritual and universal one. The poet's triumph is so evident that it should dispel most of the strictures of Samuel Johnson, in his indictment of the poem (*Life of Milton*). Johnson was certainly wrong in reaffirming his own prejudices against the pastoral form, which he rejected as false and insincere, and in claiming that in a poem like *Lycidas*, "where there is leisure for fiction there is little grief." He was obviously unfair in censuring the style, the diction, and the rhythm of a work that most critics have found without blemish in the unique magnificence of the verse measure and verbal texture. Johnson was, however, on safer grounds when protesting the "long train of mythological imagery" which overburdens a few zones of the poems, and there is no doubt that he deserves being listened to when, without mentioning it, he refers with these harsh words to St. Peter's prosopopoeia:[14]

> This poem has yet a grosser fault. With these trifling fictions are mingled the most awful and sacred truths, such as ought never to be polluted with such irreverent combinations. The shepherd likewise is now a feeder of sheep, and afterwards an ecclesiastical pastor, a superintendent of a Christian flock. Such equivocations are always unskilful; but here they are indecent, and at least approach to impiety, of which, however, I believe the writer not to have been conscious.

This celebrated page reads not too differently from the passage in which Boileau condemns "le merveilleux chrétien," or the use of the supernatural vision of our religion as a substitute for mythological fables within the epic poem.[15] But to a modern ear Johnson's statement rings truer in this context than Boileau's in his.

While accepting the critical inference of Johnson's statement, we may well deny the soundness of his argument. There is no doubt that Milton's introduction within the major poem, which is a literal pastoral, of a minor poem, which is an allegorical one, must be viewed as a grievous error, yet such an error should be seen not as a religious and moral fault, as Johnson maintains, but simply as a poetic and literary mistake. The literal pastoral is a lyrical creation; the allegorical, a satirical one. Pastoral and Christian imagery or, as Johnson would say, bucolic "fiction" and religious "truth" may happily merge, as Lycidas' apotheosis proves so well, thus disproving the critic's claim to the contrary. Such a merging, however, fails to happen when a cursing voice seeks to mingle its jarring chords with the melodious notes of a blessing one. This does not mean that the harmony of poetry proscribes all dissonance; it means only that all dissonance should contribute to the harmony of the whole. The effect of dissonance should be the achieving of what the ancients used to call, with a lovely oxymoron, a *concordia discors*. In *Lycidas* such an effect is first jeopardized by the abuse of mythological imagery, and then destroyed by the misuse of pastoral allegory, at least for a while. There is no doubt that besides rendering the central part the weakest of the three, the quantity and length of the sections involved in such abuse and misuse affect the economy of the structure, and disturb the balance of the entire poem.[16]

It is nevertheless evident that the poet achieves the effect of *concordia discors* in the first and third parts, each one of which is full of poetic and moral paradoxes, or lyrical and sentimental ambiguities. We may see an example of the paradoxes in the emphasis that the poet places, far more frequently and intensely than his classical models, on the "cruelty" of Lycidas' death.[17] As for the lyrical and sentimental ambiguities of the poem, we may cite as a single example the passage in which the poet wonders whether it would not have been better for Lycidas and himself if they had chosen:

> To sport with Amaryllis in the shade,
> Or with the tangles of Neaera's hair?

We know already that this question implies an answer totally negative: yet the poetic and emotional connotation of these names, as distinguished from their denotative meaning, far from suggesting an utter denial, betrays a wishful thought, or the vague longing of a controlled, but not repressed, desire, thus revealing, with great poetic intensity, the inner contradictions of the subject's, or of Everyman's, psyche. When all this is said, it remains true that the work is marked by both pathetic exuberance and artistic complexity, the one doing violence to the spirit of the pastoral, the other to its form. It is be-

cause of this double violence that we acknowledge in *Lycidas* one
of the summits of baroque poetry. Milton was certainly aware that
his poem was at variance with the niceties and the discretions of its
genre, and it was perhaps in order to express such an awareness, and
to produce an effect of poetic distance, that he wrote the stanza that
acts as the unforeseen coda of the poem.

Metrically and poetically, the stanza closing *Lycidas* is an odd extravagance: hence it must be viewed as an afterthought, whether or
not Milton wrote it at a later date. Its obvious function is to reveal
that, in spite of all appearances, the poem has been the utterance of
a fictional character, not to be identified with the real poet. The pretense is hardly novel. As a matter of fact it is one of the standard
conventions of pastoral poetry. What renders this case almost unique
is that normally such pretense is revealed at the beginning, by framing the song within a dialogue, or by supplying it with a proper
narrative prelude, in either verse or prose. Here, however, the revelation is made and, quite unexpectedly, only at the end of the poem.
The author surprises the reader with such belated and unforeseen
information; yet he fails to convince his audience that the voice
speaking in this coda and the one singing Lycidas' funeral elegy are
of two different persons. They are instead the two different voices
of the same person, who, after playing the role of a poet, now plays
the role of a critic. The truth of this is not denied by the beauty of
the lines which seal both the song and the poem:

> Thus sang the uncouth swain to th' oaks and rills,
> While the still morn went out with sandals grey:
> He touched the tender stops of various quills,
> With eager thought warbling his Doric lay:
> And now the sun had stretched out all the hills,
> And now was dropt into the western bay;
> At last he rose, and twitched his mantle blue:
> To-morrow to fresh woods, and pastures new.

Who speaks here is not only a poet but also a man of letters able to
see that the poem just written, in which he has worn the mask of an
"uncouth swain," is the product of an extreme cultivation and of a

peerless virtuosity. The man who had composed *Lycidas* knew that he had accomplished the miraculous feat of preserving the tradition of the "Doric lay" [18] while touching "the tender stops of various quills," may of which seemed to contradict and to transcend the pastoral norm. The poet-critic knew that after a triumph such as that of this funeral elegy, he was indeed ready, like the shepherd who had sung it on his behalf, for greener pastures, and newer fields.

5
The
Christian
Pastoral

I

Beginning with early humanism, clerics, scholars, and poets tried to interpret and to translate the ancient, pagan pastoral into new, Christian terms. The idea of a Christian pastoral haunted the literary imagination almost as much as the ideas of a Christian tragedy or of a Christian *Aeneid*. The three ideas merged in the work of Milton, where they are respectively exemplified by *Paradise Lost*, *Samson Agonistes*, and *On the Morning of Christ's Nativity*. Of these three ideas, the one that showed itself as absolutely impossible of realization was the idea of a Christian tragedy, as not only *Samson Agonistes* but Corneille's *Polyeucte* and Racine's *Athalie* so well show. The only possible Christian form of drama is the mystery play; and the mystery play ends in joyful revelation, and changes into our own redemption the passion of the Son of God. Dante, the greatest of all Christian poets, understood this very well, and called his own poem *Commedia*, which he conceived as an *Aeneid* of the soul; and which, together with Milton's *Paradise Lost*, proved that the idea of a Christian epos, of the epos of Everyman, was not a mere dream. The idea of a Christian pastoral seems to lie halfway between these two extremes; yet, if we look deeper, we see that the pastoral of Christendom is as impossible as the tragedy of Christianity. It is true that even in modern times sacred history has been intrepreted in idyllic terms. Nietzsche saw an idyll in the Gospels, and it was on this critical insight that he based his negative judgment of the prosaic simplicity of the New Testament as compared with the poetic majesty of the Old:

> In jüdischen "alten Testament," dem Buche von der göttlichen Gerechtigkeit, gibt es Menschen, Dinge und Reden in einem so grossen Stile, dass das griechische und indische Schriftenthum ihm nichts zur Seite zu stellen hat. . . . Freilich: wer selbst nur ein dünnes zahmes Hausthier ist und nur Hausthier-Bedürfnisse kennt . . . der hat unter jenen Ruinen weder sich zu verwundern, noch gar sich zu betrüben—der Geschmack am alten Testament ist ein Prüfstein in Hinsicht auf "Gross" und "Klein"—: vielleicht, dass er das neue Testament, das Buch von der Gnade, immer noch eher nach seinem Herzen findet (in ihm ist viel von dem rechten zärtlichen dumpfen Betbrüder- und Kleinen-Seelen-Geruch). Dieses neue Testament, eine Art Rokoko des Geschmacks in jedem Betrachte, mit dem alten Testament zu Einem Buche zusammengeleimt zu haben, als "Bibel," als "das Buch an sich": das is vielleicht die grösste Derwegenheit und "Sünde wider den Geist," welche das litterarische Europa auf dem Gewissen hat.

> In the Jewish "Old Testament," the book of divine justice, there are men, things, and sayings on such an immense scale, that Greek and Indian literature has nothing to compare with it. . . . To be sure, he who is himself only a slender, tame house-animal, and knows only the wants of a house-animal . . . need neither be amazed nor even sad amid those ruins—the taste for the Old Testament is a touchstone with respect to "great" and

"small": perhaps he will find that the New Testament, the book of grace, still appeals more to his heart (there is much of the odour of the genuine, tender, stupid beadsman and petty soul in it). To have bound up this New Testament (a kind of *rococo* of taste in every respect) along with the Old Testament into one book, as the "Bible," as "The Book in Itself," is perhaps the greatest audacity and "sin against the Spirit" which literary Europe has upon its conscience.[1]

Renan saw an idyll in the early part of Christ's biography, in the way of life of small Jewish communities from which he sprang forth as a Messiah, and even in the whole history of primitive Christianity, as shown by one of the most famous passages of his *Vie de Jésus* (iii):

Toute l'histoire due christianisme naissant est devenue de la sorte une délicieuse pastorale. Un Messie aux repas de noces, la courtisane et le bon Zachée appelés à ses festins, les fondateurs du royaume du ciel comme un cortège de paranymphes: voilà ce que la Galilée a osé, ce qu'elle a fait accepter. Le Grèce a tracé de la vie humaine, par la scultpure et la poésie, des tableaux admirables, mais toujours sans fonds fuyants ni horizons lointains. Ici manquent le marbre, les ouvriers excellents, la langue exquise et raffinée. Mais la Galilée a créé, à l'état d'imagination populaire, le plus sublime idéal; car derrière son idylle s'agite le sort de l'humanité, et la lumière qui éclaire son tableau est le soleil du royaume de Dieu.

The whole history of primitive Christianity has thus become a kind of delightful pastoral. A Messiah at a wedding banquet, the courtesan and the good Zacchaeus invited to his feasts, the founders of the Heavenly Kingdom like a procession of paranymphs; this is what Galilee had dared to do and forced men to accept. Greece, through her sculpture and poetry, has drawn charming pictures of human life, but with no vanishing backgrounds nor faraway horizons. Here there is a lack of marble, of skillful artisans, of an exquisite and refined tongue. But Galilee has created in the shape of popular imagination the highest of all ideals, since mankind's destiny unfolds beyond its idyll, and the light brightening its picture is the sun of the Kingdom of God.

Renan's vision is, however, a literary idealization, and nothing more. After all, the same cultural and historical environment from which there emerged the Messiah had produced prophets like St. John the Baptist, who retired where no shepherd ever dared to withdraw, into the wilderness, where sheep cannot find grass to graze and must feed only on wild honey and locusts.

Yet there is no doubt that in all Christian lands popular imagination has given a pastoral turn to the most poetic legend of Christendom, which is the story of Jesus' birth. The pastoral implications of the legend are already evident in the original texts which are the sources of the legend itself. Its most suggestive and telling details are taken from the two evangelical passages of which the legend is but a natural development. The first of these passages is to be found in the Third Gospel, which is, perhaps, of the four, both the most popular and the most poetic in spirit. It is from Luke that we learn that the wonder child was born in a stable, like a lamb; and that the angels revealed his birth first to the shepherds watching their flocks at night in the fields nearby, who in turn spread the good tidings to other men. Luke tells us how Joseph and Mary "his espoused wife, being great with child," had to leave Nazareth in Galilee, and go to Bethlehem in Judea, to pay the head tax which an imperial decree had imposed on all Roman subjects (ii.6–20):

And so it was, that, while they were there, the days
were accomplished that she should be delivered.
And she brought forth her first-born son and wrapped
him in swaddling clothes, and laid him in a manger;
because there was no room for them in the inn.
And there were in the same country shepherds, abid-
in the field, keeping watch over their flock by night.
And, lo, the angel of the Lord came upon them, and
the glory of the Lord shone round about them:
and they were sore afraid.
And the angel said unto them, Fear not, for, behold,
I bring you good tidings of great joy, which shall be
to all people.

For unto you is born this day in the city of David a
Saviour, which is Christ the Lord.
And this shall be a sign unto you, Ye shall find the
babe wrapped in swadding clothes, lying in a manger.
And suddenly there was with the angel a multitude
of the heavenly host praising God, and saying,
Glory to God in the highest, and on earth peace,
good will toward men.
And it came to pass, as the angels were gone away
from them into heaven, the shepherds said one to
another, Let us now go even unto Bethlehem, and see
this thing which is come to pass, which the Lord
hath made known unto us.
And they came with haste, and found Mary, and
Joseph, and the baby lying in a manger.
And when they had seen it, they made known abroad
the saying which was told them concerning this child.
And all they that heard it wondered at those things
which were told them by the shepherds.
But Mary kept all these things, and pondered them
in her heart.
And the shepherds returned, glorifying and praising
God for all the things they had heard and seen, as it
was told unto them.

It is from the First Gospel, on the other hand, that the visit of the
three wise men is derived (Matt. ii.1–12):

Now when Jesus was born in Bethlehem of Judæa
in the days of Herod the king, behold, there came wise
men from the east to Jerusalem,
Saying, Where is he that is born King of the Jews?
for we have seen this star in the east, and are come to
worship him.
When Herod the king had heard these things, he was
troubled, and all Jerusalem with him.
And when he had gathered all the chief priests and

scribes of the people together, he demanded of them
where Christ should be born.
And they said unto him, In Bethlehem of Judæa: for
thus it is written by the prophet,
And thou Bethlehem, in the land of Juda, art not
the least among the princes of Juda: for out of thee
shall come a Governor, that shall rule my people
Israel.
Then Herod, when he had privily called the wise
men, inquired of them diligently what time the star
appeared.
And he sent them to Bethlehem, and said, Go and
search diligently for the young child; and when ye
have found him, bring me word again, that I may
come and worship him also.
When they had heard the king, they departed; and,
lo, the star, which they saw in the east, went before
them, till it came and stood where the young child was.
When they saw the star, they rejoiced with exceeding
great joy.
And when they were come into the house, they saw
the young child with Mary his mother, and fell down,
and worshipped him: and when they had opened their
treasures, they presented unto him gifts; gold, and
frankincense, and myrrh.
And being warned of God in a dream that they should
not return to Herod, they departed into their own
country another way.

Yet the bucolic interpretation of the legend of the Nativity was not
the work of the unlearned, popular imagination, but of a conscious,
elaborate, and highly literary rewriting of the two texts just quoted.
This was done with the process called *contaminatio*—combining
those famous evangelical passages with one of the most famous pastoral poems of classical antiquity, which sanctions the bucolic interpretation of the legend of the Nativity by offering, so to speak, a
parallel or precedent on which to base it.

II

This poem is Vergil's Fourth Ecologue, a "classical" text which medieval and Christian humanism read as if it were a profane supplement to the Holy Writ, or a pagan version of its prophetic books. Written one or two generations before the beginning of the Christian era, in the year 40 B.C., the Fourth Eclogue announces the imminent birth of a wonder child who will bring peace and salvation to the world, and ends with the lament of the poet, fearing that death will prevent him from witnessing and celebrating the glories of the new, great age he has foretold. Christian humanism will see a prophecy also in this, since Vergil was destined to die in the year 19 B.C.; while, on the other hand, with the liberty the allegorical interpretation of literature usually grants itself, they failed to see a stumbling block in the fact that at the time of the poem's writing the child of whom Vergil speaks was already in his mother's womb. The Christian interpreters of the Fourth Eclogue may be excused at least in part when we consider that that poem is an exceptional piece, not only within the framework of the *Eclogues*, but also within the tradition of pastoral poetry as it had developed in classical antiquity. Vergil was well aware of this, as shown by the poem's invocation, where the acknowledgment by the poet of the paradoxical novelty of his own attempt is tempered by a note of apology. In brief, the poet tries to justify his deviation from the pastoral pattern, a deviation that may be defined as a double shift: in content, from the private sphere to the public one; and in form, from the mode of the elegy or the idyll to the mode of the ode or the hymn. Thus the poet invites the muses of Sicily, or of pastoral poetry in general, to accept once in a while a nobler subject. Only thus the eclogue he is now writing will be made worthy of the person to whom it is addressed, who is neither a humble shepherd nor a fellow poet but the consul Pollio, a protector of poetry as well as a shepherd of men:

> Sicelides Musae, paulo maiora canamus.
> non omnes arbusta iuvant humilesque myricae;
> si canimus silvas, silvae sint consule dignae.

Muses of Sicily, let us attempt a rather more exalted theme. Hedgerow and humble tamarisk do not appeal to all. If we must sing of woodlands, let them be such as may do a Consul honour.[2]

This note of apology is only natural, since the poet is now heeding other voices than those of the muses he has just invoked. He is listening to the last echoes of "the song of the Sibyl": in other words, he is following the inspiration of the Sibylline Books, which were said to retain the oracles of the Sibyl of Cumae. Thus we are warned that pastoral poetry, which normally is sentimental and nostalgic, is now about to become prophetic and oracular. The entire poem is meant as a replica of one of the Sibylline oracles, affirming that mankind has reached a turning point and that a new order of things is about to be born from the fullness of time:

> Ultima Cumaei venit iam carminis aetas;
> magnus ab integro saeclorum nascitur ordo.

We have reached the last era in Sibylline song. Time has conceived and the great Sequence of the Ages start afresh.

The instauration of the new order is conceived as the restauration of the happy state that mankind enjoyed under the rule of Saturn. Its advent is made manifest by the return of Astraea, the virgin goddess of justice, who left the earth after mankind was corrupted, and in whom Christian interpreters will all too often recognize the Virgin Mary, although this will not prevent them from seeing the Mother of Jesus also in the mother of Vergil's wonder child. The instrument of the announced palingenesis will be the expected offspring, now on his way from heaven:

> Iam redit et Virgo, redeunt Saturnia regna;
> iam nova progenies caelo demittitur alto.

Justice, the Virgin, comes back to dwell with us, and the rule of Saturn is restored. The Firstborn of the New Age is already on his way from high heaven down to earth.

The coming child will bring the Golden Age back with him, and the poet asks Lucina, the chaste goddess of childbirth, here confused with Diana, to look with sympathy at the newborn—a sun god in the likeness of her brother Phoebus, who thus will triumph again:

> Tu modo nascenti puero, quo ferrea primum
> desinet ac toto surget gens aurea mundo,
> casta fave Lucina: tuus iam regnat Apollo.

With him, the Iron Race shall end and Golden Man inherit all the world. Smile on the Baby's birth, immaculate Lucina; your own Apollo is enthroned at last.

The dawn of the new era will take place during Pollio's consulship, under which mankind will be freed from its crimes or, as a Christian would say, redeemed from its sins. The new age is referred to in mystical and astronomical terms, as a new, full cyclical series (*magnus annus*) divided into its periods or phases (*magni menses*):

> Teque adeo decus hoc aevi, te consule inibit,
> Pollio, et incipient magni procedere menses;
> te duce, si qua manent sceleris vestigia nostri,
> inrita perpetua solvent formidine terras.

And it is in your consulship, yours, Pollio, that this glorious Age will dawn and the Procession of the great Months begin. Under your leadership all traces that remain of our iniquity will be effaced and, as they vanish, free the world from its long night of horror.

The child will learn both human and divine wisdom, and will lead mankind toward a happiness made possible by the peace enforced by his father. In Vergil, that father is a human ruler or leader, and it does not matter very much whether he must be identified with Pollio or Antony, or even with the great Octavian. The Christians will of course see in him God the Father, the first person of the Trinity, or the Jehovah of the Old Testament. In the same way, in the gods and the heroes showing the path of righteousness to the coming child, they will see those ancient biblical figures who will take their place among the saints of the Christian calendar:

> Ille deum vitam accipiet divisque videbit
> permixtos heroas et ipse videbitur illis,
> pacatumque reget patriis virtutibus orbem.

He will foregather with the gods; he will see the great men of the past consorting with them, and be himself observed by these, guiding a world to which his father's virtues have brought peace.

In the lines that follow the poet describes in pastoral terms the simple tributes that Mother Earth will offer to the wonder child:

> At tibi prima, puer, nullo munuscula cultu
> errantis hederas passim cum baccare tellus
> mixtaque ridenti colocasia fundet acantho.

Free-roaming ivy, foxgloves in every dell, and smiling acanthus mingled with Egyptian lilies—these, little one, are the first modest gifts that earth, unprompted by the hoe, will lavish on you.

The poet goes on describing, still in pastoral terms, the pacifying effect of the child's advent on the animal and vegetable world:

> Ipsae lacte domum referent distenta capellae
> ubera, nec magnos metuent armenta leones; . . .
> occidet et serpens, et fallax herba veneni
> occidet; Assyrium vulgo nascetur amomum.

The goats, unshepherded, will make for home with udders full of milk, and the ox will not be frightened of the lion, for all his might. Your very cradle will adorn itself with blossoms to caress you. The snake will come to grief, and poison lurk no more in the wood. Perfumes of Assyria will breathe from every hedge.

The beneficent power of the wonder child, inspired by the approval of the wise men of old and by his father's example, will be felt more fully when he comes of age:

> At simul heroum laudes et facta parentis
> iam legere et quae sit poteris cognoscere virtus.
> molli paulatim flavescet campus arista,

incultisque rubens pendebit sentibus uva
et durae quercus sudabunt roscida mella.

Later, when you heave learnt to read the praises of the great and
what your father achieved, and come to understand what manhood is, the waving corn will slowly flood the plains with gold,
grapes hang in ruby clusters on the neglected thorn, and honey-
dew exude from the hard trunk of the oak.

Yet even his presence at first will not suffice to change man completely. The survival of man's wickedness is evoked by Vergil in
terms of all that the bucolic condemns and denies, the temptations of
profit and glory, of trade and war, of struggle and strife. Yet even
this passage will be interpreted in the key of the Christian doctrine:
especially the formula "priscae vestigia fraudis," (the traces of the
primitive deceit), which can as easily be read as if it meant "the traces
of the original sin":

Pauca tamen suberunt pricae vestigia fraudis,
quae temptare Thetim ratibus, quae cingere muris
oppida, quae iubeant telluri infindere sulcos.
alter erit tum Tiphys, et altera quae vehat Argo
delectos heroas; erunt etiam altera bella
atque iterum ad Troiam magnus mittetur Achilles.

Even so, faint traces of our former wickedness will linger on, to
make us venture on the sea in ships, build walls around our
cities, and plough the soil. With a new Tiphys at the helm, a
second Argo will set out, manned by a picked heroic crew. Wars
even will repeat themselves and the great Achilles be dispatched
to Troy once more.

Later, however, after the child has become a man, the new Golden
Age will fully triumph in this world: nature will grow by itself all
that any living creature may need, freeing not only men but also animals from the curse of work, changing into a new Garden of Eden
the whole earth:

Hinc ubi iam firmata virum te fecerit aetas,
cedet et ipse mari vector, nec nautica pinus
mutabit merces, omnis feret omnia tellus.

non rastros patietur humus, non vinea falcem;
robustus quoque iam tauris iuga solvet arator;
nec varios discet mentiri lana colores,
ipse sed in pratis aries iam suave rubenti
murice, iam croceo mutabit vellere luto;
sponte sua sandyx pascentis vestiet agnos.

Later again, when the strengthening years have made a man of
you, even the trader will forsake the sea, and pine-wood ships
will cease to carry merchandise for barter, each land producing
all it needs. No mattock will molest the soil, no pruning-knife
the vine; and then at last the sturdy ploughman will free his
oxen from the yoke. Wool will be taught no cure to cheat the
eye with this tint or with that, but the ram himself in his own
meadows will change the colour of his fleece, now to the soft
glow of a purple dye, now to a saffron yellow. Lambs at their
pastures will find themselves in scarlet coats.

All this is fated to come, because, as the Christians will say, Providence wills it:

"Talia saecla" suis dixerunt "currite" fusis
concordes stabili fatorum numine Parcae.

The fates have spoken, in concord with the unalterable decree of
destiny. "Run, spindles," they have said. "This is the pattern of
the age to come."

At this point the poet apostrophizes the coming child, inviting him
to come at the appointed hour, which is imminent. The universe waits
ready for the advent of him whom the poet calls a divine child and
the increment of the godhead:

Adgredere o magnos (aderit iam tempus) honores,
cara deum suboles, magnum Iovis incrementum!
aspice convexo nutantem pondere mundum,
terrasque tractusque maris caelumque profundum;
aspice venturo laetentur ut omnia saeclo!

Enter—for the hour is close at hand—on your illustrious career,
dear child of the gods, great increment of Jove. Look at the
world, rocked by the weight of its overhanging dome; look at

the lands, the far-flung seas and the unfathomable sky. See how the whole creation rejoices in the age that is to be!

At this point, the author expresses his fear of dying before he is able to see the full glory of the new age. Yet, were he to survive, he would sing its praise better than any other human poet, such as Linus and Orpheus; even better than Pan himself, the god of Arcady, and the highest master of the oaten flute:

> O mihi tum longae maneat pars ultima vitae,
> spiritus et, quantum sat erit tua dicere facta:
> non me carminibus vincat nec Thracius Orpheus,
> nec Linus, huic mater quamvis atque huic pater adsit,
> Orphei Calliopea, Lino formosus Apollo.
> Pan etiam, Arcadia mecum si iudice certet,
> Pan etiam Arcadia dicat se iudice victum.

Ah, if the last days of my life could only be prolonged, and breath enough remain, for me to chronicle your acts, then neither Thracian Orpheus nor Linus could outsing me, not though the one had his mother and the other had his father at his side, Orpheus, his Calliope, and Linus, Apollo in all his beauty. If Pan himself, with Arcady for judge, were to contend with me, the great god Pan, with Arcady for judge, would own defeat.

In the poem's ending, the Christian interpreters will find to their liking the image of the child smiling at his mother, as well as the reference to the divine table:

> Incipe, parve puer, risu cognoscere matrem:
> matri longa decem tulerunt fastidia menses.
> incipe, parve puer: cui non risere parentes,
> nec deus huno mensa, dea nec dignata cubile est.

Begin, then, little boy, to greet your mother with a smile: the ten long months have left her sick at heart. Begin, little boy: no one who has not given his mother a smile has ever been thought worthy of his table by a god, or by a goddess of her bed.

The Christian interpreters will not be scandalized by the final line, which they will explain away allegorically and otherwise, or will accept with the same indulgence as the allusion to Pan, whose appearance is quite natural in a bucolic poem; what appears here is only the vain ghost of that god, who died, according to the Christian interpretation of a legend related by Plutarch, at the very moment of the birth of Christ. They will rejoice especially in those passages of the Fourth Eclogue that seem to be an echo or a replica of the visions and the hopes of the Jewish prophets, especially of the passage in Isaiah describing the miracles produced in the natural world by the coming of the Messiah: (xi.6–7):

> The wolf also shall dwell with the lamb, and the
> leopard shall lie down with the kid: and the calf and
> the young lion and the fatling together; and a little
> child shall lead them.
> And the cow and the bear shall feed; their young ones
> shall lie down together: and the lion shall eat straw
> like the ox.

The modern mind, skeptical and historical, does not see anything extraordinary in this miraculous coincidence: Vergil extracts his doctrines on one side from the Platonic and the Pythagorean tradition, on the other from the apocalyptic beliefs reaching Rome from all the corners of the ancient world. As Renan says (iii):

> Ces idées couraient le monde et pénétraient jusqu'à Rome, où elles inspiraient un cycle de poèmes prophéetiques, dont les idées fondamentales étaient la division de l'histoire de l'humanité en périodes, la succession des dieux répondant à ces périodes, un complet renouvellement du monde, et l'avènement final d'un âge d'or.

> These conceptions were spreading all over the world, and had reached even Rome, where they inspired a cycle of prophetic poems, the main ideas of which were the division of mankind into eras, with successive gods corresponding to each one of them, a complete renewal of the universe; and the final advent of an age of gold.

What impresses the imagination of the Christian interpreters of the Fourth Eclogue even more than the prophecy of the imminent advent of an era of universal peace, which for Vergil was the worldly peace of the Roman order, and for them, the spiritual peace of the Kingdom of God, is the announcement that the new covenant is to be established by a child not yet born. The modern mind is not surprised by this additional coincidence, since psychological and anthropological science, especially through the joint work of Jung and Kerenyi, have proved to our satisfaction that the myth of the wonder child, of the childish or even babyish redeemer of a nation or of the entire human kind, is a permanent and universal archetype, shared by the mythological tradition of all the ancient and primitive peoples of the earth. What is more important, at least for us, is the fact, far less extraordinary in itself, that through his Fourth Eclogue Vergil introduces into pastoral poetry the paradoxical idea that a new Golden Age is at hand. By doing so, he reverses the traditional pattern, and introduces into the bucolic a metaphysical vision, and a messianic dimension, which were ignored before him. There is no doubt that Vergil was led to do so not by literary considerations but by philosophical ones. Even in this, he may have been influenced by those new religious beliefs of oriental origin, which were then penetrating Roman culture through the mediation of Alexandria, which in the ancient world was at that time an outpost of both East and West. Those new beliefs may have brought with them, in strange and garbled forms, some of the wildest hopes ever conceived by the people of God; hopes that had always been alien, and even opposed, not only to the views of classical civilization but even to its dreams. In brief, in this eclogue, which is a classical masterpiece of Latin verse as well as of that bucolic genre which was invented by Greece and perfected by Rome, Vergil suddenly introduces a nonclassical and nonpastoral element, not too different in kind from the Hebraic and biblical expectation of a divine visitation upon this earth. Without speaking of either Vergil or of pastoral poetry, Renan explains well what Vergil did in the Fourth Eclogue (i):

> Toute l'antiquité indo-européenne avait placé le paradis à l'origine; tous les poètes avaient pleuré un âge d'or évanoui. Israél mettait l'âge d'or dans l'avenir.

All Indo-European antiquity had placed Paradise at the beginning; all poets had wept over a Golden Age forever past. Israel placed the Golden Age in the time to come.

Thus, pastoral poetry, which had been always and solely sentimental and nostalgic, tried and succeeded in becoming, at least once, prophetic and oracular, and the Christian imagination, especially when trying to reconcile within itself the two antiquities, the classical and the biblical, learned this lesson only too well.

III

The two main motives of the Fourth Eclogue, combined in the double prophecy of the coming of the wonder child and of the advent of a new peace on earth for all Roman citizens (or, if we wish, for all men of good will), still inform the legend of the Nativity, to which they contribute its main pastoral charms. The redeeming child is a divine being, and yet he appears amidst men as the offspring of poor and humble parents, in a paradoxical aura of both misfortune and obscurity. He is not born in a house, or even a hut, but in a stable; he lies not in a cradle but in a manger; and in the bitter cold of winter, his little body is warmed only by the breath of the meekest of all domestic animals, a donkey and an ox. The divine nature of the child is revealed by heavenly signs, and yet the first acknowledgment that a god is born is given by the shepherds watching at night in the countryside of Bethlehem. The same shepherds, who represent all the poor in spirit, are the first human beings, besides his parents, that worship at his little feet, and they sing their simple tunes not only to celebrate his birth but also to amuse and humor him. And the pastoral mood of the whole scene reaches its triumphal climax when the rich and the powerful, the proud lords of the earth, recognize that the lowly way of life within which the child was born is higher and loftier than their own, and fully accept the Christian and pastoral commandment, according to which the exalted must be humbled, and the humble exalted. This happens when those three wise men of the East, knowing that a greater king than they has been born, follow the comet guiding them to the place of his birth and offer their royal gifts or, more simply, pay their tribute to a carpenter's son.

Pastoral traits can be found not only in the legend of the Nativity but also in the story of Christ's mission and teachings, as related by the Gospels: think of Jesus entering Jerusalem riding a donkey, or choosing his apostles among the humblest of the humble, the fishermen, of whom he makes his angler of souls; think especially of the parable of the herdsman who abandons a flock of ninety-nine sheep to find again the hundredth one, which is missing and must be lost in the wilderness. It is from this parable, so meaningful and suggestive, that Christianity later derived the most poetic of all its allegories, representing both Christ and the new faith under the figure of the good shepherd, carrying back on his shoulders the little sheep once lost. Christian symbolism seems able to translate into idyllic imagery even the highest moment in sacred history, the Passion of Christ and the Redemption of Man, the martyrdom and immolation of the Son of God. That moment, which transcends the most heroic and tragic visions ever shaped by the human mind, still allows itself to be represented under the pastoral emblem of *agnus dei*, the sacrificial lamb washing away all the sins of the world with its blood.

Yet the symbol of the "good shepherd" affected historical Christianity more durably and effectively than the emblem of "God's lamb." Thus the Church transferred the role represented by that symbol from Christ to his vicar on earth and attributed to all its ordained ministers the apostolic task of shepherding souls. Thus the pastoral, or shepherd's rod, became the sign of the priestly power over all the human herds of the earth. But religion, especially when it becomes institutionalized, cannot prevent the infidels, or even the faithful, from submitting its ideal premises, or mystical promises, to the test of fact. Pastoral literature manages successfully to avoid the ordeal of reality by escaping into dream and myth, by projecting its Golden Age into an irrevocable and irretrievable past. The Church could not always follow such an example, and this is why it saw its own pastoral allegory turned against itself. This was done by the enemies of the Church, all of them good Christians, who used for this purpose a new literary genre, mainly written in Latin, and generally known under the name of "allegorical pastoral." One could say, at least in a certain sense, that almost all pastoral poetry is allegorical, because it deals only rarely with shepherds in the literal sense of the term: in the main it uses the shepherd's disguise to give an idealized representation of the withdrawn artist, or the retired poet, of the solitary lover, or, more generally, of the man for whom private life is the highest value on earth. But the allegorical pastoral is allegorical in a specific and restricted sense: there shepherds and pastoral life do not stand for man in general, or for some universal trend of human nature, but for a particular profession, for a calling which is only of the very few. In brief, the allegorical pastoral makes fully its own the Christian symbolic identification of the shepherd with the priest. This identification is, so to speak, so technical as to suggest that the allegorical pastoral is no pastoral at all. We shall go even further and maintain that in reality it is a mock-pastoral, using the bucolic mask in order to condemn its own shepherds, rather than to celebrate them. Of all literary categories, satire is perhaps the least idyllic one, and the allegorical pastoral brings satire to the extreme limits of both invective and sarcasm.

All allegorical pastorals of this kind are in reality polemical religious tracts, written to maintain that the ministers of the Church and even the vicar of Christ on earth are not good shepherds but bad ones. They act more like temporal than like spiritual rulers, playing too often the role of shepherds of men rather than that of shepherds of souls, exchanging all too willingly the pastoral and the cross with the scepter and the sword. Instead of protecting their herds, or guiding them forward to greener pastures, they mislay and corrupt them. Their worst sin is perhaps their betrayal of the pastoral calling, a calling that demands from them, even more than from other Christians, a life of simplicity and humility, of obscurity and poverty. They replace the Imitation of Christ with the Imitation of Satan and are easily tempted into ambition and cupidity, striving after power and wealth, honor, and pomp. Thus they become both the scourge and the shame of their flocks: not shepherds but wolves in sheep's clothing, or black sheep.

In the main, the allegorical pastoral was directed against the secular clergy rather than against the spiritual, mystical, and contemplative orders, which were working more for the eternal than for the historical Church. The reasons for this are obvious, although at first sight pastoral symbolism seems more applicable to monks than to priests. The monk, after all, retreats in solitude from the world, to take care of his own soul more than that of others; from this viewpoint he resembles the literary shepherd more than the priest, who remains in the world without being of it, and who may perform his duties not only in a country parish but also in a town or in a big city, in a palace or a court. Yet the monastic calling has almost never been described in bucolic terms, either comically or seriously, allegorically or not. The reason for this is perhaps the universal awareness that while being sometimes not devoid of piety, the pastoral mode is alien from, and adverse to, any form of mysticism or asceticism. A convent or a monastery may be considered as an oasis in the desert of life, but it has nothing to do with the pastoral one. A bucolic retreat may be called a hermitage, but rather in the special and highly figurative sense that word had in eighteenth-century French. If pastoral life has any rules *clausura* is not one of them. Its great principle is moderation in the use of all good things of life, not an absolute and rigid abstention from all or any one of them. While avoiding any excessive self-indulgence, it rejects above all the mortification of the flesh. The shepherd is not an anchorite but the opposite: a wise and restrained hedonist. The only hermitage which could be established in Arcadian soil would be similar to the one envisaged by the unfrocked monk Rabelais, a kind of Abbaye de Thélème, surrounded by no walls, ruled by no other powers than those of *vouloir et franc arbitre,* so well exemplified by the motto *Fay ce que vouldrais;* and where time is not measured, since it is not man that is made for the hours of prayer but the hours of prayer that are made for man.

The residents (one would hardly say the inmates) of the Abbaye de Thélème are monks and nuns only in a metaphorical sense. In the same way, the identification of the holy men and women living in the cells of their convents or orders with shepherds or shepherdesses, would be merely a verbal one. In brief, such an identification, if made, would operate only on the plane of rhetoric rather than of imagination. It was the artificial dream to merge classical poetry with Christian belief that led the great Spanish mystic poet San Juan de la Cruz to call nymphs the saintly women of the Catholic calendar.

IV

There are many ways to decide whether a Christian pastoral is possible. One can for instance try to see what both allegory and satire may do to the bucolic framework of the so-called allegorical pastoral. One can also examine whether the form that we call pastoral elegy remains unchanged or not under the influence of the Christian conception of death. Finally one can try to study the reciprocal reaction of the evangelical with the classical element in a highly literary version of the legend of the Nativity. We shall do the last first, choosing for this purpose Milton's *On the Morning of Christ's Nativity*.

It is evident that Milton's poem is neither an idyll in the Theocritan sense nor an eclogue in the Vergilian one. In the prelude, the poet calls it an ode and, in the title of the poem itself, a hymn. The idyll and the eclogue, like the ode and the hymn, are often songs of praise, but while the former modestly celebrate human beings and earthly things, the latter proudly glorify either heroes or gods, and their virtues and deeds. Despite this, Milton derives this poem from the pastoral tradition, to which, even if only partially and exceptionally, it belongs. We should not forget that in Theocritus' canon there are not only the *eidyllia* but also the *epyllia*, the more ambitious poems reevoking in a pastoral key the passions, adventures, and undertakings of a minor god. Although the term *epyllion* means "miniature epic," those poems are rather a more lyrical and less lofty variation of that series of poems that tradition attributed to Homer and go under the name of Homeric Hymns. What is even more important to remember (even if we choose to forget the Christian interpretation of that piece) is Vergil's Fourth Eclogue, the most perfect example of the pastoral poet's willingness to heed the summons of a muse less rustic and simple than his own: "Sicelides Musae, paulo maiora canamus."

Milton was fully aware of all this when he wrote *On the Morning of Christ's Nativity*. The title itself clearly shows that the poem was conceived, like Vergil's Fourth Eclogue, as an occasional piece, and it does not matter very much that the occasion was in Vergil's case the unique event of the imminent birth of a wonder child, and in Milton's the holy day commemorating that event every year, to renew its historical reality and its everlasting meaning in all Christian souls. In brief, Milton's poem is an anniversary poem and an apotheosis at the same time, as its opening lines clearly indicate:

> This is the month, and this the happy morn,
> Wherein the Son of Heaven's eternal King,
> Of wedded Maid and Virgin Mother born,
> Our great redemption from above did bring.

As we realize from the beginning, the poem is a highly syncretic work on both the religious and the literary plane. This is manifest within the prelude itself, the very presence of which reveals the pastoral pattern of the entire composition. The most lyrical pastoral songs, which may be defined literally as songs by shepherds, are always presented by the bucolic poet as composed and chanted by others rather than by himself, who repeats those songs as he once heard them. In his prelude Milton follows this device of indirect introduction, with the difference that the announced poem (although he fails to say so) is his own. While Vergil asks his new and loftier inspiration from the bucolic Muses of Sicily, Milton addresses instead a rhetorical question to the "Heavenly Muse" of Christian poetry. In framing this question, he uses the bucolic conception of the poem as a personal offering, as a loving tribute to another being, whether man or god, but he merges this pagan idea with the Christian myth of the gifts that the wise men of the East brought to the babe who was to become Israel's King:

> Say, Heavenly Muse, shall not thy sacred vein
> Afford a present to the Infant God?

The poet wants his gift to be a rare and a new one, and since this present is going to be a poem, he wonders whether the muse of Christian poetry will make it possible for him to offer a poem more noble and precious than a simple and homely bucolic:

> Hast thou no verse, no hymn, or solemn strain,
> To welcome Him to this His new abode.

He begs the muse to make haste, so as to enable him to precede the three wise men with their rarer and richer gifts: he knows already that his poem will be a hymn or an ode, not an eclogue or an idyll, but that it will still remain a shepherd's song or offering, or, as he says, a "humble ode," to be placed modestly on the ground, with bowed head, on one's knees:

> See how from far upon the eastern road
> The star-led wizards haste with odours sweet!
> O run, prevent them with thy humble ode,
> And lay it lowly at His blessed feet.

The prelude shows its own dependence, and the dependence of the entire poem, on both Vergil's Fourth Eclogue and the entire pastoral tradition, in other ways than this. The poet is aware not only of the mythical but also of the oracular character of his own inspiration, as shown by his reference to the prophets, among whom the pagan Vergil should perhaps be included too: "For so the holy sages once did sing." In the same way, the closing of the first stanza refers to the "perpetual peace" to be brought on earth by both Father and Son, and it matters little that Milton and Vergil speak of different Persons, and of a very different Peace. Finally, the poet seems to exploit again in a new way the pastoral contrast between the lot of the powerful and the exalted and the lot of the humble and the poor, between the courts and the huts, when he describes the coming of Christ as his abandonment of his Father's mansion to be born in a stable as the Son of Man:

> Forsook the courts of everlasting day,
> And chose with us a darksome house of mortal clay.

There is in the prelude also a very different reference that prepares the ground for the dominant image of the Hymn itself. This idea is the absence on the morning of Christ's nativity of the sun, which stopped in his course "and hid his head for shame" when "he saw a greater Sun appear," realizing that "his inferior flame/The new-enlightened world no more should need." It is this very literal treatment of the Christian attribution of a solar symbolism to the figure of Christ that determines the main details and part of the structure of the whole poem. The sun's absence is significant from more viewpoints than one. While the painters of the poet's time, filled with a baroque obsession for the sharpest contrasts of darkness and light, generally preferred to paint the scene of the Nativity at night, Milton chooses instead, as emphasized by the poem's title, to reevoke the scene in the hours of early morning, at the time when "the Sun also rises." Even in this context the absence of the sun cannot be considered unnatural, since

> It was the winter wild,
> While the Heaven-born Child
> All meanly wrapt in the rude manger lies

or, more simply, the season when the weather is cold, and the sky misty and cloudy—although we know that what has eclipsed the sun is not a natural phenomenon. Yet the absence of the sun is more of a literary than a physical or metaphysical surprise. The pastoral, while humanizing nature, deifies the sun at the same time, and this is why the pastoral season par excellence is summer, when the earth dresses herself as beautifully as she can to please her divine lover. But Milton gives us a winter pastoral, lighted and heated by a spiritual sun rather than by the cosmic one. Yet he feels that he must explain the absence of the latter from the world of nature:

> It was no season then for her
> To wanton with the sun her lusty paramour.

In brief, nature is now clad in virginal attire, in a mantle of purity, in a dress of snow, thus hiding the nudity and the sins of the earth. The landscape is thus evoked in the light of the pastoral of sacred love, of what Blake would have called a song of innocence, which is however contrasted with the pastoral of profane love, with the song of experience. Winter itself seems to be endowed with the mildness of all bucolic climates and looks like a sort of new spring:

Only with speeches fair
She woos the gentle air
To hide her guilty front with innocent snow,
And on her naked shame,
Pollute with sinful blame,
The saintly veil of maiden white to throw.

The clemency of the weather coincides with the "perpetual peace" which the Father is now sending to earth to free nature from both its fright and its shame; and which the poet personifies in a feminine figure, pastoral in both the meekness of her gaze and the rustic simplicity of her symbolic garland of olive leaves. All the emblematic imagery connected with this figure (such as her "turtle wing" and her "myrtle wand") is obviously derived from the symbolism of the pastoral of love:

But He, her fears to cease,
Sent down the meek-eyed Peace;
She crowned with olive green, came softly sliding
Down through the turning sphere,
His ready harbinger,
With turtle wing the amorous clouds dividing,
And waving wide her myrtle wand,
She strikes a universal peace through sea and land.

The peace so established is described at first by the poet in worldly and Vergilian terms, as a *pax romana* rather than as a *pax christiana*, as a pause during which the sound and fury of human slaughter does not rage upon the earth:

No war or battle's sound
Was heard the world around.

But then this truce of arms expands into the truce of the elements, into the supernatural quiet of nature itself. Such enemies as winds and waters now embrace and caress each other; and the seascape

thus evoked reminds us of that supreme moment of cosmic love when
Venus was born from the foam of the waves:

> But peaceful was the night
> Where the Prince of Light
> His reign of peace upon the earth began:
> The winds with wonder whist,
> Smoothly the waters kissed,
> Whispering new joys to the mild Ocean.

What happens is in reality the suspension within the cosmos of
all motion, as well as of all strife; and this is why the sun refuses
to advance, and the stars to withdraw. Yet men are still not aware
of the event that has just taken place; they think that what they see
is but another day's dawn. This is true even of the shepherds, in
whose blessed ignorance there is more wisdom and insight than in
other men; and to whom, for this very reason, Christ's birth is revealed first. In this little scene Milton develops the pagan side of his
pastoral vision in the letter of the fables, and the Christian in its
spirit. He thus follows convention, the sympathetic attitude of the
old bucolic poets toward their poetic words, and treats with detached
indulgence the preoccupation of his evangelical shepherds with their
affairs of heart, as well as with their business. In the same way, he
accepts fully the tradition that Pan is the god of all Arcadian peoples
and lands, while using Pan himself as a figure for the Son of God,
who will redeem Jew and Gentile, barbarian and Greek. This symbolic
identification is made even more complicated by an implied reference
to the legend reported by Plutarch that at a time that Christian
readers find to coincide with Christ's birth a voice was heard shouting
across the sea, "Great Pan is dead!" (*De defectu oraculorum,* xvii).
Milton's allusion to the shepherds' ignorance of what has just happened must be read, on the literal plane, as their unawareness that
Pan has been reborn and has returned to their midst:

> The shepherds on the lawn,
> Or ere the point of dawn,
> Sat simply chatting in a rustic row;

Full little thought they then
That the mighty Pan
Was kindly come to live with them below,
Perhaps their loves or else their sheep,
Was all that did their silly thoughts so busy keep.

Like all their literary peers, the shepherds of Bethlehem are ready and willing to forget all their cares under the spell of music and song. The music they hear is the harmony of the spheres, which enraptures nature itself; and the song is but the choir of the angels, whom they see arrayed in a globe of light against the darkness of night. That "angelic symphony" has sounded for the first time as a hymn of praise to God for creating the world out of chaos itself: and if it lasted longer it would bring back the happiness and the innocence that creature and man enjoyed when they issued from nothingness as God's still unspoiled handiwork. In brief, if that divine music and song were to continue, they would restore on earth the Garden of Eden, which Milton, following the pastoral fiction, describes in terms of the Golden Age of old. Such a restoration would imply the disappearance of vanity, which pastoral poetry considers the foremost of all vices, as well as of its worst consequence, which is what pagans would call crime, and Christians sin. This would involve the abolition of punishment and retribution, or the vanishing of Hell, where man pays the wages of sin:

For if such holy song
Enwrap our fancy long,
Time will run back and fetch the age of gold,
And speckled vanity
Will sicken soon, and die;
And lep'rous sin will melt from earthly mould,
And Hell itself will pass away,
And leave her dolorous mansions to the peering day.

In the same way, the pastoral virtues of truth and justice would come back, and with them the Christian virtue of mercy, and under the sign of the rainbow, betokening the new peace between God and

man. Thus man would forever leave his mortal abode down on earth
for his Father's mansions above:

> Yea, Truth and Justice then
> Will down return to men,
> Orbed in a rainbow; and, like glories wearing,
> Mercy will sit between,
> Throned in celestial sheen,
> With radiant feet the tissued clouds down-steering,
> And Heaven, as at some festival,
> Will open wide the gates of her high palace-hall.

For all pastoral poets, the Golden Age remains forever a remembrance or a dream of the past: and only Vergil in the Fourth Eclogue
believed for a while that it was at hand, as the early Christians believed of the Kingdom of God. But Israel, says Renan, placed the
Golden Age in the future, and Christianity accepts this belief, modifying it in the sense that it will come at the end of time, and outside
of this world. Adumbrating one of the mystical ideas he develops in
Paradise Lost (the idea of the *felix culpa*, the "fortunate fall" of
Adam and Eve, which made necessary mankind's redemption and
the coming of the Son of God), Milton denies now the very hypothesis he suggested before. No, Providence (which he paganly calls
fate) has designed otherwise:

> But wisest Fate says No,
> This must not yet be so,
> The Babe yet lies in smiling infancy,
> That on the bitter cross
> Must redeem our loss,
> So both Himself and us to glorify:
> Yet first to those chained in sleep,
> The wakeful trump of doom must thunder through the deep.

In brief, the Age of Gold will be restored only after the day of the
Last Judgment, which Milton evokes in theogonic and biblical terms.
Yet the pastoral implication, in the form it takes in Vergil's Fourth

Eclogue, seduces him again, and he claims that Christ's birth is the promise and the beginning of a Golden Age which is both present and to come. After the advent of Christ, the Tempter or the Usurper (whom Milton represents in the shape of a dragon) will be held in check and will less easily sway all men:

> And then at last our bliss
> Full and perfect is,
> But now begins; for from this happy day
> Th' old Dragon under-ground,
> In straiter limits bound,
> Not half so far casts his usurped sway,
> And, wroth to see his kingdom fail,
> Swinges the scaly horror of his folded tail.

One could say that the whole poem is built on a varying relationship with Vergil's Fourth Eclogue, now converging with and now diverging from it, and that at this point it veers starkly away from its model and takes the opposite path. We may remember that the Fourth Eclogue took its inspiration from the Sibylline Books and pretends to announce the final age already prophesied by the oracles of the Cumaean Sybil. Milton answers this by stating that Christ's birth, while fulfilling the promises of the biblical prophets, has muted the voices of all pagan oracles and their priestesses and priests:

> The oracles are dumb,
> No voice or hideous hum
> Runs through the arched roof in words deceiving.
> Apollo from his shrine
> Can no more divine,
> With hollow shriek the steep of Delphos leaving.
> No nightly trance or breathed spell
> Inspires the pale-eyed priest from the prophetic cell.

Apollo was as much Pan's pastoral god: and if he can divine no more, then his poet cannot divine either. And this grieves the nymphs weeping in the woods:

With flower-inwoven tresses torn
The nymphs in twilight shade of tangled thickets mourn.

It is here that there begins the famous passage in the Hymn con-
necting pastoral and myth. We would maintain that mythology has
hardly more than a decorative function in the pastoral and that this
Christian pastoral takes the ancient gods too seriously by conjuring
them away with such strong spells. True enough, the object of Milton's curse is not only the rather harmless and literary pagan gods of
classical antiquity but also the monstrous and barbaric divinities of
the ancient East: Phoenician, Assyrian, Babylonian, Egyptian idols
against which Israel fought on behalf of both itself and its God. Milton's imagination, being both classical and biblical (rather than evangelical), was thus led to show more sympathy toward the gods celebrated by the pagan poets than toward those cursed by the Hebrew
prophets, although the former were still alive at the coming of the
Son, and the latter had been already slain by the chosen people of
the Father. This is why the gods of classical mythology seem to survive in this poem, and to remain among us, even if they stay apart,
and weep while we rejoice. This at least is what not only the nymphs
but also the good and bad geniuses of the house, the Lars and
Lemures, seem to do in this poem. But the nonclassical pagan gods,
like Peor and Baalim "forsake their temples dim," while Moloch and
"the brutish gods of Nile," Isis, Orus, and the dog Anubis, hastily
flee, somewhere or nowhere:

> Nor is Osiris seen
> In Memphian grove or green.

They no "longer dare abide" in the presence of the Babe, showing
"His Godhead true," and disappear as shadows at sunrise. The Babe,
who is the spiritual sun, falls asleep in the morning, which has not
yet been revisited by the physical sun, and this is why his couch,
surrounded by angels, is lit by the newest of all stars. The poem ends
with the closing vision of either a cradle song or a fairy tale, and all
its paradoxes seem to be summed up in the final one, or in a neat

pastoral antithesis, made by the juxtaposition of the epithet "courtly" and the noun "stable":

> But see, the Virgin blest
> Hath laid her Babe to rest:
> Time is our tedious song should here have ending,
> Heaven's youngest teemed star,
> Hath fixed her polished car,
> Her sleeping Lord with handmaid lamp attending:
> And all about the courtly stable,
> Bright-harnessed angels sit in order serviceable.

6

Dante
"Poco Tempo Silvano":
A Pastoral Oasis
in the *Commedia*

I

The brief stay of Dante the pilgrim in
the Earthly Paradise (*Purg.* xxviii–xxxiii),
which the poet locates on the very top of
the lonely and lofty mountain of Purgatory, may be considered as the single
"pastoral oasis" in the *Commedia*.[1] It is
undeniably in such literary terms, and in
no other, that Dante envisages both the
place and his stay therein: a view made
evident by the fact that Vergil accom-
panies him on that visit. This time Vergil
is not Dante's only companion; yet, even
though he will go no farther, it is quite
noteworthy that he is allowed to enter the
Garden of Eden and still to act, at least up
to its threshold, as Dante's guide. It is obvious that at this stage Vergil is to be

thought of as the author of the *Eclogues*, as well as of the *Aeneid*. The third visitor, and Dante's second companion, is another Latin poet, Statius, a converted pagan who has just ended his long purgation and who, like Dante, is on his way to heaven. The difference is that Dante is a traveler who will return to the earth at the end of his journey, whereas Statius will dwell forever among the blessed. This means in practice that the Garden of Eden is a pastoral oasis for the two Christian pilgrims, but not for Vergil, the pagan sage.

As is the case with many a pastoral oasis, the reader is introduced and admitted to it through a *locus amoenus* of uncommon length, and of extraordinary beauty.[2] Along with the three visitors, he lingers in a splendid landscape, and wanders through "la divina foresta spessa e viva" (the divine forest green and dense; *Purg.* xxviii): an immense grove immersed in a soft light, caressed by a gentle breeze, enlivened by swarms of singing birds, and refreshed by a lovely stream, running with its limpid waters between banks of grass and flowers. Beyond that stream we see the mysterious Matelda, the charming maid who is the custodian of the place. We surprise her in the act of gathering flowers, and Dante pays Matelda and her surroundings a magnificent mythological compliment, likening her to Proserpine just as she stood, while gathering flowers beside her mother, on the meadow where Pluto seized her and brought her forever to the nether world:

> Tu mi fai rimembrar dove e qual era
> Proserpina nel tempo che perdette
> la madre lei, ed ella primavera.

Thou makest me recall where and what was Proserpine at the time her mother lost her and she the spring.[3]

It is well known that Dante tends constantly to merge pagan and Christian elements, and this reference to Proserpine should not surprise too much in a context full of allusions to Venus, which an all too literally minded reader might find, at least at first sight, even more unsuitable. But besides merging the pagan and the Christian Dante tends to "contaminate" also the ancient and the modern, so that the presence of that classical reference should not prevent the reader from sharing the view, advanced by a recent critic,[4] that the meeting of Dante and Matelda is molded after a lyrical genre, the so-called *pastorela*,[5] which from Provençal verse spread to the vernacular poetry of all the Romance lands. In a *pastorela* the poet, who in the original Provençal version is also a knight, retells in the first person how once, on a spring day, going through the countryside, he unexpectedly met a country girl, generally a shepherdess.[6] The poet relates his talk with the girl; his realization that she was in a passionate mood; his sudden impulse, in tune with the occasion and the season, to make love to her. For choosing a simple and humble creature as the object of the poet's passion, the *pastorela* breaks the bonds of courtly love, and tends to end with the blissful consummation of amorous desire.

Needless to say Dante's and Matelda's encounter seeks and finds no other fulfillment but spiritual joy: an outcome no less in keeping with pastoral conventions, or at least with the noblest of them. At any rate, whether or not her apparition is analogous to that of a shepherdess in a medieval *pastorela*, it is Matelda in person, at the end of her very long account about the Earthly Paradise, that not only acknowledges the bucolic quality of the place, but even suggests that the ancient poets may have prefigured the Garden of Eden in their fabulous vision of the Golden Age:

> Quelli ch'anticamente poetaro
> l'età de l'oro e suo stato felice,
> forse in Parnaso esto loco sognaro.

Those who in old times sang of the age of gold and of its happy state perhaps dreamed in Parnasus of this place.

This implies also the reverse, that Dante is now repatterning the Garden of Eden after the bucolic visions of classical poetry, and Matelda's words should suffice to prove that this section of Purgatorio is indeed a pastoral oasis. It is with a wealth of lesser details that Dante emphasizes further this connection between the reality of the Earthly Paradise and the pastoral dream of a time or state of perfect human happiness. The most suggestive of such details may well appear the nymphlike representation not only of a spiritual being like Matelda, always treated like a real person, but even of such abstractions as the personified allegories of the cardinal virtues, which abide in both Eden and Heaven, or, as they say themselves in a lovely line (xxxi): "Noi siam qui ninfe e nel ciel siamo stelle" (Here we are nymphs and in heaven are stars).

Matelda's reference to the ancient singers of the Age of Gold sounds like a discreet compliment, addressed to both Statius and Vergil, but primarily to the latter. Her words help us to understand why Vergil himself had anticipated her own account of the Earthly Paradise. On its threshold Vergil had briefly mentioned to Dante one of the extraordinary powers or virtues that site holds in common with the Golden Age (xxvii):

> Vedi l'erbetta, i fiori e li arbuscelli
> che qui la terra sol da sé produce.

See the grass, the flowers and trees which the ground here brings forth of itself alone.

Matelda will dwell at greater length than Vergil upon this power, which is the spontaneous generation of all plants, flowers, and fruits, as well as upon two other virtues, which Vergil had failed to point out to his disciple, although they too are shared alike by the Garden of Eden and the Age of Gold. The first of them is the absolute freedom of either place from what Shakespeare calls "the penalty of Adam, the season's difference" (As You Like It, II.i), or the perturbation of the weather. After explaining the supernatural causes of the unchanging mildness of the climate, Matelda sums up that condition by the concise words: "qui primavera sempre" (xxviii), or with the traditional formula of a perennial spring, the only season of a year without cycles. And it is again worth remarking that Dante shapes such formula in a literal translation of Ovid's phrase: "Ver erat aeternum" (Met. i.107).

The second of the bountiful wonders marking both Garden of Eden and Age of Gold which Vergil has failed to mention, but Matelda chooses to emphasize, is the miraculous quality of the liquid element. It is not water that flows in the rivers gracing both landscapes, but the liquor which was the drink of the gods, as ambrosia was their food or, as Matelda says, "Nettare è questo di che ciascun dice"

(This is the nectar of which each tells). The "each" or "all" to whom Matelda alludes are again the ancient poets: yet, strangely enough, that very nectar detail of which all of them supposedly spoke is missing from the account of the Age of Gold as given in the Fourth Eclogue. There Vergil had treated that age as a thing not of the distant past but of the imminent future; the happiness announced in that poem is that of social and political peace rather than the state of nature's. It is then evident that Dante patterned Matelda's description of the Garden of Eden not on Vergil's but on Ovid's evocation of the Golden Age. It is indeed from the *Metamorphoses* (i.111) that he also had learned that in those primitive times "flumina nectaris ibant" (there flowed rivers of nectar), a prodigy accompanied by similar portents, such as streams of milk and honey.

Ovid's account is part of a fuller story, that of mankind's four ages, which he reports up to the one still with us, that of iron. His description of the Age of Gold is then not a self-contained fragment but, significantly, only the opening episode in that ancient tale of the gradual and total corruption of the human race, which the medieval Dante obviously read as an unconscious pagan prefiguration of the story of the Fall, or of the doctrine of original sin. This certainly explains why he depicted the Early Paradise not only after *Genesis* (ii.8–9):

> And the Lord planted a garden eastward in Eden; and
> there he put the man whom he had formed.
> And out of the ground made the Lord God grow every
> tree that is pleasant to the sight, and good for food.

but also after Ovid's account of the Golden Age. Yet this fails by itself to convey the meaning and purport of his or of any other poet's pastoral reinterpretation of the Garden of Eden. The Age of Gold and the Earthly Paradise may easily be correlated, but hardly made to coincide. It is evident that by turning to the *Metamorphoses*' account, rather than to that of the Fourth Eclogue, Dante wants to emphasize that the pagan Golden Age belongs to an irrevocable past.

At first sight this seems to be equally true of the Earthly Paradise, which, since Adam and Eve were forever chased from that "garden

of delights," had remained the highest and central point of the un-
inhabited hemisphere or, in Ulysses' words (*Inf.* xxvi), "del mondo
sanza gente" (of the world without people). Yet the site still exists
in time and space; moreover, Dante is allowed to linger there for a
while, and made to learn the lesser but still intemporal truths of
which that place and state are the visible symbols. Thus, at least in
a spiritual sense, the Earthly Paradise signifies a kind of ideal present,
whereas the heavenly one represents the abolition of historical and
astronomical time, or, as Petrarch would say, the "triumph of eter-
nity." While denying any identity between the Age of Gold and the
Garden of Eden, still Dante's short stay in the latter literally acts as
a kind of pastoral oasis within the economy and context of his "sacred poem." One must then seek and find the significance of such
a strange and mysterious pause in Dante's pilgrim's progress, or in
the ascent of man's soul toward Heaven.

II

Dante believed that there are prophetic dreams, and it is by one
of such dreams, prefiguring the experience he will undergo in the
Garden of Eden, that he helps the reader to understand the sense
and function of the pastoral oasis about to rise on the horizon of his
Commedia. The night before crossing the threshold of the Earthly
Paradise, his sleeping mind is visited by the vision of a young and
lovely woman, wandering through a lonely heath and gathering
flowers. While doing so, she sings this chant (*Purg.* xxvii):

> Sappia qualunque il mio nome dimanda
> ch'i' mi son Lia, e vo movendo intorno
> le belle mani a farmi una ghirlanda.
> Per piacermi alo specchio, qui m'addorno;
> ma mia suora Rachel mai non si smaga
> dal suo miraglio, e siede tutto il giorno.
> Ell' è d'i suoi begli occhi veder vaga
> com' io de l'addornarmi delle mani;
> lei lo vedere, e me l'ovrare appaga.

Know, whoever asks my name, that I am Leah, and I go plying
my fair hands here and there to make me a garland; to please me

at the glass I here adorn myself, but my sister Rachel never leaves her mirror and sits all day. She is fain to see her own eyes as I to adorn me with my hands. She with seeing, and I with doing am satisfied.

The theologians had already used the biblical figures of the two daughters of Laban, Leah and Rachel, both of whom their father gave as wives to Jacob (*Gen.* xxix.27–30), for the respective allegories of the active and the contemplative life. There is no doubt that the vision of Leah, gathering flowers like Matelda, forecasts the apparition of the latter. This consideration has led many commentators to claim that the custodian of the Early Paradise shares the traditional allegorical significance of her biblical counterpart. Such an interpretation seems confirmed by the contrasting images of the two sisters, the one moving outside, the other sitting inside the house, and by the reduction of their figures to such striking symbolic details as Rachel's "fair eyes" and Leah's "fair hands." Yet it is difficult to forget that, just like the Age of Gold, the Earthly Paradise is not the realm of activity, but of leisure. No better proof of this than the very words by which the Lord judged and condemned Adam for his trangression (*Gen.* iii.19): "In the sweat of thy face shalt thou eat bread, till thou return unto the ground": words that for man meant the curse of work, as well as the curse of death.

One must admit that working ("ovrare"), rather than seeing ("vedere"), is the single motivation of Leah's being, just as it is of Matelda's essence. Only working gratifies ("appaga") Leah's soul. Yet, if we look deeper, we shall see that working is for her a matter of choice, not of necessity. Just like Matelda, she is busy with gathering lovely and useless flowers, rather than such homely and useful products of the earth as acorns, berries, or even fruits.[7] She works not to satisfy instinctual needs, but to perform a superfluous and gratuitous act: to adorn herself, in a gesture both spontaneous and deliberate, of self-fulfillment. This means that Dante's Leah cannot be taken as an allegory of the active life, because she stands for self-contemplation, no less and no more than her sister. If Rachel sits perpetually before her mirror ("miraglio"), Leah too, at least once in a while, turns to her glass ("specchio"). Yet Leah's self-contemplation is of an outer kind, whereas Rachel's is of an inner one: which is another way of saying that the latter prefigures Beatrice in the same way her sister prefigures Matelda. And it is Matelda who takes upon herself to define the real object of the kind of contemplation which she and Leah represent. That object is not the divine mystery but the perfection and beauty of God's world.

Matelda's mood is one of serene mirth, and one could say that she plays the role of a feminine counterpart of Milton's Allegro in the pastoral oasis of Dante's journey. Yet she rejoices through contemplation, so that she seems to act at the same time, even though without melancholy, the Penseroso's part. This second aspect, however, is not as apparent as the first, and she realizes that to an uninitiated visitor her outward joy, which she conveys in song and dance, may appear unseemly, or at least misplaced. You are strangers here, she tells Dante and his companions, and you may well wonder and doubt why I am so full of mirth (xxviii):

> "Voi siete nuovi, e forse perch' io rido"
> cominciò ella, "in questo luogo eletto
> a l'umana natura per suo nido,
> maravigliando tienvi alcun sospetto."

"You are new here" she began "and, perhaps because I smile in this place set apart to the human kind for its nest, some doubt keeps you wondering."

Yet you will understand the mystery of my merriment, Matelda continues, if you recall the word of God:

> Ma luce rende il salmo *Delectasti*,
> che puote disnebbiar vostro intelletto.

But the psalm *Delectasti* gives light that may dispel the cloud from your mind.

The psalm to which Matelda alludes is the ninety-first of the Vulgate (the ninety-second of the Protestant Bible): and she refers particularly to the passage (4, 5) marked almost by its beginning by the verb she has just quoted:

Qui delectasti me, Domine, in factura tua, et in operatione manuum tuarum exultabo.
Quam magnificata sunt opera tua, Domine.

Strangely (or naturally) enough, the passage rings with a far less
enthusiastic joy in the King James version. In the latter, if compared
with the Latin text, the same passage reads, puritanwise, almost as
an understatement:

> For thou, Lord, hast made me glad through thy work:
> I will triumph in the works of thy hands.
> O Lord, how great are thy works! . . .

Here the worker is not man, but God, and what Matelda means to
say by her reference to that psalm is that in the place she oversees,
or in the state that place symbolizes, man is bound to imitate God's
magnificent artifice, and contemplate in joyful admiration the Lord's
glorious handiwork.[8]

Such a joy is obviously not the joy of the blessed—it is simply
the sense of happiness that man feels in recognizing himself as part
of the Lord's creation, as a creature who may serve God's ends even
by fulfilling the highest demands of his own nature. That such is the
truth Matelda intends to convey is clearly and fully proved by a
famous passage in the final chapter of the De monarchia (iii.16).
There Dante exposes the two purposes Providence assigns to man.
Far more important, for being the harder and higher, is the second
of the two: the contemplation of the divine vision, to which man
cannot rise by his unaided efforts but only with the help of grace.
But Providence admits also of another purpose, lower and easier, yet
worthy and noble, which consists of the unfolding ("operatione") of
man's faculties or, as we moderns would say, in the free development
of his powers. While defining man's major purpose as "the bliss of
eternal life," Dante defines the lesser one as "the bliss of his own
life."

What matters most for the present argument is that for Dante those two kinds of bliss are respectively symbolized in the two Paradises, the loftier in the heavenly, and the less exalted in the earthly one. Whereas the "beatitudo vitae eternae," Dante says, "per paradisum celestem intelligi datur," the "beautitudo hujus vitae," on the contrary, "per terrestrem paradisum figuratur." This is why the human herd needs two shepherds to lead it on the right paths: the Pope, who guides mankind toward eternal life with the help of revelation; and the emperor, who guides it toward worldly happiness with the aid of philosophical wisdom or, as Dante says, "qui, secundum philosophica documenta ad temporalem felicitatem dirigerit."

That there is a direct connection between Dante's conception of the Earthly Paradise as envisaged in the *Commedia* and the *De monarchia* passage just cited is made evident by Vergil's crowning of his disciple, just before entering the Garden of Eden, as his own ruler. While doing so, Vergil says (xxvii): "te sovra te corono e mitrio" (over thyself I crown and mitre thee), and the last word has led most commentators to believe that Vergil anoints Dante not only as the temporal but also as the spiritual leader, of himself: as his own bishop, or even pontiff, as well as his own emperor. But one must agree with a recent interpreter that the crowning and mitring which Vergil performs ideally over his disciple is patterned after the ceremonial of imperial coronation rather than after the elevation ritual of a new bishop or of a new pope.[9]

There is no doubt that Vergil prepares Dante for the experience he is about to undergo, and for the lesson he will learn in the Earthly Paradise, by making him the like of the emperor. The emperor rules over the whole of the human kind, whereas Dante now rules over the man in himself, and is at once his own lord and his own liege. It is then clear that as idea and figure the Earthly Paradise stands for the wordly and universal empire: but that as a real place or state it stands for the moral and intellectual empire of man over himself. The difference between these two sovereignties is that the first is deemed to establish the objective conditions which will bring forth mankind's collective happiness, and the second is deemed to make man's individual happiness both necessary and possible. It is not anachronistic to say that the Garden of Eden represents that legitimate "pursuit of happiness" that the American commonwealth felt should be constitutionally guaranteed to all men and specifically to its own citizens.[10]

III

The two great divisions of bucolic poetry are the pastoral of innocence and the pastoral of happiness. Dante knows that such an alternative exists and is well aware of all it implies. Those two kinds of pastoral differ in emphasis and outlook: bucolic poets deal with both of them but cannot do so at the same time. Dante must choose, and there is no doubt about his choice. It is evident that throughout this section of *Purgatorio* he intends to convey an idyllic vision of man's happiness in the present of individual life, rather than an elegiac evocation of the lost innocence of the human race. It is indeed with a verb in the past tense that Matelda speaks of Eden as an abode of innocence (xxviii): "Qui fu innocente l'umana radice" (Here the human root was innocent) whereas it is with the present of the same verb that Beatrice speaks of Earthly Paradise as an abode of happiness (xxx): "Non sapei tu che qui è l'uom felice?" (Didst thou not know that here man is happy?). These two quotes definitely prove that the pastoral oasis of the *Commedia* is conceived exclusively in the terms of the pastoral of happiness.[11]

Yet the happiness embodied in Eden can be achieved only in personal justice: a condition that justifies the parallel between the emperor and Dante, or the analogy between world rule and self-rule. Hence the presence in the Earthly Paradise, as well as in the Age of Gold, of a feminine figure standing for justice. We must agree with the American scholar who identifies Matelda with the virgin Astraea, and maintain with him that either of them is an allegory of natural justice, the one in Christian and the other in pagan disguise.[12] The circumstances that made possible the Age of Gold were a gift of the gods: a token not only of man's innocence but also of his irresponsibility. This is made clear in Ovid's account of the Golden Age (*Met.* i.89–93):

Aurea prima sata est aetas, quae vindice nullo,
sponte sua, sine lege fidem rectumque colebat.
poena metusque aberant, nec verba minantia fixo

aere ligabantur nec supplex turba timebat
iudicis ora sui, sed erant sine iudice tuti.

Golden was that first age, which, with no one to compel, without a law, of its own will, kept faith and did the right. There was no fear of punishment, no threatening words to be read on brazen tablets; no suppliant throng gazed fearfully upon its judge's face; but without judges lived secure.[13]

Justice was then a merit not of mankind, but of the age, and this is why that happy state could not last. The final sign of man's corruption was Astraea's flight from this world, signifying man's ultimate oblivion or disregard of natural justice (127–129, 149–150):

> . . . De duro est ultima ferro.
> Protinus inrupit venae peioris in aevum
> omne nefas. . . .
> Victa iacet pietas, et virgo caede madentis
> ultima caelestum terras Astraea reliquit.

The age of hard iron came last. Straightway all evil burst forth into this age of baser vein. Piety lay vanquished, and the maiden Astraea, last of the immortals, abandoned the blood-soaked earth.

For this reason the justice and happiness now symbolized in Eden must rest on man's responsibility. The Earthly Paradise is a bucolic landscape, yet the "selva antica" (ancient wood; xxviii) which makes of that landscape a garden of delights must be viewed as a transfiguration of the "selva oscura" (dark wood; *Inf.* i) of error and sin. Like many a pastoral oasis, it is a dwelling place for Naiads or Dryads; its nymphs, however, are at once heavenly stars and personifications of the cardinal virtues (*Purg.* xxx). It is a *locus amoenus* overflowing with evergreen plants and perennial flowers; but its flora still includes the bare and gray tree of knowledge, suddenly reflowering for the pilgrim's benefit (xxii), and thus turning anew into the green tree of life.

All this explains how and why Dante cannot enter the pastoral oasis or Eden until he is formally recognized the master, rather than the servant, of his will. Such is the function of the words Vergil utters during the ritual by which he crowns the pilgrim as his own ruler (xxvii):

> Non aspettar mio dir più né mio cenno:
> libero, dritto e sano è tuo arbitrio,
> e fallo fora non fare a suo senno:
> per ch'io te sovra te corono e mitrio.

No longer expect word or sign from me. Free, upright and whole is thy will and it were a fault not to act at its bidding; therefore over thyself I crown and mitre thee.

If your will is free, upright, and whole, Vergil tells Dante, then you not only *may*, but *should* do what you wish. By this command, Vergil, or rather Dante, may almost seem to anticipate the single rule which Gargantua imposed on his Abbaye de Thélème:[14] "Fay ce que vouldras" (*Garg.* lvii). All spiritual and historical differences notwithstanding, the sense, if not the tone, of Vergil's and Dante's command is the same as that of Gargantua and Rabelais: and one may even see a kind of poetic justice in the fact that whereas Rabelais, a Renaissance humanist, chose to project his vision of the freedom of the human spirit in the religious image of a monastic order, the medieval Dante chose instead to convey the same vision in the profane and classical fable of the pastoral world.

Both Rabelais's Abbaye de Thélème and Dante's Earthly Paradise stand for an activity which is of the spirit if not of the soul: for a cultivation of the self made of speculation and contemplation, of the earnest wisdom of philosophy and of the "merry wisdom" of poetry, and, we may confidently add, of both the creation and the enjoyment of music and the arts. Leah's and Matelda's garlands may suggest the lovely handiwork of either sculpture or painting; as for music, let us not forget that Matelda sings and dances before us.[15] All this proves again that the Garden of Eden is the place of both pleasure and leisure: of a distinterested and productive *otium* allowing man to exercise fully and freely not the mechanical but the liberal arts, those, as Montaigne would say, that render us free. Thus the Earthly Paradise is no place for lotus eaters: and this is why the stream crossing it with its miraculous waters is not only the river of oblivion, washing away the memory of error and sin, but also the river of remembrance, refreshing the memory of good thoughts and deeds. Hence the double name of that watercourse, called Lethe at one end, and at the other, Eunoe (xxviii).

All this implies that in Dante's view the Earthly Paradise is the ideal abode of man as a civilized being, as a child of nurture, rather than of nature. With a term which may seem misleading in meaning and prosaic in tone, one could say that its ideal indweller is the Christian humanist, or even the medieval poet or artist. This is why Vergil can penetrate the garden only up to a point, beyond which he cannot proceed, and from which he must turn back. We know very well to what place he will return: to Limbo, and more precisely to the "nobile castello" (noble castle; *Inf.* iv), where the spirits of the ancient sages forever dwell.

The noble castle of Limbo, that part of the first and dark kingdom which is indeed "an air-conditioned Hell," [16] and the Earthly Paradise, that kind of hanging garden on the lofty peak of the Purgatory mountain, may be viewed as two points on the same ideal line, but at opposite ends. Their most obvious contrasting traits are that the first is an indoor site, and the second an outdoor one. Even though it lies without the city of Dis, the noble castle is still within the pit of Hell. Like Dis, it is conceived as if it were a medieval fortress, with its walls and moats; its only natural landscape is but a "prato di fresca verdura," merely a lawn of fresh grass (*Inf.* iv). It is by an artificial light, or a "fire" of its own, that it makes itself visible in the darkness of Hell. On the contrary there is no architecture or artifice of any kind within the whole of Eden. The latter is but a forest, a meadow, a garden, a rich product of the earth, with the radious light of *plein air*. This may mean that for Dante only Christian culture is able to reconcile man with nature, the inner with the outer world.

If Eden really stands for Christian culture, we may well understand why this pastoral oasis excludes such important variants of the bucolic dispensation as the pastorals of humility and simplicity.[17] This does not mean that they are wholly alien to Dante's imagination, but that the poet turns to them in other contexts. Thus for instance the pastoral of humility makes a short-lived appearance in the

purification ceremony at the beginning of *Purgatorio* (ii), when Dante
is crowned with a garland of reeds; whereas the pastoral of simplicity briefly resounds in the Hound prophecy in the reference to the
pastoral oasis of Vergil's *Aeneid*,[18] or rather in the illusion to the
"umile Italia" (humble Italy; *Inf.* i) which Aeneas conquered, and
over which Rome was to rule.

IV

Since the Earthly Paradise symbolizes the cultivation of human
faculties in personal terms, it is then obvious why in the *Commedia's*
pastoral oasis there is no place for another variant of the bucolic
vision, the pastoral of peace. The Earthly Paradise lies within the
geography of our world, being at the center of the hemisphere of
water, but it is no part of human history, which has been unfolding
only in the hemisphere of land. The spirit of the site cannot therefore be conveyed by the pastoral of peace, which found its earliest
and highest expression in Vergil's Fourth Eclogue. The pastoral of
peace is always related to history, as proved, rather than denied, by
its prophetic inspiration. It matters little whether it prophesies political peace, *pax romana,* as Vergil meant to do in his poem, or
spiritual peace, *pax christiana,* as many baptized interpreters thought
its author unwillingly did. It is evident that Dante could hardly
avoid coping also with the pastoral of peace, at least with its Vergilian archetype, and in fact he did so in another section of the same
canticle, on the occasion of the meeting between Vergil and Statius.
Statius thanks Vergil for having helped him to become not only a
poet but also a Christian, or for having unconsciously forecast the
coming of Christ in the most famous of his "buccolici carmi" (pastoral songs; *Purg.* xxii). In this passage Statius, or rather Dante,
takes the most significant hexameters of the Fourth Eclogue:

> Magnus ab integro saeclorum nascitur ordo:
> iam redit et Virgo, redeunt Saturnia regna;
> iam nova progenies caelo demittitur alto.

Time has conceived and the great Sequence of the Ages starts
afresh. Justice, the Virgin, comes back to dwell with us, and the
rule of Saturn is restored. The Firstborn of the New Age is already on his way from high heaven down to the earth.[19]

and rephrases them concisely in a single terzina:

> quando dicesti: "Secol si rinova;
> torna giustizia e primo tempo umano,
> e progenie scende dal ciel nova."

when thou saidst: "The age turns new again; justice comes back, and the primal state of man, and a new offspring descends from heaven."

By this celebrated quote Dante makes the pastoral of peace not only a moment in history but also a moment in the biography of a Christian soul. Yet it is only after the historical restoration of the Golden Age, or after the coming of Christ, that the spirit of man, whether freed from the chain of the flesh, as in Statius' case, or still dwelling in a human body, as in Dante's, is allowed to linger again in the Garden of Eden. In brief, the pastoral of peace is a necessary prelude to the pastoral of happiness, just as the latter is a necessary prelude to the return of that lost sheep, the soul, into God's fold.

It is then evident that the Earthly Paradise, if related on one side to the noble castle of Limbo, is related on the other to the Heavenly Paradise. But whereas the souls dwell eternally in either Hell or Heaven, the spirit of man dwells only temporarily and vicariously in Eden. Like any other, the pastoral oasis of the *Commedia* cannot be but an interval or an interlude. God had created the Earthly Paradise as a nest for human nature (xxviii); yet, by yielding to temptation and committing sin, even Adam had remained there for too short a while:

> Per sua difalta qui dimorò poco;
> per sua difalta in pianto e in affanno
> cambiò onesto riso e dolce gioco.

Through his fault he had short stay here, through his fault he exchanged for tears and toil honest mirth and sweet sport.

By both choice and necessity also Dante, as Beatrice tells him, cannot stay but briefly in the same place (xxxii):

Qui sarai tu poco tempo silvano;
e sarai meco sanza fine cive
di quella Roma onde Cristo è romano.

Here thou shalt be a little while a forester, and shalt be with me
forever a citizen of that Rome of which Christ is Roman.

If Matelda's "onesto riso e dolce gioco" is the most suitable definition of pastoral happiness, Beatrice's "poco tempo silvano" is the
best motto which could be found to suggest the transitory and transitional quality of that happiness. Despite this the pastoral oasis of
Dante's Earthly Paradise prefigures the Heavenly Paradise and eternal
life precisely because it represents human life in the perfection of
its self-fulfillment. No better proof that the Earthly Paradise stands
for that kind of happiness that man may achieve unaided in this
world than the lines just quoted. We know that Dante will go back
to earth at the end of his journey, yet Beatrice's statement seems to
deny this fact. Indeed what she says is simply that the pilgrim will
attain the eternal bliss of Heaven by going directly from the place
on which they are now standing together, and on which he is at
present enjoying a brief pastoral bliss. Such and no other is the literal sense of her words. Their allegorical meaning, however, is that
man should go to the "beatitudo vitae eternae" from the "beatitudo
hujus vitae," and on the level on which she speaks it is evident that
there is no contradiction between the real and the ideal event.

If all this is true, as undoubtedly it is, then the Earthly Paradise *figures* a perfectly happy worldly life, while *prefiguring* at the same time
the blissful immortality of a soul made innocent anew. It is Matelda
that conveys even more clearly than Beatrice the second of these two
truths, when she says that God had granted the Garden of Eden to
man, or had preserved that place for all children of Adam, as "arr'
a tui d'eterna pace" (earnest of eternal piece; xxviii). Such an emphasis was necessary, in order to explain what will happen there after
Dante's meeting with Beatrice. Only on a soil which is, as Matelda
fittingly says, a "campagna santa" (holy ground) could there later
unfold the mystical and processional pageant occupying the last
cantos of *Purgatorio,* and representing in allegorical emblems the
truths of theological and ecclesiastical doctrine.

Yet, having been forester for a little while, man must become again a city dweller, this time "sanza fine" (without end). It is highly significant that in her statement, when confirming Dante in his certainty that after going through Eden the soul will rest forever in the Garden of Heaven,[20] Beatrice chooses to describe the abode of the blessed under the opposite metaphor, that of the City of God, which Christian imagination had been developing since Saint Augustine. Yet, whereas the Heavenly Paradise may turn into a celestial Rome, the earthly one will remain, at least up to the end of historical time, a pleasant orchard, or a garden of delights. This explains why Dante configures Eden after the allegory of the poets, as a Christian version of the pagan fable of the Golden Age. By giving a new substance to its conventions, and novel meanings to its commonplaces, Dante transfigures not only that ancient fable but also the whole tradition of pastoral poetry.

7
The
Poetics
of the Pastoral

I

The poetics of the Renaissance or, more
generally, of neoclassicism, abound in theoretical and critical statements about the
pastoral, telling us, with much too much
frequency, repetition, and prolixity, what
this literary genre really is, or ideally
should be. At first sight, all such statements seem to sing the praises of the
bucolic, yet there is no lack of theorists
and critics uttering adverse opinions, although they are relatively few. Far more
common and significant, however, are the
cases where the idea of the pastoral is
freely handled and shaped by the artists
themselves, not on the plane of critical
theory and interpretation but of creation
itself. The practical application of the

tenets of the pastoral creed leads quite often further than to a mere reaffirmation of the idyllic ideal, and we will examine in detail a few of those works, which, although starting from the conventions of the bucolic or the eclogue, end by transcending or contradicting the presupposition of the form. But before doing so, we shall analyze several outstanding critical statements that exemplify in a characteristic and significant manner the two contrasting theoretical attitudes mentioned above, the first an apology and the second a condemnation of the pastoral.

The most typical and inclusive of all the positive utterances is to be found in Boileau's *L'Art poétique*, in a long statement that contains some of the most graceful lines in that rather dull didactic poem. Boileau starts with a very appropriate simile, comparing the pastoral (which here he calls an "idyll," and later calls an "églogue") to a young shepherdess (ii):

> Telle qu'une bergère, au plus beau jour de fête,
> De superbes rubis ne charge point sa tête,
> Et, sans mêler à l'or l'éclat des diamans,
> Cueille en un champ voisin ses plus beaux ornemens;
> Telle, aimable en son air, mais humble dans son style,
> Doit éclater sans pompe une élégante idylle.
> Son tour simple et naïf n'a rien de fastueux,
> Et n'aime point l'orgueil d'un vers présomptueux.
> Il faut que sa douceur flatte, chatouille, éveille,
> Et jamais de grands mots n'épouvante l'oreille.

> As a fair nymph, when rising from her bed,
> With sparking diamonds dresses not her head,
> But without gold, or pearl, or costly scents,
> Gathers from neighboring fields her ornaments;
> Such, lovely in its dress, but plain withal,
> Ought to appear a perfect Pastoral.
> Its humble method nothing has of fierce,
> But hates the rattling of a lofty verse;
> There native beauty pleases and excites,
> And never with harsh sounds the ear affrights.[1]

The meaning of the image is that the loveliness of the pastoral shines best with the help of only the humblest adornments. Its beauty should be neither bare nor clouded by ostentatious luxury, by the display of precious objects. The charms of pastoral must operate through unsophisticated elegance and unassuming grace, rather than through the proud glamour of courtly fashions. In terms of style, it must tend toward delicacy, rather than grandeur, of diction: it must ring not with a resounding but with a sweet and attractive voice. Too often the pastoral seems inclined to follow, up to the limit of extravagance and exaggeration, the discreet Vergil's command "paulo maiora canamus," (iv) which the author of the *Eclogues* used however to justify a sudden shift of his own inspiration from the contemplative and the idyllic to the oracular and the prophetic. The pastoral poet often takes upon his shoulders burdens too heavy for his strength or undertakes ambitious tasks far transcending the limitations of his craft. The most frequent temptation is to raise the humble strains of the eclogue to the exalted sphere of heroic poetry, to a sublimity of feeling and diction alien to its nature, and suited only to the epic mode. The poet so tempted is unfortunately unaware of the fact that the sound of the war bugle will frighten away the peaceful dwellers of Arcadia—not only its peasants and shepherds but also the divine or semidivine beings haunting the countryside:

> Mais souvent dans ce style un rimeur aux abois
> Jette là, de dépit, la flûte et le hautbois;
> Et, follement pompeux, dans sa verve indiscrète,
> Au milieu d'une églogue entonne la trompette.
> De peur de l'écouter, Pan fuit dans les roseaux,
> Et les Nymphes, d'effroi, se cachent sous les eaux.

> But in this style a poet often spent,
> In rage throws by his rural instrument,
> And vainly, when disordered thoughts abound,
> Amidst the eclogue makes the trumpet sound;
> Pan flies alarmed into the neighboring woods,
> And frightened nymphs dive down into the floods.

If epic poetry may be represented by an eagle soaring high in the air, the bucolic may be symbolized by a domestic bird free to flee from its cage, even out into the open, but only as far as it can go on its clipped wings, which is another way of saying that its range is limited in the sense of descent as well as ascent. In brief, the pastoral must not only give up the ambition of hovering in the sky but must also avoid the temptation of sinking down to the level of the earth, to the plane of what in modern literature is called realism.[2]

After all, for Boileau and the tradition to which he belongs, the doctrine of art as mimesis means not the imitation of nature but its reduction to a vision both idealized and abstract. In the process, "nature" changes into its opposite, that is, into convention—which in turn is but the natural estate of the eclogue. It is particularly in the pastoral genre that the brutalities of an immediate experience of reality seem unnatural, and even absurd. And it is from such a standpoint that Boileau criticizes those vulgar and ill-mannered poets who prefer calling their shepherds by such rustic nicknames as Pierrot and Ninon rather than with the more natural names Lycidas and Phyllis; and who, not content with this, let them speak their vulgar dialect rather than the refined speech of the idyll, which is exactly what a modern realistic writer would do.[3] It is evident that what Boileau wants is not unadulterated reality and unvarnished truth but rather what Pope would call "nature to advantage dress'd," and he clearly implies as much in the lines (ii):

> Au contraire cet autre, abject en son language,
> Fait parler ses bergers comme on parle au village.
> Ses vers plats et grossiers, dépouillés d'agrément,
> Toujours baisent la terre, et rampent tristement:
> On diroit que Ronsard, sur ses "pipeaux rustiques,"
> Vient encor fredonner ses idylles gothiques,
> Et changer, sans respect de l'oreille et du son,
> Lycidas en Pierrot, et Philis en Toinon.
>
> Opposed to this, another, low in style,
> Makes shepherds speak a language low and vile;
> His writings, flat and heavy, without sound,

Kissing the earth and creeping on the ground;
You'd swear that Randal, in his rustic strains,
Again was quavering to the country swains,
And changing, without care of sound or dress,
Strephon and Phyllis into Tom and Bess.

To keep the pastoral in balance between the upward and downward trends, Boileau recommends the study of the great bucolic poets of classical antiquity, Theocritus and Vergil. It is from their writings, both tender and learned, that modern authors will learn how to fashion an eclogue or an idyll. Only from these models will they be taught that the artlessness of the pastoral is a matter of artistry; that its humble simplicity is not the effect of negligence but the product of an elaborate and deliberate craftsmanship. The famous advice that Boileau once gave to Racine: "Faire difficulement des vers faciles," seems to apply better to the pastoral than to any other literary form. The classical norm of the *difficulté vaincue* implies in this case the need of giving the illusion of a careless ease, of a facility without effort. It is also from Theocritus and Vergil that modern bucolic poets will learn all the possible thematic variations of the genre, which Boileau lists in full, to show that in spite of their variety the pastoral situations are traditionally limited in number and in form:

Entre ces deux excès la route est difficile.
Suivez, pour la trouver, Théocrite et Virgile:
Que leurs tendres écrits, par les Grâces dictés,
Ne quittent point vos mains, jour et nuit feuilletés.
Seuls, dans leurs doctes vers, ils pourront vous apprendre
Par quel art sans bassesse un auteur peut descendre;
Chanter Flore, les champs, Pomone, les vergers;
Au combat de la flûte animer deux bergers,
Des plaisirs de l'amour vanter la douce amorce;
Changer Narcisse en fleur, couvrir Daphné d'écorce;
Et par quel art encor l'églogue quelquefois
Rend dignes d'un consul la campagne et les bois.
Telle est de ce poëme, et la force et la grâce.

'Twixt these extremes 'tis hard to keep the right;
For guides take Virgil and read Theocrite;
Be their just writings, by the gods inspired,
Your constant pattern, practised and admired.
By them alone you'll easily comprehend
How poets without shame may condescend
To sing of gardens, fields, of flowers and fruit,
To stir up shepherds and to tune the flute;
Of love's rewards to tell the happy hour,
Daphne a tree, Narcissus make a flower,
And by what means the eclogue yet has power
To make the woods worthy a conqueror;
This of their writings is the grace and flight;
Their risings lofty, yet not out of sight.

II

Samuel Johnson did not hold pastoral poetry in great esteem, as a perusal of his critical writings amply proves. His harshest statement about this literary form is to be found in his *Life of Milton*, where it takes the shape of a critique of *Lycidas,* with a condemnation of the individual piece as well as of the species to which it belongs. Johnson begins by rejecting the common opinion that *Lycidas* is a masterful example of poetic and musical speech, maintaining instead that the poem falls far short of perfection in matters of style and technique. So, if *Lycidas* has any merits, they must be found elsewhere—more precisely, in its sentimental and imaginative content: "One of the poems upon which much praise has been bestowed is *Lycidas;* of which the diction is harsh, the rhymes uncertain, and the numbers unpleasing. What beauty there is, we must therefore seek in the sentiment and images."

The negative judgments that follow are grounded on the principle of sincerity: this poem in particular and pastoral poetry in general dress the passions they intend to convey under such an artificial mask or disguise as to fail ultimately to express those sentiments which their authors, as shown by their lack of directness, seem to have hardly felt: "It is not to be considered as the effusion of real passion;

for passion runs not after remote allusions and obscure opinions. Passion plucks no berries from the myrtle and ivy, nor calls upon Arethuse and Mincius, nor tells of rough *satyrs* and *fauns with cloven heel*. Where there is leisure for fiction there is little grief."

Johnson's critical examination proceeds logically from this starting point. Having challenged the validity of the poem through the criterion of sincerity, he develops his destructive analysis through the parallel criteria of "nature" and "truth." To these the critic adds in effect the supplementary concepts of novelty and originality, accusing the poem of being deprived of both these virtues. This lack is considered as further proof of its failure from the viewpoint of the higher values of nature and truth. It is evident that Johnson's novelty and originality are simple notions, not charged with the ideational content that the romantics ascribe to them—so much so that their absence in *Lycidas* is treated by him as a technical shortcoming, as an artistic defect. As for his general strictures about the pastoral itself, they are couched in the language of eighteenth-century rationalism. Johnson does not find fault with the formal artificiality of the genre, nor with Milton's treatment of this aspect per se; he blames both the pastoral and *Lycidas* for their intellectual falsehood, as unacceptable to our intelligence as their sentimental fallacy is unacceptable to our heart: "In this poem there is no nature, for there is no truth; there is no art, for there is nothing new. Its form is that of a pastoral, easy, vulgar, and therefore disgusting: whatever images it can supply, are long ago exhausted; and its inherent improbability always forces dissatisfaction on the mind." He concludes his criticism by condemning Milton's purely conventional use of the "heathen deities" and of "mythological imagery" and by indicting, far more harshly, the "irreverent combinations" of the poem, its "equivocations" between "trifling fictions" and "the most awful and sacred truths": in brief, all its Christian allegorical allusions, which finally end by transforming the poet into a priest, by changing the shepherd of herds into a shepherd of souls. Yet the central point of Johnson's emphatic denial of the value of *Lycidas* or, more generally, of the validity of the bucolic, is based on an ideal of decorous honesty, on the critic's belief that literature must set high standards of propriety for man's mind as well as for his heart: "He who thus grieves will excite no sympathy; he who thus praises will confer no honour."

III

The contrast between such antithetical views of the pastoral as those exemplified by the passages just quoted from Johnson and Boileau cannot be reduced to a mere diversity of individual temperament and personal outlook. Their opposition may also partly derive from the cultural differences dividing France and England and, even more, the seventeenth and the eighteenth centuries. Yet even in the seventeenth century we may find in the literature of the continent testimonials about pastoral poetry that sound more like Johnson's condemnation than Boileau's apology. One of these testimonials was given by no less a figure than Cervantes; it is found in the least typical of his *Novelas ejemplares,* the *Coloquio de los perros,* a dialogue, in Lucian's manner, between two dogs.[4] At one point the main speaker, the dog Berganza, confesses to the other dog, Cipión, to have felt some doubts about the veracity of the pictures of pastoral life that filled so many of the books read in the household of the lady friend of one of his masters:

> Pero, anudando el roto hilo de mi cuento, digo que en aquel silencio y soledad de mis siestas, entre otras cosas, consideraba que no debía ser verdad lo que había oído contar de la vida de los pastores; a lo menos, de aquéllos que la dama de mi amo leía en unos libros cuando yo iba a su casa, que todos trataban de pastores y pastoras, diciendo que se les pasaba toda la vida cantando y tañendo con gaitas, zampoñas, rabeles y chirumbelas, y con otros instrumentos extraordinarios.

> But to pick up the thread of my broken story, I repeat that in the silence and solitude of my siestas it occurred to me that, among other things, there could be no truth in what I had heard of the lives of shepherds, at least of those of whom my master's lady used to read in certain books when I went to her house. All of them treated of shepherds and shepherdesses, saying that they spent their whole lives in singing and playing on bagpipes, fifes, rebecs, and other wind instruments.[5]

Berganza, being a dog, and a very human one at that, is endowed with the practical wisdom of a picaro, with the skeptical outlook of one who must live on the good will of others or by his own wits. So he could never believe in the reality of a world where man's time is spent not in hardship and strife but in comfort and leisure, in a quest after love rather than in the search for food. Thus, to test the validity of his doubts, he had submitted them to the lesson of direct experience and had found that shepherds look and act very different in reality from the way they look and act in books:

> Digo que todos los pensamientos que he dicho, y muchos más, me causaron ver los diferentes tratos y ejercicios que mis pastores y todos los demás de aquella marina tenían de aquellos que había oído leer que tenían los pastores de los libros.

> Well, all the reflections I have mentioned, and many more, opened my eyes to the glaring differences between the lives and habits of my shepherds and those shepherds in the countryside that I had heard read about in books.

Thus Berganza develops his criticism of the pastoral in terms of a contrast between literature and life: between the sophisticated mystifications of the shepherds of fiction and the actual vulgarity and coarseness of their real-life counterparts.

Cervantes is inclined to reduce all bucolic forms to the common denominator of what he calls the *egloga,* by which he means the pastoral romance: that is, a prose narrative frequently interrupted by verse passages or lyrical interludes, conventionally presented not as the poet's inventions but as songs composed and recited by his characters. It is the frequence of such songs as well as the implication that shepherds spend most of their time making and singing them that particularly tests the dog's incredulity. Berganza seems to be aware of the existence of "folk songs": he knows that singing is a very important part of what we now call "primitive culture." Yet it is in the name of a higher idea of culture that he denies any value to the vulgar songs of the real shepherds, while denying at the same time in the name of nature all validity to the false and fictitious songs coined for them by poets. It is true that shepherds sing both in literature and in life, but in such a different way as to belie truth in one case and beauty in the other.

Here Cervantes, or Berganza for him, mocks popular poetry not only from the viewpoint of its formal shortcomings but also from the viewpoint of the uncomeliness of its language. Real shepherds use in their song the dialect or the vernacular rather than the literary idiom or even standard speech:

> Porque sil los míos cantaban, no eran canciones acordadas y bien compuestas, sino un
> Cata al lobo dó va, Juanica,
> y otras cosas semejantes; y esto no al son de chirumbelas, rabeles o gaitas, sino al que hacía el dar un cayado con otro o al de algunas tejuelas puestas entre los dedos; y no con voces delicadas, sonoras y admirables, sino con voces roncas, que, solas o juntas, parecía, no que cantaban, sino que gritaban o gruñían.

> For if mine sang, it was not songs harmonized and well composed, but "Beware of the Wolf, Juanica," and other similar ballads, and it wasn't to the accompaniment of rebecs or bagpipes, but to the noise made by the knocking of one crook against another, or by some shards placed between the fingers, and not with delicate, sonorous, and melodious voices, but with hoarse voices, which, whether alone or joined with others, seemed not to sing but to bellow and grunt.

The antithesis so established is developed in a caricatural vein, with humorous details about the coarse habits and manners of real shepherds, the commonness of their names, and the like, and ends with Berganza's assertion that the charming and happy way of life of the pastoral world is a never-never land, existing only in the imagination of literary people and in the books they write for the amusement of the idle:

> Los más del día se les pasaba espulgándose o remedando sus abarcas; ni entre ellos se nombraban Amarilis, Fílidas, Galateas y Dianas, ni había Lisardos, Lausos, Jacintos ni Riselos; todos eran Antones, Domingos, Pablos o Llorentes; por donde viene a entender lo que pienso que deben de creer todos; que todos aquellos libros son cosas soñadas y bien escritas para entretenimiento de los ociosos, y no verdad alguna; que a serlo, entre mis pastores hubiera alguna reliquia de aquella felicísima vida, y de

aquellos amenos prados, espaciosas selvas, sagrados montes, hermosos jardines, arroyos claros y cristalinas fuentes, y de aquellos tanto honestos cuanto bien declarados requiebros, y de aquel desmayarse aquí el pastor, allí la pastora, acullá resonar la zampoña del uno, acá el caramillo del otro.

Most of the day they used to spend ridding themselves of fleas or mending their sandals. Not among them were any named Amarilis, Filida, Galatea, or Diana. Nor were there any Lisardos, Lausos, Jacintos, or Riselos. They were all Antonios, Domingos, Pablos, or Llorentes, and this led me to conclude what I think must be the general belief, that all those books are dreams well written to amuse the idle, and not truth at all; for were it otherwise, there would have been some trace of that happy life of yore, and of those pleasant meads, spacious glades, sacred mountains, lovely gardens, clear streams, and crystal fountains, and of those eloquent and no less decorous love descants with a swooning shepherd here and a woebegone shepherdess there, and the bapipe of one shepherd sounding here and the flageolet of another sounding there.

He observes that if the idyllic hideouts or the bucolic backwaters described by pastoral poets were really at hand, they would leave some trace in their environment, and we would recognize them in our real landscapes. Berganza seems to imply that the rough and dry Spanish countryside is rather lacking in those *loci amoeni* where literary shepherds aim to dwell, wander, or linger in the freshness and greenness of the shade. The entire passage is obviously a debunking one; yet its real import cannot be properly evaluated without going beyond the context of the dialogue. In brief, the passage does not represent by itself all the views held by the author in this matter. One must, for instance, remember that the man who wrote these pages had followed in his youth the pastoral vogue no less enthusiastically than all the main men of letters of this age, and that he had written the pastoral romance *Galatea* after the double pattern of Montemayor's *Diana* and Sannazaro's *Arcadia*. Berganza has not forgotten this, as shown by his reference to Galatea, the shepherdess who had given her name to Cervantes' *egloga*, and by his mention of another of *Galatea*'s characters, the shepherd Elicio, in a passage not discussed here. As for *Don Quixote*, which was written shortly before the

Novelas ejemplares, it is full, as everybody knows, of bucolic episodes of the type defined by the term pastoral oasis.[6] This should be enough to prove that the pastoral vision always played a great role in Cervantes' imagination, and this is the reason why he held forever dear his *Galatea,* refusing to consider it a jejeune work or a literary sin of his youth, as shown by the fact that, with Montemayor's *Diana,* the priest and the barber save that volume from their bonfire of Don Quixote's books.

Cervantes' condemnation of the pastoral in the *Coloquio* must be taken therefore with a grain of salt, and we must not forget that the author ascribes that condemnation to an animal character, although to a very wise and articulate one. To be sure, its attribution to a canine intellect does not disqualify the statement—it merely qualifies it. One could say with a pun that the type of the humanlike dog, to which Berganza obviously belongs, plays in literature the role of the cynic: through him Cervantes expresses, at least in part, the Sancho Panza side of his mind, which here he turns not against the illusions of life but only against a literary ideal. Within the whole of Cervantes' work, Berganza's antipastoral declaration takes a position not too different from the place held within the poetry of Joachim du Bellay by his anti-Petrarchist ode, which hardly compensates for all the tributes paid by that poet to the Petrarchist cult. We must then conclude that Cervantes took an ambivalent attitude toward pastoral literature and that this ambivalence parallels the ambiguity of his outlook toward the chivalric romances, as manifested in his masterpiece. This suggests that Cervantes' main hero could easily have exchanged his chivalric calling for the pastoral one. After all, Don Quixote's fixation is bookish and literary in essence, and he would have found it not less natural to follow the commandment *eritis sicut pastores* than to take upon himself the knightly mission and task. The niece of the poor hidalgo senses that such a metamorphosis is possible, as shown by her request that the book burners do not spare from the auto da fé of his library even the few pastoral books on its shelves (I.vi):

—¡Ay, señor!—dijo la sobrina.— Bien los puede vuestra merced mandar quemar, como a los demás; porque no sería mucho que,

habiendo sanado mi señor tío de la enfermedad caballeresca, le-
yendo éstos se le antojase de hacerse pastor y andarse por los
bosques y prados cantando y tañendo, y, lo que sería peor, hacerse poeta, que, según dicen, es enfermedad incurable y pega-
diza.

"Oh, sir," cried the niece, "your worship should have them
burnt like the rest. For once my uncle is cured of his disease of
chivalry, he might very likely read those books and take it into
his head to turn shepherd and roam about the woods and fields,
singing and piping and, even worse, turn poet, for that disease
is incurable and catching, so they say." [7]

That the niece's fears are well founded is shown by Cervantes at
the very end of *Don Quixote*, when, after his return home, which
will be followed soon by his death, the protagonist tells Sanson Car-
rasco and the priest that he plans to spend the year of his forced
rest in pastoral retirement, and asks his friend to join him in his
retreat (II.lxxiii):

... que tenía pensado de hacerse aquel año pastor, y entretenerse
en la soledad de los campos, donde a rienda suelta podía dar
vado a sus amorosos pensamientos, ejercitándose en el pastoral
y virtuoso ejercicio; y que les suplicaba, si no tenían mucho que
hacer y no estaban impedidos en negocios más importantes, qui-
siesen ser sus compañeros.

... how he intended to turn shepherd for the year, and pass his
time in the solitude of the fields, where he could give free rein
to his amorous thoughts, whilst occupying himself in that pastoral and virtuous calling. He begged them to be his companions, if they had not much to do and were not prevented by
more important business.

All this amply proves that if he had not been primarily a knight
and a man of action, Don Quixote, like his creator, would have willingly accepted the shepherd's role, which for so many men of letters
of the Renaissance, adumbrates, as the niece's words clearly imply,
the poetic calling itself.

8
The
Pastoral
of the
Self

I

No reader of *As You Like It* is likely to forget the double repartee by which Shakespeare wittily closes the lively exchange between two characters of that comedy, each of whom stands for a peculiar version of the pastoral ideal (III.ii):

> *Jaques.* I'll tarry no longer with you.
> Farewell, good Signior Love.
> *Orlando.* I am glad of your departure.
> Adieu, good Monsieur Melancholy.

If Shakespeare calls monsieur the gentleman who hails a loveless solitude as the supreme grace of pastoral life, and signior the one who blesses that life for its power to join two lonely hearts together, it is only because the Christian names by which the poet had already baptized the two speakers are the French Jaques in one case and the Italian Orlando in the other. Yet it is difficult to treat as a mere coincidence this naming of the representative of the erotic pastoral as Signior Love, since the main business of the Italian poets of the late Renaissance, especially Tasso and Guarini, had been to reduce the manifold variations of the idyllic fancy to the common denominator or single archetype of the pastoral of love.

As You Like It ends with a rather Pyrrhic victory of Signior Love over Monsieur Melancholy. Yet one could say that one of the tasks of European seventeenth-century literature was to reverse that outcome or, to speak less metaphorically, to liberate the pastoral from that excessive or exclusive concern with passion and sex which had shaped the bucolic vision of the Italians. The writers of that age succeeded in doing so first by taking up its neglected variants, such as the pastorals of melancholy and solitude, which they developed in either contact or contrast with the Italian example; and then by creating a novel variant, such as the pastoral of the self, which in the end transcended all previous traditions of the genre. The achievement of this double task was the particular merit of a few masters of the literatures of England and Spain, and from this viewpoint Shakespeare would have done better if instead of a French he had given an English or Spanish name to his Jaques, and addressed him as sir or don in lieu of monsieur. One should, however, never forget that the ultimate representative of the pastoral of the self was bound to be another and less fictitious Jacques—the greatest literary figure of the eighteenth century, Jean-Jacques Rousseau, who wrote in French, and who would certainly deserve being called Monsieur Soi-Même.

Yet in a process such as the one to be described, what count most are the preliminary and transitional stages. The text that best documents the opening phase may well be the story that forms the climax of the most important of Don Quixote's bucolic interludes. That story, based on the conflict between the pastoral of love and the pastoral of solitude, ends with the victory of the latter, which for the first time is represented not by a shepherd but by a shepherdess. Since the Spanish word for solitude is feminine, one could then say that in this case it is Doña Soledad who conquers Signior Love.

II

We enter the main pastoral oasis of *Don Quixote* at the end of Chapter X of the First Part, when Don Quixote and Sancho, suddenly surprised by darkness while still in open country, decide to spend the night outdoors, in the company of a group of goatherds. Thus with the traditional motif of peasant hospitality Cervantes opens the chief bucolic episode of his masterpiece. The travelers have just shared the simple fare of their hosts when a lad by the name of Pedro, whose job is to bring provisions for his fellow goatherds, comes from the village and relates to his companions and their guests that a gentleman farmer of a neighboring village has just died and has left a strange will. From Pedro's report, which is devoid of any logical order, and even more from his answers to Don Quixote's searching questions, we learn that the dead man, named Grisóstomo, had been young, handsome, and rich. He had studied at Salamanca, from which he had brought home great learning as well as the art of writing poetry. Shortly after his return, Grisóstomo had lost his father, who had left him property in land and cattle, in goods and cash. In the goatherd's village there was a girl named Marcela, no less handsome and young than Grisóstomo, who had also lost her parents, although earlier in life, and had inherited from them even greater wealth. She had been brought up by her uncle, the village priest, a good-natured old man who had never tried to force her resolute will to marry no one. But one day, without changing her mind, Marcela did change her way of life, in a manner best described in Pedro's words (I.xii): But, lo and behold, when we least expected it, the modest Marcela suddenly appeared dressed like a shepherdess and, in spite of her uncle and everyone in the village who tried to dissuade her, off she went into the fields with the other village shepherdesses and started to tend her own flock." [1]

Grisóstomo and Marcela are the two leading characters of the pastoral fable we are about to be told, and it may well be worthwhile to examine how far they have now satisfied the stock requirements of their roles. They certainly seem to do so in full: Cervantes has endowed both of them with the supreme pastoral privileges—beauty and youth. If the author bestows on them even the blessings of class and wealth, which pastoral poetry at its most literal treats as parallel curses, it is only because, like many of his recent predecessors, Cervantes tends to relate the pastoral calling to the moral and social status of the landed gentry, and wishes to emphasize that such a calling appeals to those who are poor "in spirit" rather than in fact. This is obvious enough: yet Cervantes avoids attracting any attention to the outstanding divergence of his own story from the stock pastoral situation. It is true that literary shepherds are often born outside the pastoral state, into which they enter by an act of will, or at least by imitating the action already taken by someone they admire or befriend. In this case the divergence, almost without precedent in the whole of pastoral literature, is seen in the fact that the willing or unwilling leader, the person taking the initiative, or at least setting an example, is a woman and not a man. Now we know that in the pastoral story we are about to hear there will be not simply two leading characters of different sex but an antagonist and a protagonist, which is extravagant enough; and we also know that by an even more extraordinary exception the latter will be a feminine one.

By the way he talks we realize that the simple-minded Pedro takes it almost for granted that quite a few wealthy and well-born youths, whether boys or girls, may turn into shepherds at a moment's notice. Yet he cannot help finding it strange that at least some of them may do so for other than erotic motives. It is through Pedro's wonder at this deviation from the normal path that Cervantes betrays his awareness that he is now straying far away from the central vision of the Italian Renaissance idyll, according to which any pastoral retreat is a retreat into love, or at least into love's dream. As we know, the latter alternative occurs in the pastoral oasis of Tasso's *Gerusalemme liberata*, which Cervantes must have kept well in mind while writing these pages. That famous episode deals with Erminia's stay among the shepherds. While Erminia is a passive heroine, Marcela is an active one: she decides to become a shepherdess forever, after refusing all her old suitors and without even thinking of new ones. What is wholly novel is that Marcela, unlike Erminia, changes her pastoral retreat into a retreat from both the reality and the dream of love. It is with due emphasis that Pedro points out this fact: "Now you mustn't think that because Marcela adopted this free and unconstrained way of life, with little or no privacy, her modesty or her virtue had fallen under any shadow of suspicion. Far from it; she guards her honour so well that not one of her many suitors has boasted—nor has the right to boast—that she has given him the slightest hope of obtaining his desire."

The ironical consequence of Marcela's decision is that by acting as she did, she was bound to win all the hearts of her fellow shepherds without ever losing her own. This is why all of them had been calling her cruel and unkind; and no one had blamed her so harshly as the late Grisóstomo, who had finally died out of despair as soon as he realized that Marcela would never change her friendship into love. Although Pedro fails to say so, it is evident to everybody that Grisóstomo had put an end to his life by his own hand. If a reader asks for proof, he should be referred to the shepherd's request to be buried elsewhere than in consecrated ground. The discretion with which Cervantes alludes to all this is perhaps to be explained by theological considerations: we must never forget that the character was born a Christian, and that the author wrote in an age of religious dogmatism and fanatic zeal. Yet, besides being a Christian, Grisóstomo was a shepherd too, and any reader well acquainted with the pastoral tradition will immediately realize that his suicide is a literary transgression as well as a mortal sin. One could convey the sense of that transgression by anachronistically defining Grisóstomo as the first and last Werther to appear in the pastoral world. In brief, within the economy of the bucolic genre, Grisóstomo's suicide is no less arbitrary and unique than Marcela's decision to become a shepherdess in order to deny even more fully the rule of love.

The reader senses as much from the very tone of Pedro's words: "And the strange thing is that he has directed in his will that he's to be buried in the fields like a Moor, at the foot of that rock where the spring is, beside the cork-tree, because, the rumor goes—and they say they had it from his own lips—that it was at that spot he saw her for the first time. He has left some other requests as well, such odd ones that the clergy say they mustn't be carried out; and quite right too, because they have a heathenish smack about them." The narrator further relates that, all this notwithstanding, Ambrosio, who had been Grisóstomo's best friend, has stated his intention to fulfill his duty and do everything according to his poor friend's wishes. Pedro ends his report by informing his listeners that the following morning all his fellow shepherds will bring Grisóstomo's spoils to the spot he had chosen for his eternal rest. Hearing this, both Don Quixote and the goatherds decide to attend the ceremony.

Ambrosio, who is in charge of the proceedings, pronounces a funeral eulogy, and announces that he will burn his friend's manuscripts, as he had promised. Yet another fellow shepherd, Vivaldo, takes one of the dead man's papers containing one of his poems, and reads it aloud to the crowd. This poem is a *canción desesperada* in an extremely conventional style, and the effect of its reading over the grave of the man who wrote it is both absurd and grotesque. There is no doubt that by this and other details Cervantes wants to suggest to the reader the unseemly character of the funeral we are now witnessing. The strange obsequies of the shepherd Grisóstomo are devoid not only of Christian reverence but of pagan piety as well. It is only when Vivaldo is about to read aloud another of the poems left by the dead man that the scandal is interrupted by an unforeseen event. This was, as Cervantes says (I.xiv), "a miraculous vision—for such it seemed—which suddenly appeared before their eyes. For on the top of the rock in which they were digging the grave appeared the shepherdess Marcela, looking even more beautiful than she had been described."

As soon as Ambrosio sees Marcela, he wrathfully calls her "fiery basilisk of these mountains," and reproaches her for adding scorn to injury by her presence. To which Marcela replies that she has come only to defend herself from the accusation that she is responsible for Grisóstomo's suffering, and that she had caused his death. Marcela's long peroration begins with the acknowledgment that beauty inspires love, but also with the denial that it must return the love it inspires. The reason for this is not only that beauty is a grace which is granted without exacting the price of any responsibility toward others. What really matters is that such a grace disappears unless beauty involves the spiritual as well as the physical side. Without such adornments of the soul as modesty and virtue, loveliness cannot reside even in the most beautiful body. By yielding to man's desire, woman loses the very charms by which she attracts him. Having made these points, Marcela proclaims her moral independence in pastoral terms: "I was born free, and to live free I chose the solitude of the fields. The trees on these mountains are my companions; the clear water of these streams my mirrors; to the trees and the waters I disclose my thoughts and my beauty." Marcela affirms that she has always undeceived by her own words those attracted by her looks, and maintains that if love for her led any man to his undoing, it was the fault of his obstinacy rather than of her supposed cruelty. To Grisóstomo himself, when he declared his love for her on that very spot, far from beguiling him with false hopes or flattering promises, she had unequivocally stated her decision to lead a solitary existence, in communion only with nature and her own soul: "I told him that my will was to live in perpetual solitude, and that only the earth would enjoy the fruit of my chastity and the spoils of my beauty."

Marcela ends her speech with an eloquent plea, picturing the pastoral calling as a state by which the soul attains its ideal perfection and purity:

> If I preserve my purity in the company of the trees, why should he who would have me keep the company of men desire me to lose it? I, as you know, have riches of my own, and covet no one else's. I have a taste for freedom and no wish for subjection. I neither love nor hate any man.... I enjoy the modest company of the village shepherdesses and the care of my goats. My desires are bounded by these mountains; and if they extend beyond them, it is to contemplate the beauty of the sky, a step by which the soul travels to its first abode.

Everybody is both moved and astounded by the speech of Marcela, who leaves the scene as soon as she has uttered her last word. As for Don Quixote, acting as if Marcela were a damsel in distress, he puts his hand on his sword hilt, forbidding all present to follow or persecute her, and loudly proclaiming the justice of her argument and the righteousness of her cause. After this the funeral rites proceed according to plan, including the burning of Grisóstomo's manuscripts. Before leaving, Ambrosio announces that later he will replace the rock by which they have sealed the grave with a tombstone to be engraved with a rhymed epitaph he has already prepared. That epitaph will claim forever, as if nothing had happened, that his friend had died because of his beloved's disdain or, as Ambrosio puts it, of *desamor*. By such an ironical ending Cervantes seems to intimate the persistence of the bucolic illusion, or the persistent refusal on the part of its devotees to heed the lesson of life and to face the challenge of death.

In brief, what counts in the story is not Grisóstomo's illusion, which is at once sentimental and literary, but Marcela's spiritual and personal truth. And we find it significant that this shepherdess preaches her creed by exalting values directly opposed to those exalted in *Aminta's* first chorus. If Tasso preached sexual freedom, Marcela preaches instead freedom from love. If Tasso condemned honor, which enforces chastity and purity and makes both men and women unhappy by preventing the free play of love, Marcela praises honor, chastity, and purity as the highest of all pastoral virtues. Yet in doing so she changes those virtues into something strangely new. For her, honor is no longer a social tie controlling moral conduct from outside, but an inner power ruled by no other law than itself. Chastity and purity are not the exterior signs of the ethical will but spiritual manifestations of the integrity of the person, of the perfection of the soul. It is then by a total reversal of the pastoral casuistry of love that Marcela brings forth what seems to be one of the earliest versions of the pastoral of the self. While affirming the lofty values of the latter, she denies, however, something higher than mere bucolic love. The erotic idyll is a masculine dream: "hedonism disappointed" may often lead a rejected swain to misogyny, to that hatred for the female which is but love for woman turned sour.

Marcela seems to avoid the pitfalls of sexual hatred by her proscription of sexual love. This is what she means when she proudly states that she neither hates nor loves any man, or when she simply acknowledges that the most she can offer to any other human being is but a casual fellowship, to which she prefers the silent company of nature or the soul's intercourse with itself. Friendship is not a substitute for charity; and Marcela's way of life may well imply a denial of the Christian command to love as well as of the pastoral one. An excessive concern with selfhood ends all too often in self-love: and no other detail proves this as eloquently as the fact that Marcela attends Grisóstomo's funeral merely because it is also her trial. If she comes, it is not to pay the tribute of pity at the grave of a dead friend but to use that grave as a tribune from which to plead the cause of the self.

That plea attains its climax in Marcela's avowal that there is neither love nor hatred in her heart. Yet such an avowal reveals that, while refusing to imitate the male hating the female who fails to respond to his love, Marcela cannot avoid the far worse pitfall of misanthropy, which is the negative complement of concern with the self. Now, both self-love and misanthropy are perhaps the most important components of the pastorals of melancholy and solitude. All too often self-love dons the mantle of purity, while misanthropy garbs itself all too easily in self-righteousness. If the latter is primarily an ethical disguise, the former is predominantly a religious mask. If this is true, then we cannot take too seriously the claim Marcela makes at the end of her speech, when she says that one of her life tasks will be that heavenly contemplation which initiates a mortal's soul into its immortal bliss. It is obvious that Marcela's mysticism carries an impurity and a worldliness of its own. Before that single, final allusion to the contemplation of Heaven, she has spoken far more extensively and eloquently of the contemplation of nature, which she considers the most suitable mirror for reflecting the beauty of her own soul. In brief, not unlike the devotees of Eros, she treats her far less carnal but no less profane passion as if it were a form of sacred love.

III

There is a short English lyric which is a document of no less importance in the history of the baroque pastoral than the long Spanish prose tale on which we have just commented. That text is Andrew Marvell's *The Garden,* which deserves an intensive analysis, not only for its significance and quality but also because the poem's brevity contributes to the complexity of its statement.

The Garden opens with a baroque conceit by which the poet turns to his advantage the gnomic commonplaces of the pastoral of innocence, especially those indicting the social passions of vanity and ambition. How frequently and intensely does man exert himself (complains the poet rhetorically) to win the palm of the warrior, the oak of the statesman, the laurel of the poet, or the "single herb or tree" which is the symbolic reward of his efforts! Yet, as Marvell sententiously observes, the shadow projected by those leafy emblems of fame is far less lasting and lovely than the one produced by a grove where all plants join together to weave not coronets of glory but "garlands of repose." The only place where such a grove can be sought is the garden into which the poet has just withdrawn from the weariness and dreariness of the world. There he has found not only the two lovely sisters who are the fairest of all nymphs, peace and innocence, but also their sacred plants, which, unlike the symbolic flora of man's vanity, belong to the real vegetation of this earth. It is in their midst that the poet is now enjoying a solitude more delightful than the most tender or refined fellowship:

> Fair Quiet, have I found thee here,
> And Innocence thy sister dear?
> Mistaken long, I sought you then
> In busy companies of men:
> Your sacred plants, if here below,
> Only among the plants will grow:
> Society is all but rude,
> To this delicious solitude.

Up to the second stanza of his poem Marvell treats his own withdrawal into the garden as a flight from society. But in the following stanzas he claims that the main motivation of his escape is to find rest and relief from the labors and sorrows of love. Later, by using jointly the devices of personification and paradox, he describes his own retreat from love as if it were love's retreat from itself:

> When we have run our passions' heat,
> Love hither makes his best retreat.

Since he has chosen to convey the positive, novel experience of sexual abstention and renunciation under the imagery of the withdrawal of love, Marvell has no other alternative but to depict his own stay in the garden as love's successful attempt to find there new and different objects—not fair women but "fair trees," whose beauty far exceeds that of his sweetheart. The lover of woman has turned into

a lover of trees, and when indulging in the pastoral pastime of en-
graving their trunks, the letters he inscribes will not evoke or invoke
any absent womanly being but merely spell out the names by which
those trees are known.

Having thus changed his love objects from human creatures into
botanical ones, the poet compares himself to those gods who pursued
a maid or a nymph only to see her transformed into a flower or a
plant. Marvell builds this comparison into a striking anticlimax; reversing the meaning of the fables to which he refers, he treats the
botanical metamorphosis by which they end as if it were a consciously expected or willfully provoked outcome: the fulfillment,
rather than the frustration, of the god's desire. In brief, if a god
persecuted a maid or a nymph, it was only because he wanted to see
the creature he loved metamorphosed into a vegetable being:

> The gods, that mortal beauty chase,
> Still in a tree did end their race;
> Apollo hunted Daphne so
> Only that she might laurel grow;
> And Pan did after Syrinx speed
> Not as a nymph, but for a reed.

It is at this stage that the poet finally discards the imagery of love,
but only after drawing a last comparison between nature and woman,
which is, in regard to the latter, an invidious one. The poet now looks
not at the individual plants but at the whole grove, at the impersonal
mystery of vegetation, at a landscape completely submerged in the
anonymity and unanimity of the coloring which dominates the vegetable kingdom and the life of the earth. Yet at its first apparition the
poet cannot help contrasting nature's dye to the tints of woman's
complexion; and he insists that nature's color is more lovable than
the hues of feminine beauty, which are the colors of love:

> No white nor red was ever seen
> So amorous as this lovely green.

In the lines that follow, any erotic suggestion, even of a negative
kind, seems to disappear forever. The subject's passive and passion-

less contemplation of the garden's greenery seems now to abolish
any other substance or appearance,

> Annihilating all that's made
> To a green thought in a green shade.

Here the poem reaches its critical point, and seems to anticipate
some of the tendencies of the modern mind with its all too morbid
wish to merge with the world soul or sink into Mother Nature's
womb. Yet the two preceding stanzas prove that Marvell still thinks
in conventional pastoral terms, as is shown by the sudden metamorphosis of this all too Italian garden—not into an English park, but
into an orchard offering its juicy fruits for the asking to the joy of
man. Both figuratively and literally, nature here remains all too
fenced in; while its boundless fertility requires no human labor, its
beauty, as shown by the closing vision of the flower bed which a
"skilful gard'ner" has laid out in the shape of a sundial, may still
need the artifices of man's wit and the control of his hand. Yet it is
precisely as *hortus conclusus* that nature becomes the best abode of
the soul. If in the Golden Age or in the Earthly Paradise of yore man
could proudly wander abroad in the splendid nakedness of his body,
here he may dwell or linger outdoors in the luminous pure nudity of
his spirit:

> Here at the fountain's sliding foot,
> Or at some fruit-tree's mossy root,
> Casting the body's vest aside,
> My soul into the boughs does glide.

At this point, as if to make it move and abide in greater ease among
the boughs, the poet changes his soul into a bird. The metamorphosis
is more metaphorical than symbolic, and since the image does not
become *figura*, we should not conclude that this bird is the dove of
the spirit. Marvell's awareness that the emblem he is using was
originally religious in essence appears in the allusion to the "longer
flight" the bird-soul will undertake when its stay in this or other
gardens comes to an end. Yet such an allusion is to be taken even

less literally than Marcela's closing reference to that "contemplation of heaven" by which the soul prepares itself for its final ascent. That Marvell's is a bird of different feather than the one standing for the Christian soul is shown by its main concern—to groom its gorgeous plumage and make it shine like a rainbow in the changing light. Except for its small size, we would at first think this feathery creature a peacock. Later we realize that this could not be so for other reasons. The peacock, after all, is barely able to fly, which our bird can easily do, although at present it prefers to rest in the garden, perching on one of its trees. There, with no thought of flying away, with no other care than delighting in its own beauty, it sings aloud, as no peacock can do, of its newly found bliss. Far from being an allegory of the religious soul, which trains itself through contemplative life to fly back to its eternal abode, Marvell's bird stands for an all too human and personal psyche, which retreats from the world of society into the world of nature so as to be less distracted from the bemused contemplation of its own loveliness:

> There, like a bird, it sits and sings,
> Then whets and combs its silver wings,
> And, till prepared for longer flight,
> Waves in its plumes the various light.

By nursing and reflecting its beauty within the intimacy of a nature so enclosed as to become a private reserve, the soul changes its own hermitage into a sort of outdoor boudoir. In literary terms, this simply means that at such a turning point the pastoral of solitude gives way to the pastoral of the self. While the former rejects man's love for woman, the second repudiates all love for any object other than the subject itself. This is the reason that at the poem's end the poet looks back at pastoral love. By that retrospective glance he wants to deny the old dispensation more fully and definitely than he has done before. The poet succeeds in doing so by changing the temporal perspective, by making the new dispensation the older of the two. While in the earlier stanzas he treated the withdrawal of the self into the garden as an event occurring after the extinction of passion or the consummation of desire, now he views that withdrawal as a happening that took place in the remotest of all ages, when love had not yet made its appearance in the world.

In brief, the poet likens his own retreat to man's state in the Garden of Eden before the Fall, thus suggesting that pastoral innocence existed from the beginning of life itself. Marvell goes even further: to establish a perfect equation between the pastoral of solitude and the pastoral of the self, and to make both of them absolutely, rather than relatively, independent of the pastoral of love, he compares his own *hortus conclusus* to the Garden of Eden as it was not simply before the Fall but before the very creation of Eve:

> Such was that happy Garden-state
> While man there walk'd without a mate:
> After a place so pure and sweet,
> What other help could yet be meet!
> But t'was beyond a mortal's share
> To wander solitary there:
> Two paradises 'twere in one,
> To live in Paradise alone.

As the closing lines intimate, Marvell faces here the very issue Cervantes avoided by choosing a maidenly heroine as protagonist of his tale. Unlike the Spanish writer, the English poet builds the pastoral of the self on the cornerstone of misogyny, as well as on the more general foundations of misanthropy. Marvell the moderate puritan knew, as Milton did, that woman is a necessary evil, and that not even in Paradise will man ever live alone. Yet here he seems to think that the dream of a pure and sweet solitude may be realized within space and time, if we measure the former within the narrow range of an orchard or garden and reckon the latter within the brief span of the day, the hours of which are symbolized by the "herbs" and "flowers" of the botanical sundial appearing at the end of the poem. Marvell's acknowledgment that pastoral bliss can be only a momentary experience is made almost without regret, since the pastoral of the self must transcend that contrast between happiness and unhappiness which is at the very root of the pastoral of love. This is the reason that Cervantes ignored the tragicomic implications of the

Marcela-Grisóstomo story and that Marvell neglects the very dialectics Milton has exemplified in his famous diptych *L'Allegro* and *Il
Penseroso*. Melancholy and solitude are one and the same thing; and
the soul is at once pensive and mirthful when it keeps its own
rendezvous with itself.

IV

By rephrasing a line by Dante one could say that according to the
traditional Christian view the blessed, and the blessed alone, are
anime fatte belle, and that it is God who makes them so. On the contrary, Cervantes treats his Marcela, and Marvell the birdlike psyche
he celebrates in *The Garden*, as souls which have been born beautiful or have been made so by no other grace than an inner one. Then,
at least potentially, they are already *belles âmes* in the sense that
term will definitely acquire in eighteenth-century France, particularly
in the hands of Rousseau. Actually Rousseau's *belle âme* is emanci-
pated even more than are Cervantes' and Marvell's exemplars from
the residual controls of the mind and the will. This is particularly
true of his two main psychological archetypes, who are the Saint-
Preux of *La Nouvelle Héloïse* and the autobiographical protagonist
of the *Confessions* and the *Rêveries d'un promeneur solitaire*. Despite
his claim to be the friend of mankind, the author of those works
based his own conception of the *belle âme* on an almost hypochon-
driac misanthropy. Yet if he refused to sweeten that misanthropy
with the balm of friendship, he also refused to embitter it further
with the harsh medicine of misogyny. The task he had set out to ac-
complish was, after all, to bring back passion as the chief ingredient
of the bucolic vision of life: the test of a *belle âme* was for him an
uninterrupted effusion of feeling, overflowing and overwhelming all
its vessels and objects.

In brief, Rousseau reestablished and reinforced the broken tie between the pastoral of love and the pastoral of the self. This explains
his youthful admiration for such an old-fashioned pastoral romance
as *L'Astrée*, of which he speaks at length at the beginning of the
Confessions. This also explains his love for Italian poetry, testified
by the frequent quotations from Petrarch, Tasso, and Metastasio
in *La Nouvelle Héloïse*, as well as his passion for Italian music, especially for the opera, which in his time was but an idyll in courtly

dress. It was by turning back to the Italians that Rousseau reintro-
duced into the pastoral the concern with sex, which he fused with
the concern with the self. Sexual love is but a form of self-love, and
in the *Rêveries*, when left without a sexual object, Rousseau found
that object within himself. It was only with him that the pastoral of
the self turned once and for all into the literary vehicle of an extreme
and absolute narcissism, replacing the fables and myths of his Renaissance predecessors with the autobiographical and introspective concerns of modern literature. Rousseau transformed Narcissus, literally
and unambiguously, into Jean-Jacques, as other and later poets, no
longer committed to pastoral traditions and conventions, were to
transform him into their Werthers or Renés. And the external mirror
in which this new Narcissus would reflect his *belle âme* would no
longer be a garden or an idyllic countryside, but a nature as wild and
boundless as the romantic view of the self.

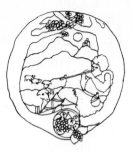

9
Pastoral
and
Soledad

Contrary to one's expectations, bucolic poetry was not predestined to sing the praises of solitude. It was only toward the end of its long historical life that the pastoral ever fulfilled what may well be the most congenial of its many tasks. The theme of solitude is almost totally absent from Theocritus' *Idylls* and Vergil's *Eclogues*, and it is never central in the pastorals of the Renaissance. Its appearances before the seventeenth century are fleeting; the role that solitude plays up to then on the pastoral stage is only that of an extra or, at the most, of a minor character. This truth, which is categorical for the Italian cinquecento, may be extended, with a few reservations or qualifications, to the whole of European pastoral poetry of the sixteenth century. No sig-

nificant exception to this rule may be granted even to Spanish literature, which had been treating that theme with peculiar intensity in a
wide range of lyrical and nonlyrical forms, originating from a unique
tradition which had begun with popular and medieval poetry, and
which reached its climax with the supreme literary masters of the
baroque age, the leading practitioners of the *estilo culto*.

The most eminent student of this tradition, the German scholar
Karl Vossler, who devoted to it a large and important work, was quite
right in claiming that even in Spain the pastoral imagination had
failed to give a genuine interpretation of its own to the theme of
solitude. Not even Jorge Montemayor, the author of *Diana*, one of
the most famous pastorals ever written, and certainly one of the
greatest in the Castilian tongue, ever was, in Vossler's opinion, a
poet of solitude: in his work, as well as in that of most writers of
the same age, and of the same kind, solitude is a fictitious value, and
this is only natural since, as the critic says, "the solitudes of all Arcadian lands are not to be trusted." [1] This generalization is particularly
appropriate to the pastoral romance, which is the pastoral of love
par excellence, and fits uniquely Montemayor's masterpiece, which is
also one of the masterpieces of that special genre. But, as we have
already said, it applies to the whole of pastoral literature, except in
some of its latest developments.

In the bucolic poetry of the ancients, solitude may briefly appear
in the love elegy, as a matter not of choice but of necessity: as one of
the many sad consequences of an unhappy love affair or, more frequently, of an unrequited love. In many such cases the unfortunate
lover goes into hiding or wandering, among deaf trees and dumb
rocks, so that no one can hear his sobs or see his tears: or, if he
chooses to reveal or confess his sorrows, so that only rivers can weep
with him, and only grottoes reecho his wails. The classical pastoral
attitude toward solitude seems to be exemplified by two passages,
one in the opening, and the other in the closing song, of Garcilaso's
First Eclogue. In the first passage solitude is viewed not as an end
but as a means, as Salicio testifies when reevoking a love happiness
he can no longer enjoy because of the inconstance of his former
sweetheart Galatea:

> Por tí la esquividad y partamiento
> del solitario monte me agradaba.

I would like for your sake the shyness and aloofness of the lonely mount.

But in the second passage solitude is treated as a kind of pain or even punishment, which the heart feels in itself when love is denied by the absence of the beloved, as Nemoroso avows while lamenting the death of his beloved Elisa, and cruel destiny

> que a sempiterno llanto
> y a triste soledad me ha condenado.

which condemned me to a perpetual plaint, and to a sad solitude.

As for those usual protagonists of the Renaissance pastoral, unrequited lovers, far from seeking solace in oblivion or escape, they feel such an urge to manifest their sufferings and to arouse compassion for their plight that they seek the companionship of fellow shepherds, who, being also fellow sufferers, are no less willing to share with others their own sorrows and complaints. This is particularly true of Montemayor's *Diana*, where no lover is loved in return, and where the casuistry of love is based on an endless chain of compassion and self-pity. Even so it is in such a work as *Diana* that we witness toward the very end of the story the apparition of the idea of *soledad*, to which the author, who was of Lusitanian origin, gives some of the meanings of the Portuguese *saudade*.

The most decisive and mysterious event of the story is the strange effect of the magic water by which the good enchantress Felicia heals forever the heart of Sireno from his desperate love for Diana, who is married to another shepherd. In a single moment both his passion and pains end forever, and the only sentiment that survives within his soul is *soledad*, by which the author means not a sense of loneliness but a feeling of privation and emptiness, trembling with vague longings, tinged with a mild sadness (vi):

Y passando por la memoria los amores de Diana, no dexava de causalle soledad el tiempo que la avía querido. No porque

entonces le diesse pena su amor, más porque en todo tiempo
la memoria de un buen estado causa soledad al que le a perdido.

And while in his memory he was going over Diana's loves, the
time when he had loved her didn't cease from causing loneliness within him. Not because his love would then give him any
pain, but because the memory of a good state engenders loneliness in the person who has lost it.

What is significant in this passage is not the reaffirmation of the
belief that loving is a good thing even if one is not loved back but
the identification of *soledad* with a psychological condition that has
little or nothing to do with actual solitude. What the words just
quoted seem to suggest is that the pastoral of solitude, or the idyllic
praise of a loneliness understood primarily as a state of mind, is not
yet possible; and that it will be possible only when both the idyll and
the elegy of love are over, when the eclogue concerns itself less with
the heart and more with the soul. In terms of literary history this
may well mean that the pastoral of solitude will emerge only when
the pastoral drama and the pastoral romance, the two characteristic
vehicles of the Renaissance bucolic conceptions of Eros, which the former tends to represent in its sensual varieties, and the latter in its
spiritual ones, yield to other, more lyrical and subjective forms. What
makes Montemayor's statement even more significant is the very
paradox by which the writer, while refraining from filling the void
left by the disappearance of love with a *soledad* understood as a
positive rather than as a negative value, seems all the same to anticipate or to announce the pastoral of melancholy, which will be the
single most important variant of the pastoral of solitude.

That the latter should develop so late is the more surprising since
solitude has always been considered as one of the conditions, as well
as one of the blessings, of the contemplative life, which in turn has
often been represented through pastoral or quasi-pastoral images. The
most significant restatement of this representation is to be found in
The Advancement of Learning, where Bacon defines the active and
the contemplative callings through two biblical figures: the first tiller
of the soil and the first tender of the sheep. It is indeed "in the first
event or occurrence after the Fall of Man" that one should see, Bacon
says (VI.vii), "an image of the two estates, the contemplative state

and the active state, figured in the two persons of Abel and Cain, and in the two simplest and most primitive trades of life; that of the shepherd (who, by reason of his leisure, rest in a place, and living in view of heaven, is a lively image of a contemplative life), and that of the husbandman: where we see again the favour and election of God went to the shepherd, and not to the tiller of the ground."

Bacon follows here in Erasmus' footsteps, and it is evident that in the context in which he speaks the contemplative estate is being equated with the call of learning, or the scholarly way of life. In brief, here Abel adumbrates, at least in part, the humanist or the philosopher. This means that Bacon uses the figure of the shepherd not for a metaphorical but for an allegorical purpose, in a way quite similar to the treatment of the same figure in ecclesiastical pastorals, the only difference being the secular rather than religious content of his allegory. If Bacon represents in pastoral terms the priest of knowledge, rather than the priest of faith, it is precisely because he hopes that the former will be granted in the temporal realm "the favor and election" which the latter enjoys in the spiritual sphere, or comparable privileges. Bacon's analogy was bound to affect but a few pastoral poets: the most significant echo of this passage, or rather the most vivid reflection of the idea therein conveyed, is in those lines of *Lycidas* by which Milton reevokes his own and Edward King's university years: lines in which the pastoral condition stands not only for the service of the muses but also for the studious life.

The factor that determined the parallel between the pastoral condition and the scholarly calling was simply that they share a unique requirement: leisure. It is of leisure that Bacon speaks, whereas he fails even to mention solitude. The shepherd-scholar, no less than the shepherd *tout court,* can exist only through the exploitation, as well as through the enjoyment, of leisure; solitude is for him a consequence of the state he has chosen rather than an inducement or an incentive. All this applies to the poet-shepherd no less than to the poet-scholar: what he needs and values most is leisure, not solitude. He appreciates the advantages of the former in a positive and absolute sense; those of the latter, only in a negative or relative way. Leisure is for him the most important of all freedoms, that of his time, whereas he views solitude primarily as a freedom from practical necessities, social obligations, or public service. This is the reason that the pastoral, especially in the Vergilian version, and in the tradition hence derived, tends to praise not so much a solitary existence as private life. In brief, it is a praise of retirement rather than of isolation—and in this the Vergilian and the Horatian tradition seem to converge. The latter, however, reechoes for many centuries Stoic and Epicurean accents, merging them with varying and different strains in a way hardly possible within a pastoral frame. It is not paradoxical to affirm that it is within the Horatian rather than within the Vergilian tradition that solitude begins to be viewed as something valuable in itself, if not yet as an absolute value. The chief reason for this is the Stoic renunciation of passions (including the tender emotions of love) and an Epicurean wisdom, which delights in the simplest pleasures. Significantly, and paradoxically, it is within some of the latest and most complex products of this tradition that the idea of solitude begins wearing a pastoral or quasi-pastoral dress.

This is certainly what seems to happen in one of the most famous lyrics of the great Spanish mystical poet Fray Luis de Léon, as well as of the Spanish Renaissance. The poem belongs to the Horatian tradition in more than one sense: first, because it is a "Horatian ode," one of the many attempts to reproduce the message, the tone, and the structure of that exemplary lyrical form in a modern setting and in the vernacular tongue; second, because it is at the same time one of the numberless reelaborations of a rhetorical topos patterned on and named after the well-known Horatian opening "Beatus ille." The topos itself consists of a formal praise of the joys of retirement as well as of a stern indictment of the false value of a life in "the world." The blessings of a retreat can after all be measured according not only to the merits of the place one retires to, but also to the shortcomings of the place one withdraws from—which is the same as saying that the topos *beatus ille* is at the same time the topos *procul negotiis*. All this implies again the celebration not so much of solitude as of privacy: the glorification not of a lonely but of a "refined" or "restful" life.

The poem, *Vida retirada*, which Fray Luis wrote in the strophic form called lira,[2] serves no other end but that of this kind of glorification, which is indeed its stated aim, as shown by its title[3] and the be-

ginning exclamation, "Qué descansada vida." Yet, despite this opening, the first four strophes tend to blame the "mundanal ruido" (the
noise of the world—exemplified by the pride of power and the vanity
of blood, the acquisition of wealth and the pursuit of fame) rather
than to praise the peace and silence of the retired life. The poet does
so only later, starting with the fifth strophe; it is indeed at this point
that the poem unfolds into a praise of the farm, or rather the fruit
orchard or vegetable garden, that the poet, or the speaker of the
poem, owns and works himself. That the poet is both the owner of
and laborer on that little plot of land is something we learn further
down, when the author gives this information almost in passing:

> Del monte en la ladera
> por mi mano plantado tengo un huerto.

On the slope of the mountain I own an orchard planted with my
own hands.

Before doing so, however, he chooses to expatiate on the beauties of
the landscape enclosing his lot. Through the exaltation of the surrounding countryside, as eloquent as that of the charming spot on
which, and out of which, he lives, as well as through the emphasis
on the peace and leisure which he can thus afford, the poet suddenly
gives to his poem a bucolic rather than a georgic turn. This is made
evident by such invocations as "O campo, o monte, o rio!" (O field,
o hill, o stream!) and by the idyllic vision of the serene repose and
placid mirth of his way of life:

> Un no rompido sueño,
> un dia puro, alegre, libre quiero.

I wish only for an unbroken sleep, for a day pure, joyful, and
free.

But the most crucial statement of the poem is to be found in one
of the central strophes, when we hear for the first time a praise, if
only implicit, of solitude—a solitude which acquires a value of its

own for being envisaged as an inscape into self-company as well as
an escape from the company of others:

> Vivir quiero conmigo,
> gozar quiero del bien que debo al cielo
> a solas, sin testigo,
> libre de amor, de zelo,
> de odio, de esperanzas, de recelo.

I wish to live with myself, to enjoy the bliss I owe to Heaven,
alone, with no witness, free of love, of jealousy, of hope, of
envy.

What makes these lines significant is the recognition that the first of
all the privations that make a quasi-pastoral conception of the idea of
solitude possible is that of an erotic attachment: a privation which in
reality is an emancipation. This seems indeed to prove that the pastoral of solitude cannot declare itself without declaring at the same
time its independence from love.

The remainder of the poem (except for a homely and therefore
quite Horatian allusion to the frugal poverty of the poet's table) is
utterly idyllic in tone. This quality marks with peculiar intensity the
last two strophes, which oppose the wretched existence of most human beings, striving after the vain goods of the world, and the quiet
eye of the retired person, enjoying in blissful peace the pure and lofty
delights of music and song:

> Y mientras miserable-
> mente se están los otros abrasando
> en sed insacïable
> del no durable mando,
> tendido yo a la sombra esté cantando.

> A la sombra tendido
> de yedra y lauro eterno coronado,
> puesto el atento oido
> al son dulce, acordado,
> del plectro sabiamente meneado.

And while the others are burning with an unquenchable thirst for short-lived power, I sing lying down in the shade. Lying down in the shade, crowned with perennial ivy and laurel, lending an attentive ear to the sweet and harmonic sound of the plectrum skillfully handled.

There is no doubt that this vision is patterned after the otherwise far different scene that opens the first of Vergil's *Eclogues*, where happy Tityrus, who, free like a bird and without a worry in the world, is now singing under one of his trees, is contrasted not with the unhappy worldlings of the city but with a fellow farmer, the poor Meliboeus, who has just been dispossessed and who is now leaving his home and his land forever. The proof that these two passages stand to each other in the relation of a model and a copy is given by a phrase that appears twice, the second time in inverted form, toward the end of *Vida retirada*. The phrase ("tendido yo a la sombra"; "a la sombra tendido") is a literal translation of the words "lentus in umbra," by which Vergil describes the relaxed position and the comfortable shelter that Tityrus has chosen for the singing in which he delights. The very fact that the Spanish poet repeats that phrase twice, in almost identical versions, reveals his intent to follow as much as possible the example of his Latin master. Vergil too draws the same picture two times, though with different words and changed details, as shown by the very first line of his eclogue: "Tityre, tu patulae recubans sub tegmine fagi" (O Tityrus, now lying at ease under the roof of a spreading beech).[4]

Even though the two figures are doing the same thing in a similar place and in an identical posture, there are still great differences between the two pictures. Whereas Tityrus busies himself not only with singing but also with playing his rustic pipe, Fray Luis's retired man is less absorbed in rehearsing his song than in listening to a melody not of his own making. The melody, as indicated by the poet's allusion to the plectrum, used with a nobler instrument than the pipe, is so pure and lofty that it could be considered an earthly idea of the harmony of the spheres, or at least as the highest kind of human music, which Fray Luis celebrates in another famous ode.[5]

As for the song he himself modulates, it stands, like the pipe playing in his model, for nothing else but poetic creation, which in both texts is viewed as both the fruit and reward of leisure. Any doubt in this regard may be easily dispelled by noticing that Fray Luis's peaceful singer is crowned with a wreath of laurel and that in this garland the laurel is mixed with ivy, the symbol of faith, which may intimate that the author represents, under a quasi-pagan mask, the figure of the Christian poet. As for the emphasis on the passive listening to music rather than on the active performance of song, it may be explained if we remember that the author of this poem was a mystic— an observation which may add persuasiveness and significance to Vossler's argument that "quietism" is one of the inspiring motifs of the Spanish poetry of *soledad*.[6] The motif seems to be present even in this poem and to manifest itself in the passionless quality of the contemplative leisure it represents and celebrates.

The most eloquent intimation that even this poem is partly shaped by a quietistic attitude is the inclusion, among the passions to be discarded, of hope, which is here understood not as the Christian virtue of that name but as pathetic longing and vain desire. But, as we have already observed, the poet assigns precedence and priority, among all the passions the retired man is happily liberated from, to *amor*, by which, as indicated by the connection with jealousy ("libre de amor, de zelo"), he obviously means profane love. That the denial of any erotic attachment is the chief message of *Vida retirada* may be proved also negatively, by the poet's failure to mention that passion in the very passage in which he directly imitates Vergil. When speaking of the serene song into which the retired man indulges while "a la sombra tendido," Fray Luis refrains from telling us what he will sing about. The omission is significant precisely because Vergil takes care to inform us of what his Tityrus sings while "lentus in umbra." It is through Meliboeus' words that we learn the subject of the carefree song of his friend, which could not be but love, nay, but a lucky love:

> . . . Tu, Tityre, lentus in umbra
> formosam resonare doces Amaryllida silvas.

You, Tityrus, lying sprawling in the shade, teach the woods to echo back your praises of your lovely Amaryllis.

This important divergence is a proof, rather than a disproof, that in its closing section *Vida retirada* shifts from the Horatian to the Vergilian mode, thus turning the ode into an idyll. There is no doubt that the poet ended, whether intentionally or not, by submitting to a process of pastoralization a poem he had deliberately started to write after Horace's "Beatus ille que procul negotiis (*Epod.* ii)[7], which is less strange than it seems, if we recall that Fray Luis's writings include a translation of all of Vergil's *Eclogues* into the vernacular tongue,[8] as well as two quasi-pastoral renderings of the Song of Songs.[9] What seems indeed exceptional, however, is that the poet gave a pastoral turn to his poem while reshaping it after many other lines of divergence and convergence, which add to its complexity without detracting from its wholeness.

The Stoic and Epicurean elements of its inspiration fit quite neatly within the Horatian frame; yet the Stoic conception of a refinement dictated by a wisdom given only to "the happy few" ("los pocos sabios") joins with a quasi-Christian interpretation of the retired life, and with the transformation into a quasi hermitage of the rural retreat. As for the Epicurean treatment of the simple pleasures of rustic life, it seems to merge with the Petrarchan exaltation of the spiritual joys which only a secluded existence can offer; and we read an echo of Petrarch's *Secretum*, or at least of its title, in Fray Luis's apostrophe: "O secreto seguro deleytoso!" (O safe and delightful hiding place!) This line indicates that, unlike Tityrus, who owes his peace of mind to such external factors as the grace of Caesar,[10] Fray Luis's retired man bases his happy quiet on something more than the little piece of land that guarantees his security and freedom. That something may not be, at least in this poem, the grace of God, but it is certainly the peace of the soul, and it seems that by calling it a "secreto" the poet turns his orchard into a *hortus conclusus*, a garden of the spirit. What the poet praises is not monastic retreat but secular retirement; yet the praise has a Christian ring or, rather, the accents of a Catholic and nonascetic mysticism. Nothing more different from the tone of this poem is that of Marvell's *Garden*, in which the voice exalting solitude speaks with the authority of Protestant self-reliance, with the rigor of puritan will.

The notes of *Vida retirada* reecho for a long time in Spanish poetry: yet there is no doubt that the baroque age celebrates solitude in novel ways and with strains still unheard. This is particularly true of Lope de Vega, who exalts solitude as an inner or, rather, subjective state, which manifests itself not only in quietude and repose but also in movement and turmoil—not without, but within life itself. Whereas Fray Luis's retired man enjoys solitude by "sitting" with himself, the person who speaks in one of the most famous of Lope's lyrical *Romances* does the same by "going" with himself:

> A mis soledades voy,
> de mis soledades vengo,
> porque para andar conmigo
> me bastan mis pensamientos.

To my solitudes I go. From my solitudes I come, since to go with myself I need only my thoughts.

If solitude is for Fray Luis the absence of feelings, it is for Lope presence of thoughts: a novely that may be expressed in literary terms by saying that *soledad* becomes also a conceit: hence the use in the lines just quoted of the plural form of the word. This is even truer of Góngora, who would write a series of sumptuous *Soledades* in which pastoral solitude ceases to be a retreat from and becomes a triumph over the world.

10
Naboth's Vineyard:
The
Pastoral View
of the
Social Order

I

In the pastoral dispensation the humble
and the poor lead a life that is almost safe
from internal disorder; yet their harmless
happiness is all too often threatened by the
encroachments of the proud and the powerful, by the incursions of those who roam
the wild, or by the oppressions of those
who dwell within city walls. Thus, for no
fault of its own, the bucolic community is
forced to taste the bitter fruits of that insecurity which should curse only those who
by living within the great world accept the
struggle for life as the condition of man. It
is also for this reason that many a "pastoral oasis" comes to an untimely end.[1]
The idyllic imagination is aware of such a
challenge, and its response is one of pro-

test, if not of revolt. The bucolic reaction to might and violence is primarily sentimental; the consciousness of its own innocence, merging with the awareness that the precariousness of its happiness is due to acts of men rather than to "acts of God," produces in the pastoral soul a sense of outraged justice.

The very concept of natural justice had been predicated not only on the inner voice of man's conscience but also on the state of nature, when mankind was supposed to be either an unruly horde or a docile herd. Hence, the important role the idea of justice has always played within the pastoral dream. After all, Astraea was the goddess under whom prospered and flourished the Age of Gold. Yet that idea remained a thing of the mind. Pastoral poetry treated justice as an ideal abstraction or as the wishful expression of a demand of the soul never to be satisfied, except perhaps in the blissful vision of a legendary past. In the Golden Age, or in the shadowy imitations of that happy state created by the poetic imagination, justice seems to work automatically, without friction or strife. But when man realizes that he is living in history, which is but a perennial Iron Age, he also realizes that justice is never achieved by itself, and that it may be denied to whoever does not fight for its sake and on his own behalf. Then he also learns that the Age of Gold is but a dream, and that he must do something to improve the base metal of the age to which he belongs.

To such base metal belonged also the time of Vergil's youth, and it was the realization of this fact that allowed the young Vergil to add a new strain to that pastoral song old Theocritus had taught him. We know how great is the debt of the author of the *Eclogues* to the author of the *Idylls*; yet if Vergil ever wrote any eclogue wholly unaffected by Theocritus' influence, it is certainly the First. The reason is not hard to seek, its theme being both historical and autobiographical. Vergil, one of the many little landholders dispossessed under the triumvirate when Octavianus rewarded his discharged veterans with confiscated farms, went to Rome to apply to the highest authority. His influential friends pleaded on his behalf so that Octavianus granted his petition and ordered the restitution of his farm. The First Eclogue is but an ideal and poetic account of these events, which the poet rehearses through a dialogue between two shepherds: Tityrus, who stands for Vergil himself, and Meliboeus, who stands for all the farmers who were expropriated without hope of redress.

Tityrus is serenely enjoying his leisure outdoors. Meliboeus, who has just been evicted, passes on the road nearby with his little herd and stops for a while to talk with his friend. Meliboeus begins by pointing out that the carefree Tityrus is indulging in the pleasant task of playing the pipe just when the speaker, like most of their fellow shepherds, is forced to abandon his land and to depart toward destitution and exile. The pathos of Meliboeus' statement springs forth from the sharpness of this contrast. His apostrophe encloses with moving delicacy the two remarks on his own sorry plight between the opening and the closing sentences, which refer at length on his friend's happy lot (*Ecl.* i):

> Tityre, tu patulae recubans sub tegmine fagi
> silvestrem tenui musam meditaris avena:
> nos patriae fines et dulcia linquimus arva.
> nos patriam fugimus: tu, Tityre, lentus in umbra
> formosam resonare doces Amaryllida silvas.

Tityrus, while you lie there at ease under the awning of a spreading beech and practice country songs on a light shepherd's pipe, I have to bid good-bye to the homefields and the plough-lands that I love. Exile for me, Tityrus—and you lie sprawling in the shade, teaching the woods to echo back the charms of Amaryllis.[2]

Tityrus, who has little or nothing to say about his neighbor's misfortune, replies that he owes his good luck to the godlike man now holding the rudder of the ship of state in his hands "O Meliboee, deus nobis haec otia fecit." (Ah Meliboeus, the man to whom I owe this happy leisure is a god.)

Meliboeus states his surprise rather than his resentment at a redress which had been denied to him and to the other shepherds, and it is with a resigned grief that he speaks of all the hardships destiny has in store for him and his herd. Then Tityrus reports in detail about his journey to Rome and the happy outcome of his entreaty,

and Meliboeus comments without bitterness on the good fortune of
his friend:

> Fortunate senex, ergo tua rura manebunt.
> et tibi magna satis. . . .

Happy old man! So your land will still be yours. And it's enough
for you.

You will spend the rest of your life on your farm, says Meliboeus,
whereas we do not know yet where and when our wanderings and
sufferings will end. We may finally settle on a poor, wild, and distant
land, while for no other merit than having fought in the civil wars a
soldier devoid of piety and pity will exploit our soil, and gather our
crops:

> Impius haec tam culta novalia miles habebit,
> barbarus has segetes. en quo discordia cives
> produxit miseros: his nos consevimus agros.

Is some blaspheming soldier to own those acres I have broken
up and tilled so well—a foreigner, to reap these splendid fields
of corn? Look at the misery to which we have sunk since Ro-
mans took to fighting one another. To think that *we* have sown,
for men like that to reap!

This melancholy outburst distracts the thoughtless Tityrus from his
selfish unconcern, and the poem ends on a note of pastoral solidarity
when the lucky shepherd offers the unlucky friend hospitality under
his roof for the night about to fall.

The dialectics of the First Eclogue is not that of injustice and justice but of disorder and order. Political rule may mitigate the disorders which military might, or the oppression of the powerful, is
bound to provoke. The victims of such disorders are the humble and
the poor, and the clemency of the sovereign or the generosity of the
best men among the rulers may sometimes set right the wrongs which
the weak and the meek must undergo. We must not forget that Vergil
composed the *Eclogues* during the times of trouble that marked the

end of the republic and the establishment of the empire. In such times, as well as in any feudal or aristocratic society, justice works only as a personal bond, as a benefit graciously granted from on high and gratefully received below. In such conditions or times justice looks more like a privilege than a right; and, like all privileges it may be granted without dessert. It is significant that in the First Eclogue Vergil depicts Tityrus as a shepherd devoid of any particular distinction, and it is even more significant that elsewhere he tells us of the poet Menalcas, whom even poetic reputation and merit failed to exempt from the enforcement of the expropriation decree.

It is obvious that in Menalcas Vergil portrays himself at the time he did not know or had no reason to expect that his farm would be restored to him. The poet unfolds such a portrayal in a passage of the Ninth Eclogue, which consists of a dialogue between Moeris, Menalcas' servant, and Lycidas, one of his friends. They walk together on their way to town, and pass most of the time reciting fragments of the poetry of their master and friend. At the start of their talk they discuss, however, the eviction of Menalcas, of which Lycidas had not yet heard. Not even poetry, Moeris sadly comments, has spared Menalcas from obeying the stern injunction to vacate his ancestral land (*Ecl.* ix):

> . . . sed carmina tantum
> nostra valent, Lycida, tela inter Martia, quantum
> Chaonias dicunt aquila veniente columbas.

But this poetry of ours, Lycidas, can do no more against a man in arms than the doves we have heard of at Dodona, when an eagle comes their way.

By avowing that even poetic laurels may be of no avail, Vergil emphasizes here that justice derives from the caprice of the rulers rather than from the rights or merits of the ruled. It was only after the peace made a few years later between Octavianus and Antony, an uneasy truce which at first raised great hopes, that Vergil could postulate the reestablishment of an order based on justice. He did so in the Fourth Eclogue, in which he conveyed that expectation through the fabulous images of the restoration of the Golden Age and of the return of

Astraea to the earth. Yet the peace and justice announced in the Fourth Eclogue were still conceived, so to speak, in aristocratic terms —as the gift of a wise shepherd of men to his herd. Only after the foundation of the empire, while writing the *Aeneid*, was Vergil able to celebrate peace and justice as the rule of a universal law.

II

Christian peace was bound to take the place of Roman peace, to deny pagan justice, and to put Christian justice in its stead. But whereas Christian peace became an idea of the future, Christian justice, at least in part, remained an idea of the past: if the former acted as a promise of the new law, the latter worked as a guarantee of the old covenant. The justice of the New Testament is indeed but a new version of the justice of the Old Testament. This is why we shall not be surprised to find in the Bible stories relating happenings very similar to those that befell such Vergilian shepherds as Menalcas and Meliboeus. One of these stories may seem to read, at least up to a point, like a scriptural variant of the First Eclogue. The gist of both tales is that the wicked and the mighty covet the property of the meek and the weak and that by means fair or foul succeed in satisfying their evil greed. The biblical story we have in mind is that of Naboth of Jezreel, whose vineyard lay close to the palace of Ahab, king of Samaria (1 Kings, xxi.2–3):

> And Ahab spake unto Naboth, saying, Give me thy vineyard, that I may have it for a garden of herbs, because it is near unto my house: and I will give thee for it a better vineyard than it; or, if it seem good to thee, I will give thee the worth of it in money.
> And Naboth said to Ahab, The Lord forbid it me, that I should give the inheritance of my fathers unto thee.

Ahab sulked in anger and grief, and his wife Jezebel consoled him and promised she would help him get his wish. She had Naboth accused of blasphemy to God and the king, and the people stoned Naboth to death (16): "And it came to pass, when Ahab heard that Naboth was dead, that Ahab rose up to go down to the vineyard of Naboth the Jezreelite, to take possession of it."

Up to this point we have a replica of Meliboeus' story, with the difference of a far more tragic ending, since Naboth loses his life as well as his land. Yet the moral seems to be the same. The lesson we are taught in both cases is that innocence and right are no safeguards against insecurity and wrong. But the biblical story does not end here; it proceeds to tell how the Lord called Elijah and sent him to curse Ahab (27): "And it came to pass, when Ahab heard those words, that he rent his clothes, and put sackcloth upon his flesh, and fasted, and lay in sackcloth, and went softly." Then the Lord spoke to Elijah, saying (29): "Seest thou how Ahab humbleth himself before me? because he humbleth himself before me, I will not bring evil in his days: but in his son's days will I bring the evil upon his house."

Now we see that whereas the moral of the two tales may be identical, their ethos is not the same. The biblical story deals with righteousness and unrighteousness even more than with justice or injustice; and this is why its protagonist is Ahab the guilty rather than Naboth the guiltless. The victim is killed, and therefore the restoration of right, or the rewarding of innocence, is no longer possible. What is still possible and always necessary is retributive justice, which brings punishment to the guilty and the wicked. Its instrument is a God who acts at once as an avenger and as a judge. This is the vengeance of God, or the justice of the Father; and it is not against but beyond that justice that the Son will preach the remission of sins, or the forgiveness of injustice. The good tidings of the gospel are the announcement that the soul may be redeemed and that man may be reborn into innocence; hence the symbol of the sacrificial lamb washing away all the evil of the world. Jesus would not have threatened to visit Ahab's sins on his offspring. Besides forgiving the repentant Ahab, he would have brought forth a bright hope for his house and for his children, and for all men of good will. Whereas the Old Testament is an indictment of man's wickedness, of his inner injustice, the New Testament is a pledge of purification and a promise that man will achieve inner justice.

The main concern of the world, however, is with both outer injustice and outer justice, and this is why even Christianity had in practice to accept the Roman view of the rule of law and of society as judge. But the rule of law was put in jeopardy by the turmoil of history, for during many centuries of external violence and internal disorder not only the state but even the church failed to play its role as judge. This made possible and even necessary the survival in the barbaric and the feudal ages of the heroic or aristocratic dream of personal justice. That dream was revived, and for a while seemed to flourish again, during the Renaissance. Some of the men of that epoch assigned to poetry itself not merely the task of reviving the dream but also that of making it true. Whereas in Vergil's *Eclogues* the gift of song was of no avail to poor Menalcas, who lost his little property like any other shepherd, now poetry seemed to share one of the main attributes of power, the one which is now called "influence"—particularly the influence to redress wrong or to set right an injustice. Some of the representatives of the new spirit extended that attribute to the humblest kind of poetry, pastoral song, which was thus supposed to uphold the rights of the poor and the meek. Only someone who was at once a man of letters and a man of arms, a humanist and a gentleman, as well as the author of a romance like *Arcadia*, merging together the chivalric and the bucolic spirit, could say of pastoral poetry what Sir Philip Sidney said in this rhetorical question in *Defence of Poetry*: "Is it then the Pastoral poem which is misliked? (For perchance where the hedge is lowest they will soonest leap over.) Is the poor pipe disdained, which sometime out of Meliboeus' mouth can show the misery of people under hard lords, or ravening soldiers, and again, by Tityrus, what blessedness is derived to them that lie lowest from the goodness of them that sit highest." In this statement pastoral poetry is viewed as an instrument of pity, which is the prime mover of personal justice, especially of the kind based on the principle of noblesse oblige, which turns justice not only into an aristocratic obligation but also into an aristocratic privilege.

III

Cervantes, greater as a poet than Sidney and his equal as a soldier, wrote in his *Galatea*, as Sidney had done in *Arcadia*, a bucolic romance of his own, and reaffirmed with no less eloquence the bonds between arms and learning in both words and deeds.[3] Cervantes was thus naturally bound to share Sidney's aristocratic vision. Yet, at least in his masterpiece, he refused, if not to relate, to join together the pastoral vision and the chivalric ideal. He made of his hero the greatest of all dreamers; but perhaps because he had himself led a hard life in a hard world, Cervantes made Don Quixote aware that social reality is far from being an idyll. Don Quixote knows that it is not the poet, this unarmed prophet, but only the armed knight that can restore justice on the earth. With pointed irony Cervantes has Don Quixote teach this lesson to a group of ignorant herdsmen—a lesson which the knight unfolds in the traditional contrast between the Golden Age of the past and the Iron Age of the present. The Knight of La Mancha is offered the opportunity to state his view on this matter shortly after the beginning of the second expedition, on the evening when he and Sancho are surprised by darkness in the fields and decide to spend the night in the open with a group of goatherds. The goatherds welcome both knight and squire at their rustic table, on which they set two wineskins, a piece of hard cheese, and plenty of dried acorns. The last remind Don Quixote of mankind's primal state, and it is with a reevocation of that primordial way of life that he opens a long address to his hosts (I.xi):

> Dichosa edad y siglos dichosos aquellos a quien los antiguos pusieron nombre de dorados, y no porque en ellos el oro, que en esta nuestra edad de hierro tanto se estima, se alcanzase en aquella venturosa sin fatiga alguna, sino porque entonces los que en ella vivían ignoraban estas dos palabras de *tuyo* y *mío*.

> Happy the age and happy the times on which the ancients bestowed the name of golden, not because gold, which in this iron age of ours is rated so highly, was attainable without labour in those fortunate times, but rather because the people of those days did not know those two words *thine* and *mine*.[4]

It is obvious that Don Quixote develops his praise of the Age of Gold through the same rhetorical device which Tasso had employed in his own praise of the same age which he uttered in the first chorus of *Aminta*, his lovely pastoral drama.[5] Yet, while converging in formal patterns, the two texts diverge in patterns of thought. Let's praise mankind's earliest times, says Tasso, not for being blessed with the spontaneous generation of the staples of life or with the eternal springtime of the climate, but for being graced with the unspoiled happiness of free love. But Cervantes is not Tasso, and Don Quixote no Amintas. The only idyllic dream which may appeal to the chaste knight is the one conveyed by the pastoral of innocence and purity, not by the pastoral of happiness and love. Besides being chaste, Don Quixote is poor and simple; for him what spoiled the Age of Gold was not sexual honor, as Tasso claims, but property and wealth. Precisely because "eran en aquella santa edad todas las cosas comunes" (in that blessed age all things were held in common), "todo era en paz entonces, todo amistad, todo concordia" (all was peace then, all amity, all concord). Maids wore no more clothes than modesty requires. Luxury and pomp were unknown, and justice ruled undisturbed precisely because judges and tribunals were not needed. But the greatest of all the blessings provided by that age was the protection it afforded to the weak, and particularly to the weaker sex. Any modest maid could then roam the wilds at will, in security and solitude, without fearing harm from masculine license and violence. Now, on the contrary, "en estos nuestros detestables siglos, no está segura ninguna" (in this detestable age of ours, no maiden is safe); no shelter can be found to safeguard our girls from "la amoresa pestilencia" (the plague of love). Yet, now that the Age of Gold is over, a noble institution has arisen in its place and taken upon itself the task of protecting damsels in distress and any other helpless creature:

Para cuya seguridad, andando más los tiempos y creciendo más la malicia, se instituyó la orden de los caballeros andantes, para defender las doncellas, amparar las viudas y socorrer a los huérfanos y a los menesterosos.

Therefore, as times rolled on and wickedness increased, the order of knights errant was founded for their protection, to defend maidens, relieve widows, and succour the orphans and the needy.

The words by which Don Quixote ends his speech: "Desta orden soy yo, hermanos cabreros" (of this order am I, brother goatherds), ring with the noble pride of a man who has consecrated his life to uphold justice, establish charity, and restore the hopes of the oppressed and the defenseless.

What makes this lofty speech ridiculous and incongruous is that it is uttered just when the chivalric ideal is on the wane; as for the age of chivalry, like the Golden Age, either it had never existed or it had disappeared a long time ago, even before the establishment of standing armies and the invention of firearms.[6] Yet what Don Quixote here announces and tries on any occasion to enact is the replacement of the pastoral dream with the chivalric dream. What makes the speech and the situation even more comic is that the new dispensation is announced to people who had never heard even of the old one. By merging the dream of justice with the chivalric dream, however, Don Quixote turns the latter into the least chimeric of all his fancies. Without doubt it is the former that gives nobility to the latter and helps to preserve that longing after innocence which is one of the main traits of the pastoral vision, which Don Quixote can never fully renounce.[7]

IV

When the Renaissance was over, it was the dream of justice that gave a new lease on life to the pastoral dream, this time by freeing it from its traditional aristocratic temper or content. Yet for a while the very survival of the pastoral dream was put in doubt. This happened when a host of new concepts challenged the dream of justice, which seemed about to be shattered, even though in the end it came out of the fray stronger than before. Such concepts were those of change, evolution, progress. It was within their context, which formed the early cluster of modern thought, that Goethe felt duty-bound to deny any further validity to the pastoral of innocence. He did so just before the end of the second part of *Faust*, in the Philemon and Baucis episode; and what makes that denial both cogent and moving is the quality of its utterance. That episode is but an affirmation of the unreality, at least within the modern situation, of the dream of pastoral justice—an affirmation which is dictated also by the pathetic awareness of the price that man must pay for the loss of that dream. Philemon and Baucis are the sacrificial victims of the new secular religion, which is the cult of power and of the self; and Goethe mourns the passing of the old couple, as well as the passing of their way of life, with a tear of pity and regret.

The episode in question unfolds in "Offene Gegend" (Open Country), and in the two scenes that follow, at the very beginning of Act

V, Philemon and Baucis are settled near the shore, close to the submerged lands which Faust has just reclaimed from the sea. Their
cottage and garden are among the dunes, and there is a chapel on a
hill nearby. The action begins with the visit of a traveler, who returns to the old place on a pilgrimage of thanksgiving. He wants to
see those two "meek people" again and to pay them his tribute of
gratitude, since many years earlier they had saved his life and rescued
his treasure from a shipwreck. First Baucis and then Philemon welcome the traveler, to whom they offer again their hospitality. Before
sitting with his hosts at the table set in the garden, the visitor advances on the dunes to recite a prayer before the boundless sea. Not
being forewarned by his hosts, he does not recognize what he sees.
Philemon, who has joined him, points out to his guest that what was
once a desolate seascape has been turned into an immense garden, into
a kind of artificial paradise and explains how this was done (11091–
96):

> Kluger Herren kühne Knechte
> Gruben Gräben, dämmten ein,
> Schmälerten des Meeres Rechte,
> Herrn au seiner Statt zu sein.
> Schaue grünend Wies' an Wiese,
> Anger, Garten, Dorf, und Wald.
>
> Wise lords set their serfs in motion,
> Dikes upraised and ditches led,
> Minishing the rights of Ocean,
> Lords to be in Ocean's stead.
> See the green of many a meadow,
> Field and garden, wood and town! [8]

The traveler is so surprised that from now on he will utter no word.
The only ones who speak during the meal are the hosts. Both of them
go on talking about the "wonder," which the naïve Philemon views
as a miracle, and the suspicious Baucis as an act of witchcraft. The
old woman ends her account by accusing the wizard or sorcerer who

has made that wonder possible, and who now is their neighbor and landlord, of coveting their property and of treating them as his subjects (11131–34):

> Gottlos ist er, ihn gelüstet
> Unsre Hütte, unser Hain;
> Wie er sich als Nachbar brüstet,
> Soll man untertänig sein.

> He would seize our field of labor,
> Hut and garden, godlessly:
> Since he lords it as our neighbor,
> We to him must subject be.

Philemon observes that their lord (Faust's name is never mentioned) had after all promised them in exchange for their grove a fair property on the reclaimed land. But Baucis, who joins superstition to wisdom, displays a lack of confidence in the flatlands which once were underwater sand. She holds fast to their property also because it is on high and solid ground. The scene ends at eventide, when Philemon leads his wife and their guest to the little shrine for evening prayer. Whether or not they must distrust their earthly master, they will trust their heavenly Lord (11139–42):

> Lasst uns zur Kapelle treten,
> Letzten Sonnenblick zu schaun!
> Lasst uns läuten, knieen, beten
> Und dem alten Gott vertraun.

> Let us, to the chapel straying,
> Ere the sunset-glow has died,
> Chime the vespers, kneel, and, praying,
> Still in our old God confide!

We thus leave the old couple with their guest, while the scene shifts from their humble cottage to their landlord's magnificent residence ("Palast," Palace) or, rather, to its pleasure garden, crossed by a rectilinear canal. There we find Faust, who has become incredibly old. He walks and ponders, when he suddenly is startled by the ringing echo of the chapel's silver bell. That sound reminds him that his realm is not boundless—that the linden grove, the smoky cottage, and the mossy little shrine are not part of his dominion. At this point he is joined by Mephistopheles, accompanied by three mighty men. They have just landed and are unloading a galley full of foreign goods. The wealth they bring in has not been earned through honest toil or zealous industry but through dishonest and adventurous commerce. Mephistopheles, who in the meantime has dismissed his henchmen, realizes that Faust is gloomily indifferent to the new riches just brought to him. To gladden the heart of his master Mephistopheles points out that their dominion of the sea is but the outcome of Faust's design to reclaim the submerged lands he had received as a feud after helping the emperor to win his wars. To which Faust replies that even though he now rules the waves he does not feel like a sovereign because Philemon's and Baucis' little grove is not his (11241–42):

> Die wenig Bäume, nicht mein eigen,
> Verderben mir den Weltbesitz.

> The lindens, not my own possession,
> Disturb my joy in mine estate.

Were that grove mine, says Faust, I would build there a lookout from which to survey with a single gaze all my masterworks and would feel no longer haunted by the sad tolling of the silver bell. Mephistopheles, who understands how Faust's mind is affected by that voice of faith and death, stirs his master to give the fatal order (11275–77):

> So geht und schafft sie mir zur Seite!—
> Das schöne Gütchen kennst du ja,
> Das ich den Alten ausersah.

Then go, and clear them out with speed!
Thou knowest the fair estate, indeed,
I chose for the old people's need.

Mephisto calls back the three mighty men to help him to execute this order, and in the third and last scene, "Tiefe Nacht" (Dead of Night), we witness that execution, which is also an execution in the dreadest sense of the word. In reality we see what happens through the eyes of Lynceus the warder, who is on night watch on the palace tower. A sudden fire breaks in the darkness and with the help of the wind burns to the ground the cottage, the chapel, and the grove, turning into ashes the old couple and any other living thing. Lynceus watches this spectacle with powerless horror; and when everything is over, sings a dirge on the way of life which had just died before his eyes, leaving behind itself but scarred stumps (11336–37):

Was sich sonst dem Blick empfohlen,
Mit Jahrhunderten ist hin.

What erewhile the eye enchanted
With the centuries is gone.

The warder's complaint wounds the ear and the heart of Faust, who inwardly repents of his reckless order and the foul deed. Yet it is only from Mephistopheles' report that he later learns that Philemon and Baucis had refused to leave their place and had perished in the flames with their guest.[9] Faust seeks to justify himself by claiming that he wanted an exchange, not a robbery, but is grief-stricken and bewails the rash order and the too rash compliance. Yet he cannot dwell too long on such thoughts; the four gray women, Want, Guilt, Care, and Necessity, enter the stage. He must now face their dreadful apparition, which precedes and forecasts his death.

The first of the many questions this episode poses to its interpreters is why Goethe chose to pattern the two victims of Faust's whim on that famous classical couple. His own Philemon and Baucis are as full of piety as their original models. Yet the old God they believe in is Christian rather than pagan. This is not the only anachronism in Goethe's version of the tale. Thus, for instance, its locale is no longer the countryside of ancient Phrygia but a Western and modern habitat which looks very much like the Netherlands, while the body of water facing the shoreline could be taken for the Zuider Zee. But it is obviously on less superficial differences than these that Goethe based the statement he made to Eckermann on June 6, 1831: "My Philemon and Baucis have nothing to do with that famous pair of antiquity or the saga relating to them. As the personages and the conditions are similar, the similar names produce a thoroughly favorable effect." Such a statement, however, is at once true and false. A comparison with the fable as told by Ovid (*Met.* viii866 ff.),[10] or rather as retold by Hederich in his mythological dictionary, the poet's direct source, shows that Goethe took into account almost all of the fable's traditional and even conventional details. Rather than ignore or discard all the elements of the story that he could not imitate, he made them serve, so to speak, as the "negatives" of his own images. Yet even in minor matters the changes which the fable underwent in Goethe's hand are considerable; for instance, in the original story there were two visitors rather than a single one; and they are two gods traveling the earth in human disguise. It is they that submerge the surrounding lands in order to punish all the other inhabitants, who, unlike Philemon and Baucis, denied the two strange pilgrims hospitality under their roof. The submerged lands appear also in Goethe's version of the fable—not only at its beginning, or rather, in its antecedents—and furthermore they are turned into the lasting creation of a human agency. Goethe's little chapel corresponds to Ovid's temple; the latter, however, had arisen only at the end of the story, by the will of the gods, never to be destroyed as Goethe's shrine is bound to be, by human hands and an evil deed. We now realize that the metamorphosis to which Goethe submitted that ancient fable worked, so to speak, according to a process of inversion, and culminated in the overturn of the fable's traditional ending—in the replacement of the idyllic passing of the old couple with their violent and gruesome death. Paradoxically it is this deliberate reversal of the fable's outcome that explains why Goethe could not avoid using the two figures which are the most typical and classical representatives of the pastoral of innocence in his all too successful attempt to prove that the latter was no longer conceivable in the modern world. Goethe knew that the dream of pastoral innocence was over, like any hope which has been proved false, and he felt that it should not be dreamed any longer. The poet's stand in this matter is the more significant since in the Arcadia episode he had treated the pastoral of happiness as a passing illusion. Still he had found it worthy of being dreamed again and anew.

Goethe had no other alternative than to use as an exemplary test of the truth he wanted to convey the very fable which was supposed to demonstrate the opposite truth. Yet, at first sight, one could claim that he could have used for the same purpose other stories than that of Philemon and Baucis, taken from other traditions than that of classical poetry. The Bible could have easily provided him with some of such stories. The first example that comes to our mind is the tale of Naboth and Ahab, in which the bone of contention is almost the same—or, in lieu of a grove, a vineyard. Goethe himself was fully aware of this possibility and even hinted at it, for he made Mephistopheles point it out on his own behalf. After receiving Faust's order to evict the old couple from their cottage, Mephistopheles turns to the audience to forewarn them of the expected outcome. He gives this forewarning by means of a biblical allusion through which he seems also to exhibit his acquaintance with sacred history or to show off his own scriptural learning (11286–87):

> Auch hier geschieht, was längst geschah,
> Denn Naboths Weinberg war schon da.

> It happens as it happed of old:
> Still Naboth's vineyard we behold!

Yet if Goethe refrained from taking in this matter Mephistopheles' hint, it was simply because he could not afford to reshape as freely as he needed, or to rearrange as arbitrarily as he wanted, the biblical story of Naboth's vineyard. One does not need to be of "the devil's party" to realize that no deus ex machina can take the place of the Christian God—that no human agency can act in his stead. It is also worth remarking that the pastoral quality of that biblical story was too slight to serve Goethe's purpose or to please his taste. Naboth's vineyard is a sign of prosperity, if not of plenty, and thus unsuited to signify the idyll of poverty, in which scarcity is the single resort, in economic, ethical, and even aesthetic terms.

That Goethe wanted to emphasize the absolute quality of the initial situation is proved by his emphatic use of the traditional opposition between the shepherd's way of life on one side and the trader's or sailor's on the other. He brings such an opposition to the extreme degree of tension by attributing Faust's ill-gotten and newly acquired wealth not merely to sharp trading practices but to piracy and privateering, as if it were a kind of war booty because, as Mephistopheles says (11187–88):

> Krieg, Handel und Piraterie,
> Dreienig sind sie, nicht zu trennen.

> War, Trade and Piracy, I vow,
> Are three in one, and can't be separated!

It is evident that Goethe expands this opposition further than it has ever been done before, within the dimensions provided by the immeasurably broader framework of modern life; and nothing could be more cogently modern than the colonial and imperialistic argument by which Mephistopheles justifies the old couple's resettlement. By employing a colloquial gallicism and a political neologism (*genieren* and *kolonisieren*), Mephistopheles seems to emphasize the topicality, or the historical immediacy, of that argument (11273–74):

> Was willst du dich denn hier genieren?
> Musst du nicht längst kolonisieren?

> Why be annoyed, when thou canst well despise them?
> Wouldst thou not long since colonize them?

Whereas he intensifies to the maximum the material attributes of Faust's dominion and power, Goethe reduces to the minimum the natural and economic attributes of Philemon's and Baucis' condition and estate. As for the humility and simplicity of their way of life, it is made even more evident if, after comparing their "little world" to Faust's "great world," we also compare the modest setting of their pastoral of innocence with the splendid background which Faust and Helena had chosen for their own pastoral of happiness.[11] If it contrasts with the lushness and opulence of Faust's and Helena's Arcadia, Philemon's and Baucis' idyllic little retreat stands out more sharply in its rusticity and bareness—or, aesthetically, in the spareness of its outline. This is why the "open country" within which that retreat is nestled fails to become a pastoral oasis and fails to be introduced or adorned by a properly developed *locus amoenus,* which would have hardly suited the occasion or the place.[12] Philemon and Baucis are good husbandmen, yet they do not belong to that kind of landholder who improves the homely nature of his estate with landscape gardening or other artificial devices. Hence the sharpening of another contrast, the one between their little grove, which is the comely product of a homely nature, and Faust's dominion, which is the artificial product of human design and particularly of land- and seascape engineering.

Yet in one sense one could and should claim even more than Goethe did in his statement to Eckermann, and conclude the analysis of this episode by maintaining that his Philemon and Baucis are radically different not only from their ancient models but also from all the other characters who have played similar roles in the pastorals of innocence and justice. Goethe's Philemon and Baucis are, for instance, ethically superior to their counterparts in Ovid for being the benefactors as well as the hosts of their visitors. They are likewise braver than Vergil's Meliboeus because they choose death rather than exile; and they are even more just than Naboth, whom we never see performing acts of love or piety. Finally, they are unluckier than any of their predecessors, not excluding Naboth, since no blow of retributive justice befalls their murderer and despoiler. Remorse does not bite deep and long enough in Faust's conscience. As for their creator, after having shed a tear on their fate, he moves ahead with his hero, leaving their spoils, or their relics, on the wayside. It is not anachronistic to affirm that Goethe sacrifices them to the glory of that "superman," Faust, or even to an almost Hegelian kind of historical justice. Historical justice, as we well know, is as merciless in forgetting the innocent victims of history as it is merciful in forgiving its makers, who are often wrongdoers.

This is the reason that of the four gray women who will haunt Faust just before his death the only one who looks formidable and inexorable is not Guilt, but Care (Sorge). Care, after all, is both the curse and the blessing of the restless. It is restlessness, or one of the major vices or virtues of the modern spirit, that turns into a new tale the story of Faust's life. But the death of Philemon and Baucis is an old story, as Mephistopheles knows, as the silent chorus is well aware. Before departing to leave Faust alone with his perplexing thoughts, the chorus finally speaks and turns to the audience to teach, in a prosaic anticlimax, the lesson of a prudence so mediocre as to turn into cowardice. It is with the gnomic wisdom of a homely proverb that the chorus points the only moral which seems to conclude, without adorning it, this sorry tale (11374–75):

> Das alte Wort, das Wort erschallt:
> Gehorche willig der Gewalt!

> The Proverb old still runs its course:
> Bend willingly to greater force! [13]

By thus denying, at the end of both of his masterpiece and his life, the pastoral of innocence, Goethe rejected in full the aristocratic dream of justice as shaped by the poetic idealism of antiquity and the Renaissance. But before him, and unlike him, the men of the eighteenth century had been unready as well as unwilling to renounce that dream of justice the bucolic ideal seemed to carry within itself. Thus the literature and the thought of the Enlightenment went back to the pastoral of innocence, only changing the old dream of justice into a new one. All aristocratic dreams tend to look back and to long after restorations history will not admit. But the new dream tended to look forward, projecting advances never fancied before. Such a new dream was later to become the democratic ideal, which is progressive, whereas the aristocratic one is regressive—two epithets to be taken not as marks of approval or disapproval but merely as neutral designations or descriptive terms. What we witness at this point, and in such change, is the gradual democratization of the bucolic view, a process which, when it reaches its climax, will shatter forever all idyllic dreams.

V

Strangely enough, some of those who contributed to the earliest phase of the process in question were members of the Roman church, mainly those Franciscan and Dominican friars who took it upon themselves to safeguard the rights of the Indians of all the New Spains of the Americas from the oppression of their Christian brethren, who were also their lords and masters. The poor Indians of Mexico, Peru, the Antilles, and many other regions of the new continent inspired in those churchmen notions at odds with the dogmas and beliefs of their church—such as those of the perfectibility and the natural goodness of man. It was those friars, rather than lay visitors or secular travelers, who were chiefly responsible for the creation of the myth of the "noble savage"; and many of them went so far as to believe that if the Golden Age was not a fable it must have indeed once flourished on the pagan soil of the New World. One of them, the good father Bartolomé de las Casas, claimed, at the very beginning of his famous *Historia general de las Indias,* not only that that happy primal state had existed in fact, but that the natives of the Spanish colonies were its last surviving representatives on earth: "gentes de la Edad Dorada, que tanto por los poetas e los historiadores fué alabada" (people of the Age of Gold, which was so much praised by the poets and the historians). Often the good fathers turned from shepherds of souls into shepherds of men, and ruled their flocks as temporal as well as spiritual leaders. When taking charge of persons rather than merely of souls they sought to establish an idyllic commonwealth, as the members of another order tried to do with the so-called Jesuit State of Paraguay. By such attempts they enacted a compromise between the aristocratic and the democratic dream. The middle path they followed was their own version of that system of government which finds its label in the term paternalism. On the European scene, and in the field of secular government, that compromise had taken the different name and shape of enlightened despotism.

The man who ideally transcended that compromise and who definitely turned the pastoral vision into a vehicle of the democratic ideal was Rousseau. He transformed into a concrete faith the vague hope that the goddess of justice would return from heaven to earth and rule again among men. The effect of this was a shifting of the dream of the Golden Age from a dim and unfathomable past to a future both foreseeable and bright. This ideological turning point coincides with one of the early fruits of Rousseau's political thought—its very pivot is to be seen in the *Discours sur l'inégalité*. At the beginning of his second *Discours* Rousseau projects his vision of the "state of nature," which he conceives and describes in terms of his own. One could say that this vision represents a fusion of the pastoral and of the Hobbesian view. For Rousseau the state of nature was ruled by physical force. Such a rule was a direct effect of natural inequality and caused mankind to live in a condition of violence and insecurity. Man was then indeed wolf to man, and this endangered both wolf and sheep. Yet the state of nature was quasi-pastoral in the sense that it ignored the vices induced by institutional life and the political order. As the violence and insecurity of primitive existence could not be endured forever, so the state of nature came to an end and was superseded by civilization, which coincided with the establishment of society and the foundation of the state. This was done by means of what Rousseau called, according to the terminology of natural law, a social contract. By such a contract primitive man exchanged the wild freedom of the state of nature for the security afforded by the protection of law.

This at first seemed to replace natural inequality with legal equality, or might with right. All citizens were supposed to be equal before the law. But Rousseau already knew that when all men are said to be equal a few deem and are deemed to be more equal than others.[14] The very creation of two classes of men, the magistrates and the common citizens, the former the law's active instruments, the latter its passive subjects, fostered the usual vices of civilization, which are vanity and lust for power, and determined between rulers and ruled a new kind of equality, worse than the earlier one, being based on civil rather than on natural law. The new inequality became intolerable when the social order replaced communal with private property. Don Quixote, in his speech to the goatherds, had already stated that the Golden Age had disappeared as soon as society introduced in human relations the concepts of "thine" and "mine," and Rousseau claims likewise that mankind's happiest epoch, which was for him the one immediately following upon the establishment of the social order, had ended at the very moment man had for the first time fenced a plot of land and said "this is mine." The institution of private property with the consequent accumulation of wealth, disparity of economic condition, and the ever increasing development of the acquisitive instinct, had provoked injustices far more cruel than those man had endured in the state of primitive anarchy. Rousseau's essay ends with the statement that the best solution of all social problems would be not to revert to the state of nature because of the impracticality and even the impossibility of such a regression, but to restore in new circumstances a situation as close as possible to the one which obtained soon after the establishment of the civil bond. In such a case proper checks and balances should be found so as to prevent the repetition of that process of corruption which is the nemesis of all social organisms.

As to transforming into a plan of action the ideal state he had envisaged at the end of the *Discours sur l'inégalité,* Rousseau wrote *Le Contrat social,* in which he gave us his tables of law. There he interpreted the claims of equality and justice in abstract and collective terms, thus sacrificing the claims of individual liberty, as shown by the paradoxical doctrine of the general will. Yet it is from the seeds of Rousseau's thought that there sprung later on French soil those strange plants which took the name of "trees of liberty." Rousseau's ideas paved the ground not only for republican liberty and democratic justice, but also for socialist equality—in brief, for all the radical or revolutionary ideas of modern history. There is no doubt that Rousseau and many of his disciples fostered the formation of those ideals with the instrumental help of the pastoral view. This happened only at the beginning; yet the fact remains noteworthy. The bucolic vision is after all fundamentally static, and as such alien to the notion of social and political change. Its inner nature implies an utter denial of the idea of revolution itself. Yet we now know that revolution may in some cases spring forth from its direct antithesis, which is not evolution but involution, as the two great revolutions of modern history, the Russian and the Chinese, so eloquently prove.

The most important of the contributions of the pastoral ideal to the early development of revolutionary ideology is the myth of the Golden Age. Revolutionary ideology, however, used that myth not as an ancestral memory or a moral example but as the promise of a brave new world. Rousseau was perhaps responsible for this metamorphosis even though he conveyed it in vague and confused terms. Rather than of the Age of Gold, he had spoken of the state of nature and had avoided identifying the former with the latter. He viewed the Golden Age (even though he never used this term) in the earliest stage of the social system. It was that stage that he wanted to see restored; or rather what he wanted was the instauration of a new and reasonable equivalent in a future as near as possible. Yet this view made it possible for others to transform a backward-looking dream into a forward-looking one. This was done primarily by some of the radical thinkers who followed in Rousseau's footsteps, especially after the revolution. The most eloquent statement of this conception may be read in a Saint-Simonian manifesto, entitled *De la réorganisation de la société européenne,* which the master himself framed at the dawn of the century, with the collaboration of his disciple Augustin Thierry:

L'imagination des poètes a placé l'âge d'or au berceau de l'espèce humaine parmi l'ignorance et la grossièreté des premiers temps: c'était bien plutôt l'âge de fer qu'il fallait y reléguer. L'âge d'or du genre humain n'est point derrière nous, il est au-devant, il est dans la perfection de l'ordre social; nos pères ne l'ont point vu, nos enfants y arriveront un jour: c'est à nous de leur en frayer la route.

The imagination of the poets placed the Golden Age at the dawn of the human race, amidst the ignorance and rudeness of primitive times. It is rather the Iron Age that should be banished there. The Golden Age of mankind is not behind, but before us; and it lies in the perfection of the social order; our fathers have not seen it, our children will one day reach it; it is for us to prepare the way.

The most important statement in this passage is perhaps the concluding one, which implies that we should not merely speculate about the forthcoming Golden Age but also help to make its advent faster and easier. This seems to anticipate the postulate which Marx formulated in the second of his theses on Feuerbach: that the task of thought now should be not to interpret the world but to change it. At this stage the pastoral view is transcended once for all. That view aimed at contemplating man and nature and at idealizing both of them. And even though it might sometime turn into a retrospective or a prospective dream, it was primarily introspective in temper, choosing as its natural habitat the Platonic cave of the self and taking inner or private life as its main concern. The bucolic ideal, which tended to avoid roaming in the open spaces or in the wilderness, was even more bound to shy away from the walled squares of the great cities, where rebellious masses may raze Bastilles or behead nobles and kings.

Yet, as Goethe understood, the bucolic ideal was denied and destroyed by the bourgeois spirit even before it was denied by the revolutionary spirit. Marx and Engels stated this truth in these ringing words of *The Communist Manifesto*, which appeared only a few years after the second *Faust:* "The bourgeoisie, wherever it has got the upper hand, has put an end to all feudal, patriarchal, *idyllic* relations" (emphasis added). Yet the pastoral myth survived, even though only as a myth. As such it affected the ideologies of the anarchists, of those whom Marx called utopian socialists, and of many social visionaries and political idealists. The fable of the Golden Age was still to be frequently used, either as a negative or as a positive argument, by many minds rejecting the revolutionary ideal, or protesting its failure to fulfill its purest goals. The most significant representative of the former is Dostoevski, who thrice used the vision of the ancient pastoral happiness of man, as it had been suggested to him by a painting he had seen at Dresden (Claude Lorrain's *Acis et Galatheé*).[15] In each case he projected that vision into a dream and turned that dream into a nightmare to prove that the inner necessity of that ideal of perfection by which the revolutionary spirit tempts and threatens the human soul turns it into its very opposite or into a corruption never dreamed before. A lesser Russian writer, far nearer to us in time and mood, the poet Sergei Esenin, represents no less eloquently the other alternative. Unlike Dostoevski, he saw the revolution come, and welcomed it; but shortly after its coming he condemned the new order after which he had yearned for bringing into the Russian countryside a new Age of Iron instead of a new Age of Gold. It was in a pastoral key that Esenin sang of the revolution before and after its advent. Yet when the poet felt that the revolution had disappointed him by failing to keep its promises and to fulfill his dreams, he attuned to the mode of the elegy a lyre once attuned to the mode of the idyll. It was in 1789 that Chamfort, a writer who was also destined to end as a disappointed victim of the upheaval he had fostered, coined the famous revolutionary slogan: "guerre aux château, paix aux chaumières!" Esenin was probably unaware of that slogan; yet most of his poetry sounds like a single pastoral elegy, like a constant bucolic complaint, lamenting that the Revolution, after razing the manors of the landlords to the ground, is now waging war on the humblest villages of that Arcadia, the Russian countryside.[16]

11

"Arkadisch Frei Sei Unser Glück!": Goethe and the Pastoral

I

Many are the works of Goethe that deal with pastoral or quasi-pastoral subjects or relate to the bucolic tradition in spirit and form. In most of them the tie is partial, and in many the poet tends to treat the pastoral convention in a mocking vein, through the devices of parody, irony, and even travesty. Thus, when he was still a young man, he imposed a bucolic theme on the unshapely mold of the plebeian farce, producing in his *Satyroe* a deliberate caricature of Rousseau's and Herder's worship of the natural and the primitive. In his maturity, he assumed the mask of Tasso's most passionate shepherd, and chose the vehicle of the pastoral elegy in order to justify to a worried friend, in the poem *Amyntas*, his love for such a humble and simple nymph as the tenderly loving, and tenderly loved, Christiane Vulpius. Almost at the same time he gave pastoral overtones to *Hermann und Dorothea*, which he wrote in Homeric style, as a modern and middle-class Odyssey, but which in the end he reduced to the more fitting scale of a bourgeois idyll.

Yet, as one would expect, it was in his masterpiece that Goethe reconveyed and reinterpreted the pastoral view with the greatest intensity. In his striving after any sort of self-gratification and self-realization, Faust could hardly avoid being confronted with the bucolic conception of human bliss. One of the main episodes of the second part of *Faust* is indeed the hero's attempt to achieve pastoral happiness: an attempt that unfolds in what seems to be an actual, even if short-lived, reestablishment of the Age of Gold. The full significance of his attempt cannot be assessed without contrasting that *Faust* episode with a scene from *Tasso*, in which that reestablishment is utterly rejected for being dangerous or impossible. The character uttering such an uncompromising denial is not the protagonist of that drama but his feminine antagonist, Eleonora d'Este; yet there is no doubt that in this matter and in this context it is she, and she alone, who represents Goethe's views.

Goethe wrote *Tasso* not only to convey but also to transcend the personal tragedy of the artist. Goethe himself had succeeded in reconciling the conflict between the poet as a private person and as a public figure, and this is why it would be wrong to consider *Tasso* a self-portrait. Yet his portrayal of the legendary figure of the Italian poet is based on self-experience—on the author's awareness of how easy it is for the artist to yield to his inner urges, and how hard it is for him to comply with social demands. To this psychological awareness Goethe joined a literary one. He knew that many poets, ancient and modern, had adopted idyllic fables or donned pastoral costumes in order to give expression to their desire to heed the lawless summons of the self rather than to observe the checks and restraints imposed on the individual by all human commonwealths.

Goethe also knew that most of these poets had embodied that desire in the dream of free love, and had represented that dream through the fable of the Golden Age. That dream had haunted the imagination of Rousseau, and it was under the spell of Rousseau, and in the mood of the Sturm und Drang, that Goethe wrote a first partial version in prose of the drama about the Italian poet of whom Rousseau had been so fond.[1] Goethe was also aware, at least as much as Rousseau, that no writer or artist had ever expressed the dream of free love and the fable of the Golden Age as poignantly as Tasso had done in his pastoral drama *Aminta*. But when he wrote the final version of his play Goethe was no longer a man and poet of the Sturm und Drang. This is why he represents the urges and desires of his hero not with lyrical identification but with dramatic detachment. By setting against those desires and urges the moral or social views of the other characters, Goethe submits to public criticism the pathos and self-expression of the artist as man.

Goethe does so with particular emphasis in the first scene of the second act, which is at once a reaffirmation by Tasso, and a repudiation by Eleonora d'Este, of the Italian poet's view of love. Eleonora mildly and tenderly reproaches Tasso for his sullen misanthropy, for his unsocial rejection of all companionship. Eleonora is well aware that the poet's refusal of affection and friendship is due to an unrestrained longing for a passion or love ignoring all social barriers and ethical bonds. Tasso himself had projected that longing in the nostalgic vision of the Golden Age as evoked in *Aminta*'s first chorus;[2] and Eleonora ends her reproach by referring to that vision, which she disowns as an alluring but deceitful dream (II.i):

> Auf diesem Wege werden wir wohl nie
> Gesellschaft finden, Tasso! Dieser Pfad,
> Verleitet uns, durch einsames Gebüsch,
> Durch stille Thäler fortzuwandern; mehr
> Und mehr verwöhnt sich das Gemüth, und strebt,
> Die goldne Zeit, die ihm von aussen mangelt,
> In seinem Innern wieder herzustellen,
> So wenig der Versuch gelingen will.

If we follow this way, we shall never find companionship, Tasso! This path waylays us, and makes us wander without end through lonely groves and silent glens; and more and more the spirit spoils itself, and seeks the Golden Age it misses from without and tries to restore from within in an attempt that hardly can succeed.

Tasso seems to take Eleonora's allusion not as a warning but as a compliment. The effect produced by the reference is far from the one she intended: Tasso eagerly seizes it as an occasion or pretext for indulging once more in his dream; and immediately reevokes, with moving eloquence, a happiness which should be of here and now, rather than of never, or of a time long past:

> O welches Wort spricht meine Fürstin aus!
> Die goldne Zeit wohin ist sie geflohn?
> Nach der sich jedes Herz vergebens sehnt!
> Da auf der freien Erde Menschen sich
> Wie frohe Herden in Genuss verbreiteten,
> Da ein uralter Baum auf bunter Wiese
> Dem Hirten und der Hirtin Schatten gab,
> Ein jüngeres Gebüsch die zarten Zweige
> Um sehnsuchtsvolle Liebe traulich schlang;
> Wo klar und still auf immer reinem Sande
> Der weiche Fluss die Nymphe sanft unfing;
> Wo in dem Grase die gescheuchte Schlange
> Unschädlich sich verlor, der kühne Faun
> Vom tapfern Jüngling bald bestraft entfloh;
> Wo jeder Vogel in der freien Luft,
> Und jedes Thier, durch Berg' und Thäler schweifend,
> Zum Menschen sprach: Erlaubt ist was gefällt.

O what a word you utter, oh my Princess! Whereto has flown the Golden Age after which every heart longs in vain? Then over the free world men would be spread like peaceful herds in mirth; an ancient tree on a flowery meadow would offer its shade to the shepherd and the shepherdess; a youthful thicket under its light twigs would conceal the secrets of tender love; quiet and clear over the clean sand the river would softly embrace the nymph; the frightened snake would hide among the grass without doing harm; the daring faun would flee, chastised by the fierce youth; in the free air every bird and every beast erring through the plains and through the hills would tell all men: What pleasing is, is just.[3]

Although this passage does not closely follow *Aminta's* chorus, it closes with a reaffirmation of that "happy and golden rule" of nature which the Italian poet had stated at the close of one of the central stanzas of that chorus. Goethe's "Erlaubt ist was gefällt" is a quasi-literal translation of Tasso's "S'ei piace, ei lice" (What delights, is lawful).

Faced with this outburst, Eleonora has no alternative but to put Tasso in his place, and she does so by denying any validity to the poet's dream. The Age of Gold cannot be reestablished because it never existed; if the values its vision claims to represent ever had any reality, they may forever return, not in the low sphere of passional license, but in the exalted one of moral freedom, as an ideal bond or spiritual friendship. By such a bond or friendship two separate souls may join together in the contemplation of the beauty of the world. This is why the law of nature must yield to the law of society or, better, to the norms of civilization or culture, which puts decorum in the place of passion or caprice:

> Mein Freund, die goldne Zeit ist wohl vorbei:
> Allein die Guten bringen sie zurück;
> Und soll ich dir gestehen wie ich denke:
> Die goldne Zeit, womit der Dichter uns
> Zu schmeicheln pflegt, die schöne Zeit, sie war,
> So scheint es mir, so wenig als sie ist;
> Und war sie je, so war sie nur gewiss,
> Wie sie uns immer wieder werden kann.
> Noch treffen sich verwandte Herzen an
> Und theilen den Genuss der schönen Welt;
> Nur in dem Wahlspruch ändert sich, mein Freund,
> Ein einzig Wort: Erlaubt ist was sich ziemt.

The Golden Age, my friend, is gone, gone by: only the good will ever bring it back. Allow me to confess my thought to you: The Golden Age, with which the poet still is wont to flatter us, it seems to me, did once exist as it hardly does now; and if it did, it was certainly such that it can always be restored to us. Yet kindred hearts may meet and share the joy of the lovely universe; but in your motto you should change a word, my friend, a single word: What is decent, is just.

Here Goethe makes Eleonora use for her own purpose the antithetic tenet by which G. B. Guarini sealed in his *Il Pastor Fido* the stanza he wrote as a palinode to *Aminta*'s chorus, to deny the law stated by his own predecessor and rival. Eleonora's "Erlaubt ist was sich ziemt" is indeed a not unfaithful rendering of Guarini's "Piaccia s'ei lice" (May it please if it is lawful). By saying that man should follow the rule of decorum rather than that of pleasure, Eleonora, and Goethe with her, seems here to affirm that any restoration of the Golden Age is impossible.

Faust is a very different creature from Goethe's other heroes or heroines: his ethos transcends the conflict between responsibility and irresponsibility, as his imagination transcends the conflict between reality and dream. Yet it is quite significant that at a given moment of his development Faust seeks to restore the Golden Age in an action that may be viewed at once as a pageant, as a vision, or as a magic portent. It is evident that we must examine the purpose and purport of this action or experience to find the reason that Goethe resurrected in *Faust* the vision of Tasso, which he had denied in that drama of his youth.

II

Faust's restoration of the Golden Age takes place in the course of the Helena and Arcadia episode (pt. II, act III), culminating, as we shall see, in a magnificent *locus amoenus* in the best classical and pastoral manner.[4] This, however, is not the only time that that topos appears in Goethe's masterpiece. The very first scene of the second part of *Faust* is but an extended *locus amoenus*, as shown by its title, "Anmutige Gegend" (Pleasant Landscape). It is obvious that before studying the second, we must study the first of these two *loci amoeni*, the more so since this one, unlike the other, is neither classical nor pastoral. A further reason for studying this scene is that it deals with a situation for which we may also find a precedent in Tasso, this time not in his pastoral drama but in his epic masterpiece.

What happens to Faust in the opening scene of Part Two is in fact not too different from what happens to Erminia in Canto Seven of the *Gerusalemme liberata*.[5] That poor damsel in distress flees away from both love and war, and after spending the night in a lonely forest she wakes up to find herself in a lovely place where nature rules in beauty and peace. The landscape in which Faust awakens, however, is not mediterranean and southern, but Alpine and northern, as shown by landmarks like mountains and waterfalls[6] and by the presence of romantic sprites like fairies and elves, including Shakespeare's Ariel, who seems to lead them. The physical and spiritual geography of the locale is such that it excludes any human settlement, whereas Tasso's countryside is the kind that naturally turns into a pastoral habitat. Erminia soon discovers that it is indeed so, and she joins as a welcome guest the local pastoral community, within which she rusticates for a while, seeking rest and relief from all care and passion, and reacquiring the sense of security and purity she had lost.

Like Erminia, Faust is now a fugitive from the ordeal of life, and it matters little that in the ordeal, unlike Tasso's heroine, he had played an active role rather than the part of a victim. What is the matter is that, like Erminia, he needs oblivion and regeneration, and he finds them in the bosom of nature, with no help from any fellow creature or even from natural man. While awakening in that landscape, he feels reborn not to security and peace but to success and adversity, to adventure and strife. Whereas Tasso's *locus amoenus* inspires and prepares Erminia's decision to seek escape in privacy and solitude, and to withdraw, at least temporarily, from the world, Goethe's "anmutige Gegend" helps Faust to free himself from all private concerns—even from the memories of Gretchen's "little world"—and to choose to test his powers in the arena of public life, in history's and culture's "great world."[7] Thus, if Erminia's pastoral paradise is but a gateway to innocence, the Alpine paradise within which Faust suddenly achieves his spiritual and physical regeneration becomes, as Eden turned out to be even for Adam, a gateway to experience.[8] For this very reason the "anmutige Gegend" fails to be followed, as the *locus amoenus* in Tasso's poem is, by a pastoral oasis, which, had it been bound to appear within the same context, could not have been conceived in terms other than those which obtain within the framework of Erminia's story: that is, as a pastoral of innocence.

It is true that almost at the end of the play, at the beginning of act V ("Offene Gegend"), there appears a brief pastoral of innocence, in the Philemon and Baucis episode. Yet this episode does not become a pastoral oasis precisely because the protagonist of the poem does not partake of its blessings. As a matter of fact, Faust is not content with behaving as an outsider in regard to that old couple's pastoral "little world"; he acts as its enemy and its destroyer; he is certainly responsible, even more than his henchmen, for Philemon's and Baucis' violent death ("Tiefe Nacht"); and therefore for the tragic or at least antibucolic ending of that episode.[9]

While attracted by the pastoral dream, Goethe was always insensitive to that dream when the object of its longings are security and peace, or the rewards of archaic simplicity and primitive purity—which is another way of saying that he viewed the pastoral of innocence as utterly unreal for denying two of the values he held most dear, civilization and history. Yet halfway between "Anmutige Gegend" and "Offene Gegend," in act III, Goethe introduces the pastoral oasis of which Faust is both the creator and hero. As we have already hinted, this pastoral oasis unfolds at once as a return to Arcadia and a restoration of the Golden Age. This implies no contradiction in regard to what has just been said concerning the Philemon and Baucis episode. Faust's own pastoral oasis is both necessary and possible, since it is not a pastoral of innocence but, according to Faust's heart's desire, a pastoral of happiness. In this pastoral, Goethe magnificently reechoes, in terms of a present reality, Tasso's regretful exaltation of the Golden Age of old. In this we may recognize the mysterious operations of poetic irony and poetic justice: Faust's *Et in Arcadia ego* may indeed be read as a palinode of Goethe's earlier denial, through the words of Eleonora d'Este, of the dream of the Italian poet.

III

Of *Faust's* pastoral oasis we may repeat what we have stated about the pastoral of happiness and of love.[10] Such a pastoral is but a midsummer dream, the dream of the midsummer of life. By that dream middle-aged man projects his yearnings after a youth which is no longer his, and after a love which may still be his. This is why the object of that dream is almost always a fresh and simple girl, which is what is meant by either a shepherdess or a nymph. One of the most brilliant novelists of our time, Vladimir Nabokov, seems to have understood so well the pastoral essence of an older man's desire for feminine youth as to call his Lolita a "nymphet." [11] The gist of this is that the object of pastoral love must be lovely, but not necessarily beautiful: she must be endowed with fresh charms rather than with a dazzling pulchritude. Hence a love tryst loses all pastoral quality when the ages and roles are reversed—when the younger and naive partner turns out to be the male and it is an older and more experienced female who takes the lead. In such a case the woman tends to be a glamorous beauty, or a mature paramour, and there is nothing pastoral in the poetic works representing the love situation in such terms, as is the case with the fable of Venus and Adonis as, for instance, Shakespeare and Marino handled it.

In Goethe's pastoral oasis Faust, who certainly is no common pastoral swain, still plays more or less the traditional masculine role, but the woman he loves is anything but the embodiment of girlish simplicity and feminine immaturity. This is probably the first time that Helena, whom Greek imagination had forged as a mythical creature and then reshaped into a heroic and tragic figure, enters the humble enclosures of the pastoral world. The paradox of Helena's presence in Faust's pastoral oasis is to be seen not only in the circumstance that, far from being young, she is ageless, but also in the fact that she is a grand heroine and a great queen. This may well be not the only time that a lady of high degree, or even of royal station, enters the pastoral world, but it is certainly the only one in which such an exalted personage shares full bucolic privileges without the pretense of coy simplicity, without discarding, at least fictitiously, her noble garments and donning rustic clothes in their stead. Yet, in a pastoral oasis like the one Faust chooses to establish, it is obviously Helena who is needed, and in all her magnificence and pomp. No Phyllis would have served in her place, since what Faust needs is not freshness and youth, which Gretchen once gave him, but the supreme beauty that only a Helena can give.

We know very well that the nymphs or shepherdesses of most love

pastorals are but fantasies or fancies; yet, even if they fail to represent particular women, they stand for the eternal feminine, or for a
generality that is a reality as well. This is why, even when willing
to acknowledge the purely imaginary essence of their bucolic scenery
or idyllic background, pastoral poets are generally unwilling to avow
the unreality of the feminine figures peopling the legendary Arcadias,
or the fabulous Golden Ages, of their eclogues. The most they do is
admit the conventional idealization of those creatures through the
fictitious rusticity of their behavior, apparel, or manners. The pastoral is often a mask, or even a masque, but there is always a living
face, or a living person, beneath its mummery or pantomime. These
considerations may help us to recognize another and even stranger
paradox in Goethe's pastoral oasis. That oasis is in fact more of a
real habitation (not a mere name) than is generally the case, since
it coincides with an Arcadia reevoked in actual geographical and historical terms. Goethe's Arcadia exists in man's annals as well as on
man's maps; its outlines are marked not only by ancient groves and
classical ruins but also by the castles built on its rocks by barbaric
invaders and Christian crusaders, both of northern blood.[12] It is in
one of these castles that Faust takes his residence, ruling from its
bulwarks the surrounding countryside, since that castle is also a
fortress, as hinted by the word "Burg," which designates as well as
describes it. On the other hand Helena, who is the guest of Faust's
"Burg," and who later rules over all Arcadia as its only queen, appears and dwells within the pastoral oasis of Goethe's poem not as a
woman of flesh and blood but as a reincarnated ghost. Faust had conjured her back to earth by magic, and it matters little that later she
joins him by free will. She remains a phantom, and her return to
Sparta and Arcadia remains a phantasmagoria, which is more ideal
but no less unreal than the "Mummenschanz" at the Imperial Palace,
with the travesty of Faust as Pluto and the Emperor as Pan. Yet that
phantasmagoria is literally conceived in bucolic terms, which means
that Faust's and Helena's pastoral oasis may be illusion but is not
deceit.

As we have already said, this pastoral oasis is, from beginning to
end, but a pastoral of happiness—it reflects the bliss of two creatures,
whose only business is love, whose only concern is each other, whose

only world is a timeless paradise of their own. Goethe conveys this ideal state in a splendid operatic duo, merging the aria and the recitative in a unique harmony. This duo is the climax of Faust's and Helena's first meeting, which takes place in the inner courtyard of Faust's castle ("innerer Burghof"). Their dialogue is really a monologue, since the two partners speak on behalf of each other or, rather, of the single couple their twin beings jointly form. Two loving hearts reciprocally reecho each other's inner voices; this is why Helena is always able to seal with the proper clause each of the sentences Faust utters only in part. Helena finds in every case the rhymed response uniquely fitted to Faust's cue, and the poet could not have found a more suitable device than this kind of amoebean song or, as Faust calls it, "Wechselrede" (alternate speech), to express the oneness of a loving pair in feeling and thought (III.9378–83):

> *Faust.*   Und wenn die Brust von Sehnsucht überfliesst,
>   Man sieht sich um und fragt—
> *Helena.*   wer mitgeniesst.
> *Faust.*   Nun schaut der Geist nich vorwärts, nicht zurück,
>   Die Gegenwart allein—
> *Helena.*   ist unser Glück.

> *Faust.*   And if the breast with yearning overflow,
>   One looks around, and asks—
> *Helena.*   Who shares the glow.
> *Faust.*   Not Past nor Future shades an hour like this;
>   But wholly in the Present—
> *Helena.*   Is our bliss.[13]

No love poetry emphasizes the solitude and the oblivion of two happy lovers as intensely as the erotic pastoral. Even when they are not alone in their paradise, they forget society and the world. It is also in order to reduce everything to the absolute of love that the pastoral of happiness tends to despoil man and woman of all superfluous attributes, especially those that are social rather than personal in character. Eros is really nude in the pastoral, by which we mean that he appears there in the naked innocence of *amour-passion* rather than in the specious garments of *amour-vanité*.[14] From this viewpoint the most antibucolic pair of lovers in history and poetry are Antony and Cleopatra—not only for their tragic end but also because they stage their passion in the great theater of the world. In this, at least at first sight, Goethe's Faust and Helena resemble Antony and Cleopatra more than any other historical or legendary pair. Yet after their first meeting even they leave the inner courtyard of Faust's castle, "surrounded with rich, fantastic buildings of the Middle Ages," and seek the proper background ("Schauplatz") for their love in a suitable bucolic setting, with "caverns," "grottos," and "arbors" (9586), which turn the place into a real bower of bliss. Their pastoral oasis, strictly speaking, begins only then and there; yet, from a broader viewpoint, it opens earlier, as soon as they meet. If this is true, then the scene of their love is crowded with a double retinue of attendants, thus assuming the aspect of the most antipastoral of all institutions, the court.

Whereas the tutelary virtues of Arcadian life are humility and simplicity (it is not only the Christian shepherd that is poor in spirit), Faust and Helena enjoy their happiness under canopies of luxury and pomp. And whereas the classical eclogue, while gracing the shepherd with the gifts of the Muses, frees him from the burden of an inquiring intellect or a searching mind, it is evident that Faust will not renounce, even here, the privileged curse of speculative thought. All this proves that Goethe's pastoral oasis is conceived at least in part according to an antipastoral and even anticlassical canon: in the Renaissance terms of pride and splendor, of glamour and grandeur. Splendor and grandeur mark the nature of the place, and this is why the Helena episode culminates in a *locus amoenus* of an exuberance that no earlier treatment of that topos ever approached. Yet it is worth remarking that this *locus amoenus* is not the description of a landscape directly apprehended by the senses, immediately perceived by the poet's or the character's physical eyes. It is while still in the walled-in courtyard of his "Burg" that Faust depicts, through the second sight of both imagination and memory, the dazzling beauty of the surrounding countryside. Here we have more than an "anmutige Gegend": just because he gazes only with the eyes of the spirit, Faust does not limit his contemplation to the range of human eyesight. Instead of restricting himself to a narrow spot, as is the case with most *loci amoeni,* he embraces the whole of Arcadia. Faust's praise of the land that is, more than any other, the land of the sun ("das Land, vor aller Länder Sonnen"; 9514) is so magnificent that a few critics have called it a paean. In this paean Faust first exalts Helena's "Vaterland," which he has just turned into a larger kingdom for the Queen of Sparta, and divided among his own dukes, who will be her vassals; and then exalts the Golden Age, which he has decided to restore within its borders, as he says in an apostrophe addressed to the queen of that happy land (9565), "Der ersten Welt gehörst du einzig an" (For thou belongest to the primal world). Faust's words bless the time and the place with a prosperity and an opulence that even Renaissance poetry had not fancied in its wildest dreams. After describing the fresh springs and rich meadows populated by herds of grazing cattle and the ancient woods with their robust oaks and graceful maples pregnant with sweet juices, Faust's praise turns all of Arcadia into an immense horn of plenty, inexhaustibly filled with the generous bounties of an all-benevolent Mother Nature (9546–49):

> Und mütterlich im stillen Schattenkreise
> Quillt laue Milch bereit für Kind und Lamm;
> Obst ist nicht weit, der Ebnen reife Speise,
> Und Honig trieft vom ausgehöhlten Stamm.

> And motherly, in that still realm of shadows,
> The warm milk flows, for child's and lambkin's lips:
> At hand is fruit, the food of fertile meadows,
> And from the hollow trunk the honey drips.

Nature's boundless generosity is but a reflection of Faust's will power, or even will to power: it is by the fiat of his willful dream, rather than by the grace of the gods, that the Golden Age is restored in Arcadia, or in the personal fee he has turned into a realm for his queen. It is by expanding the topos of the lovely landscape beyond all measure, as well as by extending that commonplace from the sphere of direct representation to that of an evocation to be literally understood in the magic meaning of that term, that Faust and Goethe turn

Arcadia into a *locus amoenus* which is at once more ideal and more real than any of its antecedents in pastoral literature. Yet, if even the most enduring Age of Gold cannot last forever, so even the oldest and greatest of all the lands of the heart's desire has to be at least relatively restricted in space. Unlike that pastoral land Sicily, Arcadia, as Goethe takes care to remark, is "landlocked" (9570); it coincides with the central region of the Peloponnese, or with that peninsula's hinterland, to speak in geopolitical terms. It is quite proper for Arcadia to be a fair distance from the seashore and salty waters: a condition or location that pastoral poetry views as another of its blessings, since it makes it even easier for its shepherds to avoid being tempted, as traders and coast dwellers always are, by the adventures and perils of the sea.

As a matter of fact it is Faust himself who utters a high praise of the spiritual values of the Arcadian way of life, settled and sedentary, for being close to the soil and rooted in a fixed place. Such praise is to be found in two of the lines he addresses to Helena (9570–71):

> Gelockt, auf sel'gem Grund zu wohnen,
> Du flüchtetest ins heiterste Geschick!

> To tread this happy soil at last incited,
> Thy flight was towards a joyous destiny!

If Faust speaks so, it is because Arcadia, or any settled land, stands in Goethe's mind for society and civilization or, as Yeats would say, for "Doric discipline." [15] It is not without reason that Faust chooses to emphasize not that Sparta is close to Arcadia but that Arcadia is "in Spartas Nachbarschaft" (in Sparta's neighborhood; 9569). The very presence of Helena on that "happy soil" indicates moreover that for Goethe Arcadia is the symbol not merely of culture but also of its highest object or product, which is beauty, particularly the beauty of classical art and ancient poetry. That this beauty is lasting and vital is shown by Helena's ideal resurrection and by her brief return to her homeland. But that such beauty may still not be an eternal and universal presence is proved by Helena's second death, by her final and irrevocable return to the netherworld. Hence the contrast between Helena and the creatures of myth, which are really immortal, and the even more important contrast between the solid and the liquid element, between land and water, between Arcadia and the Aegean sea. Indeed, if earthly Arcadia stands for culture and beauty, the fluid Aegean stands for nature and life.

Since the Italian Renaissance a few pastoral poets have felt that, unlike the sailor's, the fisherman's way of life does not differ too greatly from the shepherd's. Sannazaro and Rota were the first to compose, the former in Latin and the latter in the vernacular, "piscatory eclogues." Such a conversion is natural and easy when we think that the fisherman, unlike the seafarer, tends to remain near the shore and that the body of water on which he entrusts, briefly and relatively safely, his frail vessel, is often protected by human works and circumscribed by natural walls, as is for instance the case with Sannazaro's and Rota's seascape, which is the Gulf of Naples. Whereas that blessed spot of the Tyrrhenian Sea may appear as idyllic as any Arcadian or Sicilian landscape, there is nothing idyllic in the Greek sea as evoked by Homer and Goethe. This is why the Aegean scene closing act II as well as the "Classical Walpurgis Night" ("Klassische Walpurgisnacht") is anything but a piscatory analogue of the pastoral oasis of act III. The former, as a matter of fact, is but a literal and poetic antithesis of the latter. There are hardly any nymphs in Faust's Arcadia; only after Helena's return to Hades the Trojan women attending her as a tragic chorus refuse to follow their mistress and change themselves into Dryads, nymphs of plants and trees; Oreads, nymphs of hills and caves; Naiads, nymphs of springs and brooks; and Menads, nymphs of vineyards. But as long as the human happiness of Faust and Helena lasts, there is no place in Arcadia for supernatural creatures or immortal beings.

The sea, however, is full of those: first among them the Sirenes, who are far from being, as Ulysses well knew, mere saltwater Naiads. They sing the alluring chant of the sea, which is the chant of natural life, or of an existence that transcends the limits of the species as well as the individual.[16] Only in the sea is there everlasting permanence, because there is perpetual change, whereas Arcadia and the Golden Age are but points in space and time, and unable therefore to outlast the transformations of the human and historical world. In contrast, the ever changing sea remains immutably the same in the universal "Stirb und werde"[17] of prehistorical chaos. Hence the culmination of the Aegean scene in the triumph of Galathea. Galathea, this marine Venus, is really "the divine counterpart of Helena";[18] and this is why, unlike Helena, she is granted a triumph which is at once the triumph of life, transitory in each of its metamorphoses, but eternal as an elemental force and cosmic power.

IV

Helena cannot triumph precisely because she represents beauty rather than love; the poem's and her pastoral oasis is bound to end as soon as she shares with Faust a love based not on beauty alone. Such is, of course, the love for their son, Euphorion. At this point Goethe violates one of the main conventions of the pastoral, and the violation is so deliberate as to reveal on his part a deep understanding of that tradition and its message. The pastoral of innocence, even though it tends ultimately toward *amour de soi,* willingly admits of parental and filial love. The pastoral of happiness, on the contrary, even when it leans toward a platonic idealization, or a spiritual sub-limation, of the erotic impulse, hardly allows any love that is not rooted in sex. This is the reason that children vaguely but frequently appear in the pastoral of innocence as members of an idyllic family or bucolic clan, but that they are almost always absent from the pastoral of happiness, and particularly from the erotic eclogue. Pas-toral couples seem to have no offspring, and they manage to avoid the scourge of childraising when unable to prevent the curse of childbirth. The traditional love pastoral is full of adolescents, but empty of youngsters below the age of puberty.

It was with the voice of a modern that one of the most precocious members of the generation which came to the fore just after the pub-lication of the first part of *Faust,* the romantic Novalis, said in a lovely aphorism: "Wo Kinder sind, da ist ein goldenes Zeitalter" (Where children are, there is an Age of Gold).[19] Goethe, however, knew that one of the most traditional symbolic functions of the fable of the Golden Age was that of signifying adult love. This means that he also knew that by introducing a child within Faust's and Helena's bower of bliss, he would bring havoc to the pastoral oasis of his poem. There is no doubt that Euphorion plays the role of a destroyer, causing the ruin of others through his own ruin. His apparition is the beginning of the end of his parents' happiness. Pastoral bliss is over as soon as the lovers' duo turns into a family trio. Yet Helena thinks that this will bring even a greater beautitude (9699–702):

> Liebe, menschlich zu beglücken,
> Nähert sie ein edles Zwei,
> Doch zu göttlichem Entzücken
> Bildet sie ein köstlich Drei.

> Love, in human wise to bless us,
> In a noble Pair must be;
> But divinely to possess us,
> It must form a precious Three.

This formation of "a precious Three" occurs just after Faust and Helena withdraw into their bower. Now they are wholly "abgesondert von der Welt" (separated from the world; 9588–89); and at first their only companion, or rather servant, is Mephistopheles, who since the "Klassische Walpurgisnacht" episode has looked and acted like an old hag, under the assumed shape of one of the daughters of Phorkyas. Yet to any "idyllischem Liebespaare" (twain idyllic lovers; 9587) even a single servant, especially if she or he is a Phorkyas-Mephistopheles, should be *de trop*. Yet the real *terzo incomodo*,[20] although a welcome one, is their newborn son. Unlike Adam and Eve, who became man and woman inside but father and mother outside the Garden of Eden, Faust and Helena seem to reconcile in their paradise the conflicting demands of conjugal and parental love. It is there that they engender their son; it is there that they see him instantly grow from infancy into childhood. Yet even such a miraculous child introduces in that pastoral Eden the antipastoral feelings of parental duty and parental concern. These feelings seem to change his father and mother into a domestic couple, prosaic, bourgeois, and commonplace. Instead of being fully absorbed in the contemplation of each other, Faust and Helena watch uneasily their son's mischief.

We know that Euphorion stands for many things: but above all for modern poetry, and even for the figure Byron. We thus understand why he rejects all that Arcadia represents. He prefers the adventure and war of the world at large to the peace and quiet of that secluded spot. He starts jumping over the rocks and reaches the top of the cliff in order to see, beyond the valleys and ridges of Arcadia, the vast expanse of the sea. His daring frightens his father and mother, yet such normal and natural fears seem absurd and ridiculous in the case of Faust and Helena, whereas they would be moving in the case of any Hermann and Dorothea. Faust's and Helena's parental recommendations and warnings, echoed by the chorus, which unexpectedly joins them, are in fact predicated on the rules of golden mediocrity, on the norms of peasant prudence and earthbound security. One of their admonitions to Euphorion is that he should stick to the safe way of life of the settled flatlands (9741–42):

> Ländlich im Stillen
> Ziere den Plan.

> Rurally quiet,
> Brighten the plain!

We realize now that Faust's pastoral oasis is a dream, and we may well believe with a modern poet that it is "in dreams begins responsibility." [21] All the same, a genuine pastoral oasis is no place for responsibility; the pastoral outlook is bound to yield to the antipastoral view of life as soon as Idleness or Leisure gives way to Care or Solicitude.[22] While worrying about the dangers threatening their defiant son, Helena and Faust suddenly look like an aging and careworn couple unable to cope with the problems of belated parenthood. But, unlike them, Euphorion will remain forever young: he will die in the fullness or, rather, in the freshness of his powers, as a favorite of the gods. Euphorion indeed destroys himself while seeking to imitate Icarus. He tries to fly, but fails in the attempt; he falls from high, through the insubstantial air, at the feet of his parents, on that solid ground from which he had wanted to free himself. When this happens, Helena behaves like a tragic mother, annihilating her physical being in a forlorn grief. She leaves Faust but her garment and veil and joins forever her son in the abode of the dead.

Thus Faust's and Helena's pastoral of happiness, like Philemon's and Baucis' pastoral of innocence, seems to end in tragedy. This appears to contradict the general spirit of the work, which is not a tragedy, despite its subtitle.[23] It appears to contradict also the principle, stated by a distinguished critic, that Goethe's creation tends constantly toward "the avoidance of tragedy." [24] To this one could object that Goethe, like Dante, while rejecting the tragic as the ultimate meaning of being, may still accept it as one of the episodic outcomes of life. Yet it is their tragic ending that denies permanent validity to the two pastoral episodes of Faust; both are superseded by the realities of human experience. They would have disappeared anyway, almost of themselves: in the first case, through the natural rather than violent deaths of Philemon and Baucis; in Faust's and Helena's case, through love's surfeit. The rule of all pastoral oases is to be but a temporary state, a pause, an interlude. As for the pastoral of happiness, it can endure no more than its due even when it joins the pastoral of beauty to the pastoral of love. Yet, transitory as it is, the stay in Arcadia represents an ideal moment in Faust's life, and in Goethe's poem. It would be neither anachronistic nor arbitrary to define that stay as *Faust*'s Apollonian hour. It is after all one of the protagonist's utterances that gives one the right to do so (9558–59):

> So war Apoll den Hirten zugestaltet,
> Dass ihn der schönsten einer glich.

> So was Apollo shepherd-like in feature,
> That other shepherds were as fair and fleet.

Apollo is a very human deity, and this explains why he is the patron of shepherds: far more so than Pan, who lives in Arcadia as a symbol rather than as a tutelar god. It is just for being a dreamland that Arcadia cannot be the land of myth. The creatures of the fable can enter its confines only when it is no longer the land of heart's desire, and happiness, love, and beauty are no longer its rulers. When Arcadia ceases being pastoral, it turns into wild and reckless nature. We realize that the pastoral dream is forever ended when we foresee the forthcoming triumph of Bacchus, as announced at the episode's close. After joining the lament for Euphorion's death, the members of the chorus turn into creatures of the wild; and the metamorphosis ends with the chant of those of Helena's attendants who have changed into Menads (10030–35):

Und nun gellt ins Ohr der Zimbeln mit der Becken Erzgetöne,
Denn es hat sich Dionysios aus Mysterie enthüllt;
Kommt hervor mit Ziegenfüsslern, schwenkend Ziegenflüsslerinnen,
Und dazwischen schreit unbändig grell Silenus' öhrig Tier.
Nichts geschont! Gespaltne Klauen treten alle Sitte nieder,
Alle Sinne wirbeln taumlich. . . .

Now the ear is pierced with cymbals and the clash of brazen bosses,
For, behold, is Dionysos from his mysteries revealed!
Forth he comes with goat-foot Satyrs, whirling goat-foot Satyresses,
While amid the rout Silenus' big-eared beast unruly brays.
Naught is spared! The cloven hoofs tread down all decent custom;
All the senses whirl bewildered. . . .

The drink of Arcadia is milk, as nectar is of the Age of Gold, and this means that the pastoral disappears when wine is drunk in its stead. The tragic feeling stirred by Euphorion's end fails to develop: even before the dirge for his death is over, we hear the wild strains of the dithyramb. This means that both the pastoral and the tragic view of life are replaced by the sacred disorder of the satyr play: Apollonian restraint withdraws, and all falls prey to the Dionysian urge. Contemplation and ecstasy are replaced by intoxication and orgy. The pastoral, which Goethe always viewed as a passing human triumph, and which for this reason he always refused to identify with the socially or culturally primitive, is overwhelmed by a primordial force which is teutonic rather than georgic. Hence the sudden irruption on Arcadian soil of creatures which are half animal and half divine, and as such real monsters. This irruption, explosive as it is, is in a certain sense an anticlimax, like the intervention of a deus ex machina. Yet it helps us all the same to resolve once for all Faust's earlier doubt about the real essence of the inhabitants of that Arcadia which now is no longer theirs, of that Golden Age which now is no longer ours (9556–57):

> Wir staunen drob; noch immer bleibt die Frage:
> Ob's Götter, ob es Menschen sind?

> We wonder; yet the question still remaineth,
> If they are men, when Gods they seem.

We know now that they are more men than gods, and this is why they ultimately fail to obey the command Faust once uttered (9573): "Arkadisch frei sei unser Glück!" (Our bliss become Arcadian and free!) In that command Faust simply rephrased the motto of Tasso in his *Aminta*, which Eleonora d'Este had rejected also on Goethe's behalf. When we first hear it, that command sounds like Goethe's retraction, like his acceptance of Tasso's claim that man should seek to restore the Age of Gold. But in the end we realize that that command was a hypothetical rather than a categorical imperative. The irruption on Arcadian soil of the monsters of the fable, treading down all decent custom under their cloven feet, serves as an ultimate reminder that the Goethe of *Faust*, though in a far broader and deeper sense, shares the belief of the Goethe of *Tasso*, that only "what is decent, is just."

12
Gogol's
Old-fashioned Landowners:
An
Inverted
Eclogue

I

There is a famous story by Nikolai Gogol that the author himself admitted to have written in a pastoral key: more particularly, as a kind of modern version in Russian, or rather in Little Russian terms, of the ancient tale of Philemon and Baucis. The story, entitled *Old-Fashioned Landowners*, opens the first volume of the collection *Mirgorod*, which appeared in 1835, a few years after *Evenings on a Farm Near Dikanka* (1831–1832) and shortly before *The Inspector General* (1836), which in its turn was to be followed at a longer interval by *The Overcoat* (1840) and the first part of *Dead Souls* (1842). Ideally, if not chronologically, the story seems to occupy a central position in Gogol's work, lying halfway between the folksy humor of his early Ukrainian tales and the bitter mockery of his masterpiece.

Old-fashioned Landowners is centered around an old couple distinguished and, as is always the case with Gogol, up to a point characterized by the curious names of Afanasy Ivanovich and Pulcheria Ivanovna Tovstogub. The narrative is but a long evocation of the simplicity of their life and, at the end, of the equal simplicity of their deaths. The acknowledgment that the story unfolds within a pastoral, or quasi-pastoral, framework is made at the beginning of the tale, which, as commonly in Gogol, takes the shape of an introductory statement in general terms, concerning in the present case "the modest life of those solitary landowners . . . who in Little Russia are generally called old-fashioned."

The opening passage starts by depicting the "faraway villages" of those landowners in the charming picturesqueness of their ruins, as well as in the seductive attractiveness of their way of life, now about to fall into oblivion and neglect. And it is in the sentence referring to the subtle and yet overwhelming power of suggestion which those places and their inhabitants still exercise on the visitor or the traveler that Gogol makes the acknowledgment mentioned above: "Without realizing it, you pass with all your feelings into *this humble, bucolic life.* . . ." (The italics are naturally ours, and we may add parenthetically that the "humble" of our version fails to do justice to the *nizmennyj* of the original, an adjective meaning "plain" and "flat" as well as "humble" and "low.") As if that hint were not enough, the writer hastens to point out the resemblance existing between the two old people of his story and the protagonists of one of the most lovely pastoral myths which antiquity bequeathed to us through Ovid and his *Metamorphoses:* "Were I a painter, and should I wish to represent Philemon and Baucis on canvas, I would not choose other models than these."

The statement limits its claim to a similarity in character as well as in situation; yet critics and readers have all too often been inclined to take Gogol's word at something more than its face value. The early Belinski, for instance, changed the abstract similarity into a concrete identity when, in his critique of this tale, he addressed Gogol's readers with the following apostrophe: "And now contem-

plate the life of Philemon and Baucis. . . ." The task of this essay is
to reexamine whether the frame of reference of *Old-fashioned Land-owners* is pastoral in a genuine or in a specious sense, and to determine whether the parallelism between these two sets of characters,
suggested by the writer and asserted by the critic, is based on a relationship of either concordance or discordance.

The first (or perhaps the last) question to ask in such an inquiry
is whether the author's glowing praises of the bucolic condition
flow from an earnest feeling or derive instead from a sentimental
affectation, either self-conscious or not. If we do so, we must however heed an important warning: the criterion of sincerity, which
has at its best only a doubtful aesthetic value, is rather a poor yardstick to measure the quality of an inspiration choosing as its vehicles
the bucolic, the eclogue, or the idyll. Even when it flows most spon-
taneously and naturally, pastoral inspiration tends to adopt conventional forms, and it would be wrong to deduce from this alone that
the pastoral attitude is a sentimental pretense, a literary pose, or a
poetic sham. The bucolic imperative, *eritis sicut pastores*, fulfills itself not on the plane of experience but of contemplation alone, and
the artificiality of its masks or disguises is but a consequence of the
pastoral dream's inability to materialize itself. Thus, if the nature
of pastoral attitude lies in the very conventionality of its ideal assumptions, it would not be too paradoxical to affirm that the test of
Gogol's sincerity should be seen in his observance of the conventions
of the genre rather than in his neglect of them.

Some of the most important of such conventions concern the perspective through which the bucolic poet looks at the pastoral world.
He may choose to look at it with an insider's insight, or with an outsider's outlook: by pretending to be an actor, or merely a witness;
by playing the role either of a shepherd or of a shepherd's friend.
It is obviously easier to sing of shepherds than to behave like one:
to contemplate the bucolic way of life from without, rather than
from within. This is the preferred alternative in all modern versions
of the pastoral, although it is not uncommon even in the older ones;
and it is also the solution chosen by the author of this tale or, more
precisely, by its narrator, who speaks as someone who once, or more
than once, journeyed to an Arcadia of his own. As often happens in

pastoral literature, Gogol however merges the fiction of the pilgrimage with the idea of a recurring retreat: "Sometimes I love to descend for a while to a sphere of life unusually solitary, where no wish ever crosses over the hedges surrounding the little yard."

Thus, through the double frame of the journey and the retreat, Gogol succeeds in changing the land of his heart's desire into a place which is *in*, but not *of*, this world, and which exists as a sort of dream, and perhaps as a nightmare. He locates that place in a region out of the reach of our experience through its remoteness not merely in space but also in time. Even in this, Gogol's invention runs true to type, since the "pastoral oasis" is often conceived as a charming and lonely province, divided from the centers of activity and life by historical barriers as well as by geographical ones. Gogol's awareness of this is made evident by the key words in his story, which are the epithet *starosvetskij*, meaning literally "of an old world," rather than merely "old-fashioned," and the noun *ugol*, signifying "nook" or "corner," and endowed with some of the connotations of the English "backwater." While the adjective refers to the inhabitants, the noun alludes to the habitat, and both imply that the way of life they suggest is both inaccessible and irrevocable. Gogol states explicitly as much when he declares: "All this has for me an ineffable charm, because I don't see it anymore, and we hold dear the things from which we are separated." Yet, paradoxically, when rehearsed in the author's imagination, the stagnating existence led by the people vegetating in those old-fashioned corners makes look unreal the feverish and convulsed existence of our all too real, all too human world: "The life of their owners is so quiet, so quiet, that for a while you forget yourself, and think that the passions, the desires, and all the agitated products of the evil spirit, troubling the world, do not exist at all."

II

Gogol opens the narrative section of his story by giving us a double portrait of Afanasy Ivanovich and Pulcheria Ivanovna Tovstogub, and such a portrait, both physical and moral, begins with their very names. Names are very important in Gogol's fiction, as well as in pastoral literature, where, however, they are conventional rather than characterizing devices. Pastoral names, while trying to convey at first an impression of rusticity and commonness, end by producing the opposite effect of rarity and preciosity, of an elegant strangeness. The names of the two old-fashioned landowners are, however, so vulgar and coarse as to suggest not merely the plain and the ordinary, but rather the bizarre and the grotesque. This implies that Gogol's intent, whether conscious or not, was not to replace the artificial with the natural, the poetic with the prosaic, or even the serious with the ridiculous. By giving his characters names that are more absurd than funny, the author seems to project his invention beyond the boundaries of realism. That such is the case is made evident by the mannerism of the representation, and especially of the portrayal of the old couple. Even when choosing to depict the blessings rather than the ravages of time, no realistic writer would depict old age with traits like the following one: "The soft wrinkles on their faces were so gracefully placed that a painter would have done well to paint them."

This detail may suffice to prove that the spirit of the tale "demanded," to use for our own purpose a famous formula by Ezra Pound, not a group of marble but "a mould of plaster." We must therefore not be surprised by both the rigidity and the softness of the figures: they are lifelike and lifeless, hardly disguising their ghostly unreality under the artificial geniality of their doll-like faces. The old man especially looks like an automaton, and seems to be an anticipation, in far smaller size, of the wooden and stolid Sobakevich, one of the most monstrous creations of *Dead Souls*, although the stolidity of Afanasy Ivanovich is mollified by a smiling benignity reminding us of the sugary sweetness of Manilov, another of the characters of Gogol's masterpiece. To be sure, the author may have emphasized the puppetlike joviality of Afanasy Ivanovich's face in order to develop again the traditional contrast between the careworn countenances of those who live in the turmoil of the world and those who spend their lifetime in obscurity and quiet. Yet the distortion of the representation destroys any feeling of sympathy and tenderness: and notwithstanding the author's statements to the contrary, we suspect from the very beginning that his couple of characters is unlovely, as well as unlovable.

This, however, fails to deny by itself the bucolic quality of Gogol's invention, which, in its turn, seems to be enhanced by the description of the material side of the protagonists' way of life. The bucolic dispensation is grounded, so to speak, on an economic utopia, which reduces all pastoral well-being to the spontaneous fertility of the soil. In every eclogue the earth offers freely and generously its gifts, growing all fruits and crops without the toil of our hands or the sweat of our brows. Perhaps all the difference between the bucolic and the georgic lies only in this: that the peasant or farmer, unlike the shepherd or the herdsman, plows and tills his fields; that, not merely content with enjoying the fruits of the earth, he wants to exploit his plot, to sell his produce, and to change into wealth his labors and hardships. Afanasy Ivanovich and Pulcheria Ivanovna are neither shepherds nor laborers but landowners and gentleman farmers; yet we never see the tenants or serfs tilling their soil and tending their crops, as if their property would yield food by itself, like a little Arcadia lost in the vastness of the Russian Empire.

In the terms of economic science, one could say that there the process of production is taken for granted, and that the author directs our attention to the process of consumption alone. Thus, paradoxically, Gogol produces a quasi-pastoral effect through the very opposite of the pastoral situation, which is certainly based on the spontaneous generation of the staples of life, but where self-sufficiency operates on the level of mere subsistence, so that the threat of scarcity is made void only through the rule of self-restraint. In contrast with this, here we witness instead the triumph of largeness and affluence, and the author's awareness of this fact is made evident in the passage where he defines the manners and customs of his old couple as a characteristic example of that type of life which was once led "by old, native, simple, and yet, *well-to-do* families" (emphasis added). Yet, despite all this, Gogol does not break totally the pastoral scheme, because he uses the theme of abundance and prosperity to emphasize the moral rather than the material well-being of the protagonists. What Gogol gives us here is his own version of the agrarian dream: a dream according to which a moderate prosperity is not only a generous gift of nature but also a reward for the simplicity of the soul, and for its innocence. Such a simplicity and innocence are exemplified here, as in all agrarian utopias, by a way of life free from the taint of the acquisitive spirit as well as from the curse of money.

Pastoral or quasi-pastoral economy is patriarchal in the literal sense, since it coincides with home economics, and its rightful manager is the paterfamilias. Here the situation is, however, subtly and comically reversed, since the master of the house (or, more exactly, the writer of the story) lays all the burden of the household on the shoulders of Pulcheria Ivanovna. The pastoral, whether it deals with material or with emotional and spiritual happiness, is a typically masculine dreamworld, and this divergence from the normal pattern is important enough to suggest a deviation not only from the letter but from the very spirit of the bucolic ideal. This impression or suspicion will be further strengthened as soon as we learn more of the manager, and of her way of doing things.

Pulcheria Ivanovna's husbandry shows, first of all, an excess of foresight, which is hardly a pastoral virtue, since shepherds are wont to follow the bad example of the grasshopper of the fable, spending all summer in song and dance, rather than the edifying behavior of the ant, who labors and toils to collect food and fuel for a rainy day as insurance against poverty, famine, or a cruel winter. As a matter of fact, Pulcheria Ivanovna goes further than that and converts prudence into thoughtlessness by preparing provisions so far in excess of the necessary amount as to render them useless: "Pulcheria Ivanovna was a great housekeeper, and collected everything, sometimes even without knowing herself what to do later with all this." In brief, the provider degenerates into a hoarder; and in this respect the old woman already anticipates two of the most vicious and disgusting characters of *Dead Souls:* the widow Korobochka, covetous and mean, and the miser Plyushkin, who lives like an insect on the filthy heap of the odds and ends he saves as if they were useful or precious things.

The concrete symbol of Pulcheria Ivanovna's safekeeping is the immense and overflowing storehouse, the main object of her cares, and the only building on the property giving the impression of beehive activity: "the administration of Pulcheria Ivanovna consisted in an uninterrupted opening and shutting of the storeroom, in salting, drying, and baking an immense quantity of vegetables and fruits." The storeroom is the fat belly of the house, and, like all fat bellies, has its own parasites: "the magazine would not have been big enough if the servants had not consumed a good deal of produce." The very presence of such a horn of plenty suggests that the farmland growing all the produce that fills, interminably and inexhaustibly, its entrails, is a Land of Cockaigne, which in its turn is but a monstrous caricature of Arcadia's blissful fertility. Both commonwealths base their economy on consumption alone, yet the Land of Cockaigne carries not only fruits but even sausages and hams on the branches of its trees. Thus, unlike Arcadia, the Land of Cockaigne is the utopia of the picaro, a projection of hunger's dreams, the wish fulfillment of the starving man's obsession with food. This is why, while in Arcadia nobody steals, thieving and pilfering is the rule in this peculiar world, although even this hardly scratches Pulcheria's hoard: "in spite of how much the guests or the phlegmatic coachmen would steal, the blessed land produced everything in such an amount, and Afanasy Ivanovich and Pulcheria Ivanovna needed so little, that all those terrible depredations were scarcely felt in the household."

Using Veblen's terms, one could say that this little world is ruled by the principle of conspicuous consumption, although the formula cannot be understood in this case as meaning ostentatious waste. Yet Gogol must speak with tongue in cheek when he claims that the old couple "needed so little," which really means that they needed nothing, except all sorts of food. Thus, the greatest understatement of this story may be seen in the narrator's assertion that "according to the old custom of old-fashioned landowners, they were very fond of eating": an ironic understatement which is perhaps due to the equivocal intent to emphasize and to attenuate at the same time the realization that what is taking place here is an exception to the pastoral rule, according to which human needs must neither sink below the minimum nor rise above the modicum level.

Thus, in an existence like this, generally dominated by an absolute passivity, there takes place every day a series of epic deeds and gargantuesque feats, seemingly out of keeping with the nongolden mediocrity, or outright meanness, which is its regular norm. The arenas of such undertakings are the kitchen and the table: two fields of activity to which the narrator devotes the main section of his tale. And the account of the extraordinary, if not exceptional, eating habits of this couple takes the form of a detailed and orderly report of a typical day of their life.

The day starts, bucolically enough, with an early rising and a light breakfast. After this, the master goes outdoors to take a walk; but in the yard he meets his overseer, and stops to discuss farming matters with him. The talk does not go any further than the walk, and the old man returns to the house. As soon as he crosses the threshold, he addresses his wife with an inquiring statement which, along with her reply, we will hear repeated in hardly different terms all the day long: "Perhaps it is time, Pulcheria Ivanovna, to eat something . . . ." The old woman phrases her answer in the shape of a rhetorical question, negative only in form, as shown by the modifying clause following it: "But what to eat at this time of the day, unless. . . ." This conditional word serves merely as an opening for a series of very practical, and highly persuasive, suggestions. Needless to say, the proposals are accepted without further ado, and, what matters most, they are enacted on the spot.

After a replica of the same performance, the two old-fashioned landowners are ready for the main meal of the day, taking place at noon, and consisting of a heavy and elaborate dinner. This is graced by a lively conversation, convivial in the literal sense, since it deals, appropriately enough, "only with matters strictly related to the dinner itself." When the dinner is over, the master finds time for a little nap; and, as soon as he wakes up, he feels ready for another light repast. In mid-afternoon, while the mistress takes care of her affairs, the landlord occupies himself with the important business of watching from his window the constant opening and closing of the storeroom, which thus reveals continuously its insides, only to hide them again. In this section of the tale the belly symbol combines with a mouth image, since the action of the storeroom's door seems to suggest the operation of two devouring jaws.

Soon enough the two old people meet again, and the gentleman greets his lady with the ritual address, calling forth the usual repartee from his partner: "What could I eat now, Pulcheria Ivanovna? What indeed, unless. . . ." A new list of recommendations follows, with the customary effect. All this is easier done than said, and in a while

Afanasy Ivanovich takes another bite before sitting down to supper. Supper is served at 9:30; and, although Gogol chooses not to dwell at length upon it, we may rest assured that the old couple is not fasting at so late an hour. But soon the day is over, and Afanasy Ivanovich and Pulcheria Ivanovna retire to their rooms and go to bed.

At first "an absolute peace" seems to reign "over that little corner, so quiet and active at the same time"; but the old man wakes up in the middle of the night and walks back and forth in his room. He groans, and the old woman asks him why. The master answers that he is suffering from a bellyache. The mistress, quite in keeping with her medical opinions (she is for instance a great believer in the thera-peutic virtues of strong spirits rather than of grasses and plants), advises him to have a little snack. The patient complies, and a new refilling of his stomach seems to bring him prompt relief. The two old people doze off again, and the wheel of time comes to the end of its circle, to turn again at daybreak.

Here we have the mock-heroic treatment of a way of life which is based not on "days" and "works," but on "days" and "meals." Yet it would be wrong to think that the eating feats of the old pair are evoked by Gogol as a kind of perpetual kermess. What we witness is not an orgy, but only a routine. We are shown self-indulgence without self-gratification; we watch the triumph of greediness, not of gluttony or gourmandism. The only thing that counts is the quan-tity of the intake, not the quality of the food; and this is why we have failed to mention any of these numberless dishes, since they are apparently unable to arrange themselves into the pattern of a menu. The author himself has nothing to say about how any one of the many courses he names may either look or taste, so that the fare remains as flavorless for the reader's imagination as for the palates of the protagonists. In such a world, eating is an automatic activity, vegetal absorption and animal rumination, not a passion or a vice. Gaster, of whom Rabelais made a god, could not become in such a world even a demon or a monster: here eating is neither a blessing nor a curse; it is nothing more than habit, and nothing less. From this standpoint, Gogol's tale is a denial of the pastoral dispensation, where the innocent pleasures of eating are enhanced by frugality, by what one might call the hedonism of simplicity.

The way of life represented in *Old-fashioned Landowners* differs from the pastoral scheme in other matters than the eating habits of its two characters. Thus, for instance, one of the main paradoxes of this story is to be seen in its being a pastoral unfolding within the four walls of a house, rather than beyond them. The indoor quality of Gogol's invention reminds us of genre painting, especially of those Flemish interior scenes, revealing through a window the closeted happiness of a couple of old burghers. And at least here, the author of this tale never seems to feel the appeal of northern nature, which is so strong in Flemish painting, as shown by its willingness, as in Brueghel, to go outdoors and to give us the pastoral of winter in the poetry of ice and snow. Such an example, of course, is rarely followed by pastoral poetry, which prefers in general a mild climate, warm weather, and a sky without clouds. The traditional pastoral seems to dream of only one season, which is a perpetual summer or an ever-lasting spring, where shepherds and their herds sport *en plein air,* and where blue waters and green shades protect them from the fierce rays of the sun. But this story, being both a Russian and an indoor pastoral, seems to know no other warmth than that of an intolerable and artificial heat. If the two landowners are constantly, and abnormally, overfed, so are their lodgings constantly, and abnormally, over-heated. This is especially true of the bedrooms; and, as if this were not enough, the old man sleeps customarily over the oven, in Russian peasant fashion. One of such ovens is to be found in every room, as if to multiply in a series of reflected images the vision of an immense stomach, blindly and sleepily digesting its own food.

The cozy rooms of the house, all too small and low, are not only stuffy, but filthy too. In contrast with the perfect neatness of a shepherd's hut, with its clean furniture and its spotless walls, the habitation of the two old-fashioned landowners is dirty and messy. An awful number of flies (another parasite symbol) cover the ceiling with a black cloud. While a shepherd's hut contains but a few charming things, often the handiwork of the shepherd himself, who is always an artisan, if not an artist, the only objets d'art adorning this household are several nondescript portraits and engravings, which the flies have soiled awfully; and a few dark prints pasted on the dusty walls, which everybody takes for large stains or faded spots. While a pastoral dwelling is always full of chatter and song, the only singing to be heard here is the shriek of the doors, moving on their old and rusty hinges. It is to these doors that the writer devotes the most charming passage of the story, claiming that each one has a voice or speech of its own. Except for them, everything in the house is indifferent, inarticulate, and dull, since the home itself is ruled not by leisure but by boredom and sloth.

Such boredom and sloth seem to disappear when the masters practice hospitality, which is the highest of all pastoral virtues. There is no bucolic narrative failing to play up this theme: so, for instance, the story of Philemon and Baucis is built on the very fact that they are the only ones among their neighbors to welcome two unknown travelers, who could easily be mistaken for highway robbers, while they are instead Jupiter and Mercury incognito. To be sure, the visitors dropping in at the Tovstogubs' are not disguised gods, but ordinary people, like the narrator himself: or perhaps like the perpetual traveler of *Dead Souls*, the pleasant rascal Chichikov.

Whoever the guests, the old couple gives them a royal welcome, as if they were beings nobler than themselves, putting at their disposal the best they have, which mainly means their table and their beds. Each guest must at least stay overnight; and the masters of the house show him their usual selves, since his presence does not change their manners, but simply makes them more pleasant and good-natured than ever. Yet the arrival of a guest at least changes the rhythm of their life: "then everything in their house would take on a different aspect. One could really say that the two old people lived for their guests. They tried to treat them continuously with everything their property produced." Like Philemon and Baucis, on such occasions they throw wide open their far fuller and fatter larder, offering something more substantial than cheese, milk, or berries. And without ever being compelled, like the old Phrygian couple, to sacrifice their only, and dearly loved goose, they see to it that their guest is handsomely treated, which means that he is forced to gorge himself; and while doing so, he is also entertained by the naive talk of his host. In brief, in all this section of his tale, Gogol deals with the theme of pastoral hospitality through the perspective of a caricatural exaggeration, and reduces it to mere absurdity by its very excess

III

The two most important divisions of the pastoral are the pastoral of innocence and the pastoral of love. There are other divisions, such as the pastoral of solitude and the pastoral of the self, but they are only variants of the two main branches. Of these two, the pastoral of innocence claims a sort of primacy or priority, since bucolic love is but a quest for innocence in happiness itself. At any rate, the two categories seem to merge together when the subject of bucolic inspiration is a happy ménage. Strangely enough, the ecolgue looks with sympathy at conjugal love only when the marriage, as well as the pair, is an old one. From this standpoint, the fable of Philemon and Baucis is so exemplary as to become an archetype.

According to such an archetype, the pair must be not only old, but also childless. The couple of Gogol follows the traditional pattern also in this respect: "they never had any children, and all their affection was concentrated on each other." It is significant that the author speaks of affection rather than of love; and we wonder whether the fire of passion ever burned in those two hearts, now filled only with ashes. Yet, in the absence of a child, even a pet can do. It is quite natural that a pet should later appear in a story like this, although, against what one might expect, that pet is not going to be a dog. The dog, after all, is the pastoral animal par excellence, a useful servant of his master, and a loyal guardian of his herd. But in this case, as we have already said, we have to do with an indoor pastoral, so that the dog is quite naturally replaced by a sleepy and lazy cat, of the common gray breed, and of the female sex. Obviously she is the pet of the woman, and of the woman alone. Pulcheria Ivanovna explains very well the reasons for her preference: "A dog is unclean; a dog makes damages; a dog breaks everything; a cat is a quiet creature and hurts nobody."

Gogol makes it quite clear that even Pulcheria's affection is a matter of habit, which is the only power ruling this small world: "I cannot say that Pulcheria Ivanovna loved her very much, but she had grown attached to her out of habit, merely by seeing her constantly around," or lying in a ball at her feet. Yet this very image recalls the vision of the child in the womb, and there is no doubt that the cat plays in the story the role of a missing, and perhaps even missed, child. In disagreement, or perhaps in agreement, with such a filial role, the cat will soon break the bonds tying her to her motherly mistress and will leave the house to live her own life, as the quasi-prodigal daughter she was destined to be.

All this part of *Old-fashioned Landowners* seems to be almost a caricature of *The Postmaster*, perhaps the most beautiful and influential of all Pushkin's tales, with the only difference that in the Pushkin story the abandoned parent is a father, and that here the cat acting as a prodigal daughter will fail to return home, even if only for a visit, after her parent's death. Yet, even if this idea has come to him from Pushkin's story, in the treatment of this episode Gogol seems still to be aware of another pastoral theme: the abduction of a simple country maid, or the seduction of a naive provincial girl, either by a courtly fop or a city slicker, bringing temptation and corruption into a happy and innocent circle up to then untainted by the vices and passions of the world. Here too the poor creature is allured and deceived by an outsider, or rather by a band of them. The parallel between the destiny of the cat and the fate of all too many country wenches is drawn by the author himself: "they succeeded in seducing her, as a detachment of soldiers seduces a foolish peasant girl." Yet the parallel ends here: because Pulcheria Ivanovna's pet was carried away by a feline breed not corresponding in any sense in human terms to the type of the worldly libertine or the wicked city man. Her corrupters were wild cats of the woods, who, as Gogol hastens to point out, "must not be confused with those braves that run on house roofs. Being town-dwellers, despite the roughness of their mores, they are far more civilized than those that inhabit the woods."

It is such a band of wild cats, hiding in a thicket near the house, that ensnares the poor pet and turns her into a member of their gang. Here the deviation from the bucolic situation is to be seen in the daughterlike cat's decision to abandon her state of sheltered innocence, not to follow the deceitful illusions of glamour and pomp, but to lead an existence of fierce struggle and of an equally fierce insecurity. The action of the little beast could be compared to the action of a girl of good family, fleeing from security and respectability to join a gypsy tribe, or to become a tramp or an outcast. Gogol himself interprets and translates the cat's experience in human, all too human, terms, as shown by the reasons by which he motivates her unwillingness to become domesticated again. One of these very reasons, by way of example, is but "the romantic notion that to love in poverty is better than to live in a castle. . . ."

Romantic love, which may be considered as either a variation or a deviation of pastoral love, plays after all a minor part in this sad event. The real, or the deeper, motive of the cat's escape is the "call of the wild": the appeal of the barbaric freedom of the natural world. Thus, after all, the cat's behavior is not patterned after the bucolic attitude toward nature, which is passive and contemplative, as the terms "idyll" and "idyllic" most properly mean. The pastoral is attracted by orchards and pastures, by hills and groves; and it feels very rarely the more robust charms of the great outdoors. At any rate, it stops short of that kind of nature which transcends the scope of human thought, and the measure of human things. In brief, the pastoral resists with success the overwhelming temptation of the wilderness. Within the sphere of the eclogue, nature remains humanlike and homelike, and as such it is ruled by the spirit of calm rather than by the demon of strife. In the bucolic dream, society becomes a little more natural and nature a little more social than they are in reality. This is after all the very meaning of the myth of the Golden Age, where mankind lives under the blessings of a happy and brotherly peace. But the cat of Pulcheria Ivanovna chooses to live in a new Age of Iron, cursed by the cruelty ruling animal life, by the very ferocity that her wild cats show, for instance, to little birds: "all generous feelings are alien to them; they live from robberies; and they strangle little sparrows in their nests."

The evident function of this episode is to suggest what the German romantics would have called "the nightly side" of nature and life, but the irrelevance of the occasion (the loss of a pet) reduces the representation of an all-present evil to the proportions of a miniature or a vignette. Through the perspective of irrelevance, which Gogol adopts quite frequently in his work, all the tragic implications of this small adventure are lost, and this story within the story is kept within the right limits of a half-humorous, half-pathetic anecdote.

In a life based only on routine the most insignificant happenings or circumstances, especially if unforeseen, may have the most shattering impact. So the mistress sees in the loss of her pet (an event playing in this story a role very similar to the loss of his new cloak on the part of the protagonist of *The Overcoat*) not only an awful calamity, but the very sign of her death: "It is my death that has come for me, she told herself, and nothing could distract her from this thought." A few days later Pulcheria gets sick and takes to bed. Afanasy Ivanovich thinks naturally of the sovereign remedy, and asks whether she would like something to eat. Pulcheria cannot take any food: and the patient's loss of appetite is the clearest symptom of the gravity of her condition. In what looks like the most pathetic passage of the entire tale, the old woman makes all preparations for her death. Her only regret is that of leaving her husband alone and, above all, unprotected and shelterless: "you are like a baby," she tells him: "you need to be loved by those who take care of you." So she entrusts him to the attentions of Javdoxa, her housekeeper, to whom she recommends that her husband be treated as if he were a child. Her most important recommendations regard his clothing and his food: "Look to it that in the kitchen they prepare the dishes he likes, and that his underwear and clothes are always clean. . . ." The passage ends with the death of the old woman, followed by the scene of her funeral, through which we glimpse the dumb grief of the old man.

The narrator resumes the story with his visit to the survivor after a five-year absence. The old man too is approaching death, and his decrepitude seems to be reflected in the house and the property, which are falling into neglect and ruin. The author describes at length the senile degeneration of Afanasy Ivanovich, reduced to the state called in psychological jargon regression to infancy and colloquially second childhood. The death of his wife has left him not so much a widower as an orphan, crying because his mother-wife is no longer there to nurse and to feed him: "he sat insensibly, insensibly held his spoon, while a stream of tears flowed, flowed, and flowed, like an inexhaustible spring, on the napkin covering him." The narrator sums up the impression of his last visit to his former host with his first unguarded words. Now the author breaks the veil, or lifts the mask covering his vision, baring for the first time the naked face

of truth: "five years of all-exterminating time: and this already insensitive old man, an old man whose life had apparently never stirred
a strong emotion within his soul, whose entire existence seemed to be
reduced to sitting on a high chair, to eating pears and dry fish, to
telling good-humored stories: and such a long, such a burning grief!
What has greater power on us, passion or habit?"

At this stage, such a question cannot but be rhetorical. The heart-
break of a child may surpass in intensity the measure of every human
despair, but it will pass. Thus, when Gogol says that "all passions
look childish in comparison with that long, lingering, unfeeling
habit," he reveals a state far worse than any real human grief. Pain
fails to become a habit even in the elegy, and in tragedy itself. If
the elegiac imagination conceives of human existence in terms of a
blooming and withering flower, the tragic view maintains that "ripe-
ness is all," even when facing the finality of either ruin or death.
Both elegy and tragedy sing of our decline, and therefore of our
growth. But in this story there is neither flowering nor withering,
neither maturing nor decaying, because nothing grows or develops.
The pastoral differs from both elegy and tragedy because it is the
fable of stasis, but Gogol's is only a fable of regress.

The last visit of the narrator is followed by the news of his friend's
death. "Quite strangely, the circumstances of his demise were similar
to those of Pulcheria Ivanovna's end." The old man too had been
warned by an ominous sign: during a walk in the garden, he had
once heard the voice of his wife calling him from afar. And soon
after, he had died, to be buried beside her. Instead of ending the
story with this second funeral, Gogol prefers to close it with the
arrival of a young and distant relative, who is the two old-fashioned
landowners' only heir. He will totally ruin the property under the
pretense of reforming and improving it. Yet he too will settle soon
enough in the groove of routine, even if he chooses vice's path rather
than virtue's.

The story, as well as the life-cycle of its protagonists, has now
come to a close, and only at this point will the reader well acquainted
with the fable of Philemon and Baucis be able to conclude that the
similarities between the two tales, even if obvious, are slim and few.
In both cases, we have an old man and an old woman living together

in love and peace, satisfied with what they have, and asking for nothing from either God or man. Both couples are without children and kindred, so that the most important happening in their eventless existence is the arrival of one or more guests, whom they treat generously and welcome as friends. The differences are many, and often relevant: we have already discussed several of them in detail without however fully disposing of them. We have already pointed out that while one couple is very poor, the other is rather rich, although we must acknowledge that this economic contrast is, per se, less significant than it may seem. After all, standards of prosperity differ widely in space and time, varying with changes of climate and milieu. As for the social difference, it is but a variant of the economic one: the modern pastoral, bourgeois and realistic in temper, had already replaced pastoral communism with capitalistic property, transforming the shepherds and herdsmen of old into country squires or agrarian landlords. All such distinctions, after all, emphasize only external and superficial divergences: and the same thing could even be said of the contrast between the frugality of the Phrygian couple and the self-indulgence of the Russian pair, if it would not involve (as it does) something more than a mere diversity in both mores and means.

When all this is said, we still feel that *Old-fashioned Landowners* and the Ovidian mythological fable occupy the two opposite ends of the same poetic, and moral, scale. They differ in other matters than contingencies and circumstances. Thus, for instance, the existence of Philemon and Baucis cannot be understood in terms of the alternative between passion and habit or, rather, of the reduction of all vital values to the second element of that alternative. In their souls, passion has eased itself into a serene calm, not into a living death. Their hearts, not deadened by habit, are still able to feel, and their eyes still look at the world as if it were fresh and new. They enjoy both the "days" and the "works," and thus change idleness into leisure, which is the opposite of sloth. In all they do, they follow the golden rule of moderation, and humbly accept the law of nature, the law of alteration and alternation, with its visible symbols, the ever-changing seasons of the year. Thus they age nobly and gracefully, since their bodies grow old but their souls remain young.

It is obvious that such luminous wisdom is not only unattainable, but even inconceivable, in Gogol's gloomy world. Yet the greatest of all signs of contradiction between the fable of Philemon and Baucis and the story of Afanasy and Pulcheria Tovstogub is to be seen not so much in the manner of their lives as in the manner of their deaths. The pastoral hero accepts death as a sad but not somber event, with the consoling awareness that his fellow shepherds will bring offerings of flowers to his grave, where the inscription *Et in Arcadia ego*, carved in stone, will remind the passerby that there lies a shepherd who once played his oaten flute and tended his flock. Yet the destiny of the old pair sung by Ovid will be even better than this. Philemon and Baucis had led a life of such purity that the gods decided to bless them even in death. When their hour came, both of them were transformed into plants: the old woman into a linden tree, and the old man into an oak. And the two trees joined their branches so as to give a pleasant shadow to the temple which Jupiter, to reward their hospitality, had erected on the place of their hut. Thus Philemon and Baucis return forever to the earth from which they were born: yet their vegetal metamorphosis is a triumph of life rather than of death. This is pagan piety at its best: a piety which in Gogol's tale is not replaced by any Christian creed or belief. The most significant trait of *Old-fashioned Landowners* is its absence of religious feeling: its lack of faith, as well as of charity and hope. Faith is replaced by superstition, which is blind to the sacred, and sees the ominous rather than numinous in the mystery of the world.

It is not in the visit of the gods nor in the wonders produced by that visit, with the final metamorphosis of the two characters into trees, that we must see the real miracle of the fable of Philemon and Baucis; that miracle is but the simultaneity of their death. Goethe recognized in this the meaningful climax of the whole tale, and this is why he refused to change its ending in the highly arbitrary version of the Ovidian fable which he gave in his *Faust*. To be sure, in Goethe's version Philemon and Baucis die together as victims of a manmade curse rather than as objects of the gods' grace. Goethe could not do otherwise, being unable to accept the pastoral dream except as a momentary idyll, which the demonic power of life will destroy at will, so Philemon and Baucis die in a fire when Faust tries to have them ejected from their hut, which was built on the marshland he planned to reclaim and to change into fertile soil for the good of mankind. In brief, Goethe replaced Ovid's apotheosis of Philemon and Baucis with their sacrifice or martyrdom, making of their double death not an act of justice and grace but almost a historical necessity. But Gogol instead broke the pattern of the double death: and this is the most eloquent proof that he aimed not at a transfiguration, but at a defiguration of the mythological characters he pretended to translate into modern, and Russian, terms.

IV

In his famous critique of *Old-fashioned Landowners*, which is part of a long essay on Gogol's shorter narratives, the great Belinski failed to unveil the mystery of this story precisely because on one side he took too seriously Gogol's sense of reality, and on the other interpreted all too simply and literally its highly complex literary relation with its classical model, or ideal source. That, all this notwithstanding, Belinski could still write such a revealing page as the one that follows does great credit to his critical insight:

How powerful and profound is the poetry of Mr. Gogol within its external appearance of plainness and pettiness! Take his "Old-World Landowners." What do you find there? Two parodies of humanity, who in the course of several decades drink and eat, eat and drink, and who then, as has always happened, die. Where is the fascination in that? You see all the banality, all the ugliness, of this bestial, misshapen, ridiculous existence; but at the same time you take a real interest in the characters of the story, you laugh at them, although without spite, and then you sob with Philemon over his Baucis, you share his profound, unearthly grief and you are enraged at the worthless heir who squanders the property of those two simpletons! And then you have such a realistic conception of the actors in this stupid comedy, you see their whole life so clearly—you who perhaps have never been in the Ukraine and have never seen such scenes or heard of such people! Why is this?... Because the author has found poetry even in this vulgar and stupid existence... You weep for people who only ate and drank and then died! Oh, Mr. Gogol is a true wizard, and you cannot imagine how angry I am at him for almost having forced me to weep for people who only ate and drank and then died! [1]

The importance of this eloquent page is not to be fully denied even by its many errors and faults. Belinski is certainly wrong in praising *Old-fashioned Landowners* for a pathos which is not there, and which is instead replaced by a conscious bathos, by the bathos of life rather than by that of art. Yet the writer seems partly aware of this, as shown by his acknowledgment that the characters of Gogol's story are "two parodies of humanity," a definition which reveals again the keenness of an intuition contradicting his judgment. We think that the critic is wrong for being angry at the author, rather than at himself, for weeping where there is no place for tears, or even for laughter, as Belinski himself seems to guess when he speaks of this story as if it were a "stupid comedy," to use his own words. Yet the actors of that comedy are not as realistically conceived as he claims them to be, although even here he recognizes that you may never have met people like them, either in the Ukraine or elsewhere. Still, when all has been said, after recognizing all the merits of this page, both penetrating and opinionated, we must still conclude that it leads to an ultimate misunderstanding of *Old-fashioned Landowners*. This is evident from the very beginning of his essay, where Belinski establishes a false connection between the sense of Gogol's art and Gogol's sense of life. The misunderstanding is compounded by the critic's all too ready acceptance of Gogol's identification of its two characters with their Ovidian models: "The perfect truth of life in Gogol's tale is joined with the simplicity of the invention. He does not lie to life, nor libels it. . . ." We will not quarrel with Belinski's assertion that this story is endowed with what he calls "the perfect truth of life," because we do not wish to reopen the vexing question of Gogol's realism. We cannot, however, agree with the critic's praise of "the simplicity of the invention," since the structure of the tale, as we have tried to show, is exceedingly elaborate and complex: its main quality, in composition as well as in diction, is a kind of queer quaintness. We will see later whether it is true, as Belinski maintains, that Gogol neither "lies" to life nor "libels" it: although one could say at this point that Belinski casts doubt on the validity of such a statement by his very realization that Afanasy and Pulcheria Tovstogub are "two parodies of humanity." Belinski failed, however, to realize that they are two parodies of literature as well: a failure due to his inability to see that the author of this story deals very deceitfully with the reader, and that he treats now ambiguously, now high-handedly, the literary frame of reference he feigns to use.

After a full reading of the story, we may recognize the clues, and even the proofs, of the perverse turn of its author's mind, in the very passage where he stakes his claim that his narrative partakes of the pastoral or the idyll. It is worth while to quote this passage again: "Were I a painter, and should I wish to represent Philemon and Baucis on canvas, I would not choose other models than these." The statement seems unequivocal, and sounds convincing enough, especially if we consider that it is being made at the very moment the writer is sketching the old couple's physical and moral portrait, even if in doing so he employs the pen in lieu of the brush. Yet Gogol's assertion could also impishly mean that the two people he is drawing would look like Philemon and Baucis only if they were *not* painted with words. Even more significantly and strangely, the entire sentence could be read in such a way as to imply that the verbal portrait being offered to the reader should be treated as an original, rather than a copy after another master. Does Gogol intend perhaps to convey that the old couple celebrated by Ovid should now be reshaped after his own? We do not know.

What we do know is that by giving us a prosaic version of the fable of Philemon and Baucis, Gogol has done something more than translate that fable into the key of realism: he has destroyed the spirit of the fable, while following the letter of the pastoral convention and form. This simply means that the destruction of both the idyllic and mythical components of the story of Philemon and Baucis has been achieved by means of parody—a literary perspective or device which may be simply defined as a caricatural imitation of a preexisting form. The caricatural imitation of parody ends by creating an effect of estrangement and incongruity, which in this case derives from a *contaminatio* of the pastoral convention with elements alien, and even opposite, to it. The impression so induced in the mind of the reader may be suggested by Gogol's description of the carpet of the old couple, "with its birds looking like flowers, and flowers looking like birds."

What happens in the entire story is however slightly different: those which are made to look like flowers or birds are things far less nice than either flowers or birds. D. S. Mirsky recognized the hidden vulgarity of this little world when he summed up his brief critique of this piece by saying that "the vegetal humours of the old pair, their sloth and gluttony, their selfishness, are idealized and sentimentalized." [2] Yet here and elsewhere Gogol employs idealization and sentimentalization in order to create an artistic illusion or an aesthetic paradox, not to suggest a moral or psychological anticlimax. In literary terms, *Old-fashioned Landowners* is not a satirical piece but merely a parodistic one. The secret of parody is confusion, and here idealization and sentimentalization are used as mystifying and stultifying devices. *Old-fashioned Landowners* (and perhaps also *Ivan Shponka and His Aunt*, a story in *Evenings on a Farm near Dikanka* which anticipates already the climate of this tale), gives us the first glimpse of the method which Gogol will fully adopt only in *Dead Souls*, where however the pathetic tone is consciously false, and used for unambiguously comic effects.

The perspectives of idealization and sentimentalization dominate any genuine bucolic inspiration, with the aim of ennobling the simple and natural way of life which that inspiration chooses as its main concern and object. But the idealization and sentimentalization of the two old-fashioned landowners are equivocal, and end by belittling even more their all-too-little world. The truth of this will become evident as soon as we compare Gogol's picture with other quasi-pastoral representations of the life of the landed gentry as given in Russian literature. In Tolstoy's *Childhood* that way of life is sentimentalized in a genuine sense, and transformed into a gently humorous idyll. In Turgenev's *Nest of Gentlefolk* that way of life is described as something beautiful already on the wane, and its passing is evoked in the tones of a melancholic complaint, in the terms of a romantic elegy. As for Goncharov's *Oblomov*, which sees in that life not only the blessings of a pastoral idleness and leisure but also the curses of torpor and sloth, the picture has almost epic grandeur, and far transcends the miniature proportions of Gogol's false idyll. Thus Gogol's pseudopastoral does not lead us into the realms of innocence and happiness, but into those of inertia and indifference. As such, it does the opposite of what Belinski thought it did: it "lies" to life, and "libels" it. The picture seems full of "sweetness," but there is no "light" in it. "High seriousness" is replaced not only by mock gravity, but by mock levity as well.

The reader of *The Inspector General* will certainly remember that as an epigraph for that play Gogol chose an old Russian proverb that says: "Don't blame the mirror if your face is awry." The epigraph has all too often been interpreted as a warning, as the justification of the artist's right and duty to describe the ugliness of life as he sees it. But Gogol is not a satirical writer, because he is not a moralist; what is twisted in his work is not reality, but the imagination reflecting it. Here the crooked mirror of his art gives us but a distorted version of the pastoral vision, slandering forever an ancient fable, and perverting the sense of life that inspired it. This tale is a further proof that Gogol, despite his conservative and even reactionary leanings in politics and in religion, was one of the greatest subversives of literature and iconoclasts of art. Thus he really was, although in a different sense from what Belinski meant by those words, a "true wizard."

13
Tolstoy's
Domestic Happiness:
Beyond
Pastoral
Love

I

In 1856, while waiting for his official dis-
charge from the army, Leo Tolstoy fell
in love with a girl far younger than himself. She was a wealthy orphan by the
name of Valeria Arseneva, and lived in
Sudakovo, not far from Yasnaya Polyana.
As a friend of her family, Tolstoy had
accepted to act as her legal tutor. We know
the full story of this infatuation through
the writer's diaries and letters,[1] and there
is no doubt in our mind, as there was
hardly in his, that in this affair Tolstoy
played an undignified role, and made a
fool of himself. Tolstoy felt attracted by
the freshness and youth of his ward, and
thought seriously of marrying her. Valeria
attended the coronation ceremonies of

1856, and her tutor reacted with distaste at a letter from her praising snobbishly and glowingly the worldly and courtly splendor of the occasion and of the attendant festivities. Tolstoy finally used Valeria's sentimental friendship for a music teacher as a flimsy pretext for being jealous, and even for insulting her. Although he never proposed, he behaved in such a manner as to make Valeria and her relatives believe that an early wedding was possible, and even probable. Soon enough, however, he brutally put an end to a liaison which had been less than a troth and more than a flirt.

Precisely because he knew that he was not in the right, he sought both solace and revenge by composing a story to prove to his and everyone else's satisfaction that, had he wed the girl, the marriage would have ended in failure, or turned out to be a mistake, and that the bride alone would have been responsible for such an outcome. This story was *Domestic Happiness*, written in 1858 and published in 1859.[2] For a while the author thought of withdrawing, and even of destroying, the manuscript, which in one of his diaries he described as "a shameful abomination." Tolstoy's hesitations were due not only to moral scruples but also to literary doubts, which very few of his critics have shared. Most of the interpreters and readers of that tale have decided otherwise: and their enthusiastic approval is well represented by the opinion of Romain Rolland, according to whom *Domestic Happiness* is as perfect as a piece by Racine.[3] Rolland was undoubtedly right, and it matters little that he mistakenly identified the heroine of the tale with Sonia Bers, Tolstoy's future wife, or that he misread the story to the point of seeing in it "the miracle of love": a definition that would have been more fitting if the narrative had stopped halfway, since the rest of the story deals, at least as much as with the miracle of love, with the lesson of life.

If there is no doubt that the tale is a little masterpiece, it is no less evident that it is, as masterpieces often are, an ambiguous creation. Its ambiguity lies in the antithetical contrast between its two parts, one evoking love before and the other after the marriage. The opposition between the components of this diptych may be summed up by saying that the first is written in the key of a pastoral romance; the second, of realistic fiction.[4] To be sure, the term "pastoral romance" as applied to the opening section of *Domestic Happiness* should be understood figuratively rather than literally, as a reminder that its inspiration is genuinely idyllic. Obviously the author reshaped that inspiration according to modern ideas, values, and tastes, and replaced the formal conventions (but not the inner spirit) of the old-fashioned pastoral with a more concrete feeling for psychological reality, and with a more direct concern with human experience. Yet he tempered likewise the moral and practical realism of the closing section with classical measure, mature detachment, and lucid wisdom. He finally gave a superior unity to the composition by the device of having the story told by the girl, and from her point of view, not only in the first but also in the second part, even though the latter may seem to present the outlook of the masculine partner.

This device seems paradoxical if on one hand we take into account the autobiographical origin of the story, and keep in mind on the other the perspective, and even the bias, of the pastoral vision, which places woman in the foreground just because it is preeminently a man's wishful dream. The very fact that *Domestic Happiness* is the only story by Tolstoy in which a woman speaks in the first person may suffice to suggest the author's stand toward the pastoral or quasi-pastoral conception of love: a conception which he could envision only by projecting it outside of both his own sex and himself. There are good reasons to believe that the psychological motivation that dictated the story combined with a polemical intent: that Tolstoy wrote *Domestic Happiness* also as a protest against the credo of feminine emancipation, which was gaining ground even in Russia, in the wake of the success of the novels of George Sand. It would be remiss to fail to remark in this context that George Sand had often chosen to convey the nobility of passion by describing it in pastoral terms.[5] One could then say that whereas George Sand had the masculine mask of her pen name to proclaim the rights of woman, Tolstoy took on in this story the mask of his heroine to proclaim the rights of man—or that in the two parts of the tale he made Masha speak both for and against George Sand.

The great business of George Sand was romantic love, which is a more modern and more dramatic, more intensive and more inclusive manifestation of the erotic version of the pastoral dream. We must never forget that in all his life Tolstoy rejected that kind of love with all his being, on instinctual as well as on ethical grounds. It was not only his mind, or even his conscience, but also his sexual temperament that prevented him from accepting and experiencing that kind of love. In his later years, when he tried to liberate himself from what in his old age he was once to define as "the tragedy of the bedroom," [6] he practiced, or at least preached, abstention and asceticism, which is the Christian but certainly not the pastoral or romantic solution of the sexual problem. Yet, as he proved in so many masterpieces, he was able to understand and to express romantic love in others as few writers have done before or after him. Even so he always selected feminine characters as the only possible vehicles or objects for the representation of that kind of love: as he did in the case of the Valeria-Masha of *Domestic Happiness*, whose girlish psychology he unveiled with uncanny insight. Nor must we forget that in all such situations he used the masculine partner not to convey through him the lesser role which man plays in a liaison of this kind, but the masculine side, the male's conscious denial or unconscious rejection of romantic love. In *Domestic Happiness* this task is entrusted to Tolstoy-Sergey Mikhaylych, even though the latter acts as the willing foil, or plays but an antagonist's role, in regard to his feminine counterpart, who is at once the heroine of the tale and the narrator of the story.

II

Masha starts her tale when she is seventeen years old, which is the perfect age for a maid or a nymph. Shortly before, having been fatherless for a long time, she lost her mother, and now she is an orphan, feeling lonely and afraid before life and the experience of adulthood. In this too we may see a common pastoral theme, that of the young maiden who needs protection and help for being left alone in the world. Although an orphan, Masha is not poor, because even in a modern Arcadia excessive prosperity and excessive poverty are equally unknown. As a matter of fact, both she and Sergey Mikhaylych are members of the leisure class, or, more literally, of the Russian landed gentry just before the end of serfdom. The heroine of such an idyll could not but reside in the country, and she lives indeed on the country estate left by her family to her and her younger sister, with no other companion or adviser than a trusted governess. Both the sister, who is only a child, and the governess, who is an elderly woman, count for little in the story, in which the latter plays the role of a discreet confidante, and the former that of a silent witness. These three women have just spent, closeted in the solitude of their house, a winter of discontent, when suddenly comes springtime, the bucolic season par excellence, bringing in its stride not only the promise of a milder weather but also the stirrings of a new life.

Such visitation coincides with the visits of their neighbor Sergey Mikhaylych, a man thirty-six years of age, or old enough to have been a friend of Masha's father. He had already appeared in the house to assist Masha at the time of her mother's death, and now he reappears regularly to see whether everything is going well with the two girls, whom he considers his wards. Yet he is obviously interested only in the elder of the two, who in turn has no eyes but for him. Masha reports all that Sergey Mikhaylych does and says in her presence, yet she says nothing of his aspect, whether he is good-looking or not. This oversight may be due either to the modesty of the storyteller or to the self-consciousness of the writer, or possibly to both. Since the narrative is partly autobiographical, it is not too indiscreet to remind the reader that Leo Tolstoy was never handsome and that he was painfully aware of his plainness. This, and the fact that masculine beauty is not a pastoral requirement, justifies the surmise that Sergey Mikhaylych must have homely traits, if not an outright ugly face. But besides resembling his creator, morally as well as physically, Sergey Mikhaylych resembles many of the masculine characters that Tolstoy later reflected in the introspective mirror of his art. This is hardly surprising, since one's self-image is the only model that a writer, even more than a painter, has always at hand.

As for what seems to be Masha's self-portrait, it is, as we know, but the fictional likeness of a girl who had posed for the artist, unconsciously and unwillingly, only once in her lifetime, to disappear from his sight forever, and all too soon. For Tolstoy the man Masha was Valeria Arseneva, or a real person, different from any other girl he knew, yet the disguised or masked portrait he gave of her in *Domestic Happiness* foreshadows several of his future feminine characterizations, most of which are also based at least in part on persons no less real and unique. This means that Tolstoy tended to represent the same feminine ideal in many of the fictional women he refashioned or created anew, as he tended to represent the same masculine type, or human ideal, in quite a few variants of a single self-image, hardly changing with the passing of time. In brief, Masha and Sergey Mikhaylych, even though they fail to reproduce themselves in Tolstoy's future works as a couple, anticipate two types that regularly occur in the creations of his maturity. If we compare the hero and the heroine of *Domestic Happiness* to their more familiar equivalents in Tolstoy's two supreme masterpieces, we shall better understand the specific as well as the generic significance of these two prototypes.[7]

Masha resembles Natasha, the heroine of *War and Peace*, as well as Kitty, the lesser of the two heroines of *Anna Karenina*, at least in her virginal longing, in the whole of her maidenly nature. Yet she differs from both at least in this: that before marriage she feels far surer of her feelings than either one of them, but after marriage she loses that sureness, whereas Natasha and Kitty gain it all at once, and in full. If Natasha and Kitty never feel disappointed in their mates, it is also because in their girlhood they had met other men and fallen in love with them; hence their disenchantment with romantic love.[8] If Masha does not turn into another Anna Karenina it is because, until the story is almost over, she never sheds the illusion that marriage and romantic love should or might coincide. The greatest difference, however, lies in their social environment: Natasha, Kitty, and even Anna are surrounded by a swarm of relatives, acquaintances, and friends (in Anna's case, even by cronies), which means that they are part of a large family circle, or of a broad social set. But Masha is an orphan living in utter solitude; except for her sister and governess, she is literally alone in the world.[9] During her betrothal she does not meet, even casually, any other man—had she met one, she would have hardly noticed him. Thus she seems to stand before the man she will marry just as Eve stood before Adam, lonely and intact, in the chaste nudity of her soul.

The man before whom she stands has already reached the threshold of middle age, and lived twice her life span. With slight variations in age, Tolstoy portrayed the same psychological type in the Nikolay Rostov of *War and Peace*[10] and, above all, in the Konstantin Levin of

Anna Karenina. The type in question is that of an eccentric country squire, reserved and even boorish, embodying within himself the original and natural man. Such a character hates the conventions of the world and denies the values of society; lives following no other norms but the laws of nature, and no other dictates but those of his inner voice: a voice that speaks on behalf of his temperament as well as of his conscience. A character of this kind is not only an idealization of the author's actual personality but also the embodiment of a human ideal the writer had found ready-made outside of himself. He had found it in the works of Jean-Jacques Rousseau, in which it remains all too often a mere ideal, or an object of the writer's abstract preaching, seldom projected into vital fictional beings. Yet the masculine protagonist of *Domestic Happiness* resembles at least one of Rousseau's minor figures, Julie's husband in *La Nouvelle Héloise.* Sergey Mikhaylych is a creature of flesh and blood, while his model is pale and lifeless; yet in many of his traits, especially as a wise husbandman of his estate and his passion, he looks very much like the Rousseauian character bearing the quasi-Russian name of Wolmar. Needless to say that at first, at least in the mind of Masha, he plays the same role as Julie's lover, the far younger Saint-Preux. At any rate, in the atmosphere of *Domestic Happiness* or, more generally, of Tolstoy's ethos, there is hardly room for a ménage à trois; in that story there is no place but for a single man and a single woman, who stand not only for themselves but also for the eternal Adam and the eternal Eve. If we are not told their surnames, it is because they are not needed. The man is called also by his patronymic, as if to indicate that he acknowledges the ties of the family while rejecting the shackles that bind most of his fellow men to society and the world. As for Masha, she is always called by her Christian name alone,[11] as if to emphasize her orphanhood, solitude, and singleness: a state which implies both danger and freedom, since it allows her to choose her own bonds.

III

The bonds she chooses are, as we know already, those of romantic or pastoral love. Precisely because the story is told by her, we must accept her outlook, and describe the initial situation in bucolic terms. The situation is that of a seventeen-year-old girl falling in love with a thirty-six-year-old man, and of a thirty-six-year-old man falling in love with a seventeen-year-old girl. The situation is a typical projection of the pastoral imagination, so typical as not to admit of the reverse, or of a liaison having woman as the senior partner. (In this connection it is worth remarking that Tolstoy made the situation more extreme, and thus more typical, by aging his hero, or by making Sergey Mikhaylych eight years older than he was himself at the time of the actual affair.) According to the erotic code of the pastoral, when the woman is older than the man, her love remains unrequited: which, far from rendering the situation pathetic, as it would do in the case of a man, simply renders it ridiculous, or even grotesque.[12] But when the senior partner is a man, the liaison is possible, probable, nay unavoidable: love this time will be returned, although the man, besides being no longer young, is not even handsome. This is how it should be, since the prime mover of pastoral love is youthful feminine beauty, which is endowed with such innocent power and unconscious charm as to entice at all ages the spirit and senses of man. "You have youth and beauty," says Sergey Mikhaylych to Masha at least twice, at the very beginning of the tale, thus paying to its heroine the most obvious of all compliments, so obvious as to have been paid innumerable times by the sons of Adam to the daughters of Eve, and to serve as a fitting epigraph for all love pastorals. Those two qualities, which combine together to make the supreme attraction of a maid or a nymph, cannot be separated from each other, so that youth does not count without beauty, and beauty is of no avail without youth.

So the attraction between the young maid and the older man is reciprocal, and is based on a spontaneous reaction, on a love freely given and freely returned. Feminine youth longs for security and protection, whereas mature manhood seeks virginity and purity and yearns for a fruit fresh and intact, which life has not yet soured or spoiled. This too runs true to the idyllic pattern, since pastoral love often originates from familiarity and friendship. Masha avows to have at first loved Sergey Mikhaylych "from old habit," as a family friend or an older relative, like a father or an uncle. Without implying the slightest suggestion of incestuous feeling, one might say that their love starts with filial overtones on Masha's part and with paternal ones on Sergey Mikhaylych's. What is more significant is that the older partner loves this woman-child for being a simple and natural creature, whom he hopes to reshape in his own image, at his own will. One of the most extreme bucolic views is the rejection not only of manners and conventions but also of fashions and even of clothing, which are viewed as an unnatural disguise, as a kind of makeup hiding the real person under a false mask.[13] Youth must be simple and even bare; beauty, unadorned and unaffected. Hence Masha should not have felt surprised at Sergey Mikhaylych's "complete indifference and even contempt for . . . [her] personal appearance," for the manner in which she was dressed and groomed, even though he would seem silently to blame even more than her ladylike finery her "affectation of simplicity."

The idyll, which had started with the spring, turns by summer into a genuine passion, which, however, on the girl's part feeds not on reality but on dreams. As pastoral life at its best, that passion manifests itself in a constant communion with nature, according to the changing moods of the hour and the varying hues of the landscape. As if afraid to destroy this silent music, to break the miraculous sympathy so established between themselves and the world, the two lovers speak softly and in whispers. It is with the almost mystical term of "wild ecstasy" that Masha tries to define the instants when this feeling of perfect harmony attains its peak. Then physical sensations and spiritual emotions seem to blend into a sense of magic bliss. They seem to obtain such a "wild ecstasy" in the charming episode in the orchard, when the girl climbs on the cherry tree to pick its fruits, while the man watches from below. Without a shade of libertine frivolity, and in an aura of absolute purity, the scene reminds one of a real-life happening that Rousseau relates in the *Confessions* (iv), and which is known to the readers of that book as "l'idylle des cerises." In that idyll Jean-Jacques simply shares a basket of cherries not with a single nymph of his choice but with two maidens met by chance in the woods. The scene Tolstoy evokes is no less idyllic, but its inspiration is nobler and deeper: what we witness in these pages is almost an agape, whereas in Rousseau's we watch little more than a picnic.

Masha, in a perfect bucolic mood, considers the bliss she is now experiencing as the natural state of man ("it seemed so necessary

and just that everyone should be happy"), and thus she wants that
bliss to last without change or end in the flux of time ("that . . . [her]
present frame of mind might never change"). This desire to arrest
the fleeting instant is the characteristic trait of a thoughtless bliss:
the wish to remain within the enchanted circle of an everlasting youth
is a sign of immaturity, or the symptom of a crisis in growth. What
bewitches Masha is the narcissism of adolescence, or the self-love of
a youthful soul. As such, it is a morbid state, which, when acute and
brief, may even contribute to man's psychic health. But when it out-
lasts youth and becomes a chronic ailment it turns into that idolatry
of the self that marked the older Rousseau. Then introspection becomes an irresponsible adoration of all the movements of one's soul,
and the person loves himself just for being what he is.[14] It is self-
contemplation and the contemplation of her love that make Masha
play in the first part of *Domestic Happiness* the role of an *Allegra*,
enjoying her emotional bliss not only without doubt but also without
thought. Beside and against her Sergey Mikhaylych seems to play
the role of a *Penseroso* simply because he cannot cast away all his
doubts or ignore his thoughts.

IV

The end of the first part brings the pastoral romance to its climax.
Masha has created around herself a kind of magic wall, as if "the
world of the possible ended there." So full of happiness as to be
afraid of life, she goes to the little church to pray, and prepares herself for an early wedding. Her preparation is only psychological, and
it contrasts with the practical attitude of her governess, for whom
preparing for a wedding means preparing a trousseau, and all the
rest is "sentimental nonsense." But nothing troubles the soul of
Masha, and on the morning of her wedding day she sees a sign of
the peaceful serenity of her life in the spotless purity of the sky: "In
the clear sky there was not, and could not be, a single cloud." This
image is but one of the many by which the writer develops one of
the main motifs of his story: a complex and coherent seasonal symbolism, which unfolds according to a quasi-archetypal pattern. Masha
had lost her mother in autumn, the season of falling leaves, and the
orphan's sense of dejection had lasted all winter, the season of ice
and snow. Her protector, the man to whom she was bound to give

her heart, had first appeared briefly in late winter, as if to announce that life was at hand. Spring had then come, and love had silently sprouted in two hearts, one still too young, and the other not yet old enough. That love had bloomed in the glory of summer, joining them with troth's vows. When the wedding takes place, the year's cycle has made a full turn, and we are again in the fall season, which stands for both maturity and decline, thus alluding to the age of the bridegroom, and to the consummation of conjugal love.

During the honeymoon the newlyweds become fully oblivious of the world and find that reality is not inferior to the dream. But the honeymoon ends with the beginning of winter, which brings again to Masha a mood of monotony, sadness, and solitude. "So two months by," says she, "and winter came again with its cold and snow; and, in spite of his company, I began to feel lonely, that life was repeating itself." Business, that great enemy of pastoral mirth, which is founded on leisure, claims again the daily attention of Sergey Mikhaylych. The betrothal had been, so to speak, an outdoor idyll, but the cold season and married life make of Masha a stay-at-home, without a responsibility of her own, since the household runs like a clock under the strict supervision of her mother-in-law. The mistress of the house that Masha has entered as a bride represents the matriarchal or patriarchal order, or a way of life within which, at least ideally, there is no conflict between youth and age, love and marriage, innocence and happiness. When a newly married couple takes its place within such an order, groom and bride are expected to live quietly and to age gracefully in their little corner, and to turn at the end of their lives into another Philemon and Baucis. Before marrying Masha had thought that happiness meant unchangeability: that where and when there is bliss time seems to stand still. During her betrothal she had indeed believed that only in immobility love could last and grow. But now that she is married and settled the motionless bliss of conjugal love turns into a kind of deadly inertia, and she is frightened when she discovers that her love, "instead of increasing, stood still." When the honeymoon is over, married life turns out to be a letdown and a disappointment, especially if compared with the early days of their troth: "To love him was not enough for me after the happiness I had felt in falling in love." Masha's change might be described by saying that once she had confused pastoral and romantic love, whereas now she thinks that they are two different things, and seeks the second in lieu of the first: "I wanted excitement and danger and the chance to sacrifice myself for my love." Now that life seems to flow indifferently past her, Masha resents her husband's quiet acceptance of a mode of being in which life itself seems to be at a standstill. What repels the young wife more than anything else is the patriarchal way of life, based as it is on the forces of tradition and habit: "I suffered most from the feeling that custom was daily petrifying our lives into a fixed shape. . . ."

Masha's restlessness is another sign of immaturity, and youth's immaturity is never so evident as when it claims the rights of adulthood. It is just when Masha declares that she wants no longer "to play at life," but to live, as her husband does, that without knowing it she treats life as if it were a plaything. Sergey Mikhaylych yields to her pressure, as if he knows in his heart that the time has come for Masha to visit the great city, to get into high society, to enter the wide world. Thus he decides that they will spend the season in the capital. Just before Christmas they settle in Petersburg, for a test which for him is a trial, and for her a triumph. Masha looks so "unlike the other women," with the fresh charm of her "rural simplicity," that she wins the acclaim of the worldly, and shines among them like a new, bright star. Her husband, reduced to playing the role of an escort, disappears like a dim shadow in the radiance of her halo. When she stands out in the glamour of her beauty and the splendor of a gorgeous dress, "he effaces himself in the crowd of black coats." And whereas Masha drinks with intoxicating joy the heady wine of success, Sergey Mikhaylych tastes the bitter fruit of disappointment, resentment, and even jealousy.

Yet it is only when Masha forces him to stay in the capital a few days beyond their due for the sake of attending a reception in honor of a foreign prince wishing to make her acquaintance that the hidden disagreement between husband and wife turns, for the first and last time, into an open rift. Sergey Mikhaylych limits himself to avowing, in a few and clear words, the repulsion he has been feeling while watching his wife share day by day "the dirtiness and idleness and luxury of this foolish society"; yet Masha takes that hardly unexpected outburst as an injustice and an insult. Wife and husband return home apparently reconciled, but what seems a peace is but a truce, even though neither party ever dares or cares to break it. From that time on they live morally estranged under the same roof. The husband devotes again all of his time and thought to the management of the estate, while "fashionable life," as Masha confesses, takes full command of her. Even the facts of life, such as the birth of a child and the death of her mother-in-law, fail to disenchant Masha from her infatuation with the false values of the world. After three years she convinces her husband that they should spend the summer abroad. In Baden, the famous German water resort, Masha's vanity is flattered again by the allurements of social success. But all veils fall from their eyes when what had started as an innocent flirt with an Italian marquis turns into an attempted seduction which for an instant brings her to the brink of ruin.[15] She saves herself in time, but the horror and shame at her weakness, which had led her almost to the end of the path of corruption, deprives Masha of her self-esteem as well as of the hope to regain her husband's love or even respect.

V

After tasting the ashes that life's "forbidden delights" all too often leave in our mouth, Masha returns home to wither and languish in the utter loneliness of a silent despair. With no help from her husband, who refuses to intervene either in word or deed, behaving with a discretion so extreme as to look passionless, she slowly realizes that the fruit of good and evil may be picked only from the tree of knowledge. Still tortured by the delusion of her youthful hopes, aware that the affection of her husband has turned into a strange and remote aloofness, fearing that "he had no longer a heart to give" and doubting that she will ever be able to live for others now that she is no longer able to live for herself, Masha finally succeeds in overcoming her dejection after a long, unplanned talk with her husband. It is indeed more a question of a conversation than of a confession or an explanation. Through this exchange husband and wife are able to communicate again, without wrath or bitterness, and it is with a few quiet words that they seal again the peace of their hearts.

During this talk Masha avows her wrong, while still wondering whether she was fully responsible for it: "Is it my fault that I know nothing of life, and that you left me to learn experience by myself?" In her self-questioning she seems to blame also her husband, at least for having failed to guide her: "Why did you never tell me that you wished me to live as you wished me to?" Sergey Mikhaylych's reply to this query is worthy of Rousseau's Wolmar: "All of us, and especially you women, must have personal experience of all the nonsense of life, in order to get back to life itself." As for Masha's fear that she is no longer able to love, Sergey Mikhaylych reassures her by saying that "each time of life has its kind of love," and that the hour has come for them to love each other as husband and wife, not as betrothed or newlyweds.

The wise Sergey Mikhaylych puts Masha on guard against committing again the same error, which is to confuse times and kinds of love. "Let's not try to repeat life," he tells her, knowing that it can be repeated only in dreams. Yet he forgives Masha in the best possible way, by giving her hope, and by sharing her sense of guilt: "Our quest is done. . . . " At this point the adolescent narcissism of Masha disappears once for all. From now on she knows that love is not a passive image reflected in the mirror of the soul but the action or motion of a heart turning toward other objects or beings outside of itself. Her trial is now a thing of the past: from now on she will be the full partner of her husband: "That day ended the romance of our marriage; the old feeling became a precious, irrevocable remembrance; but a new feeling of love for my children and the father of my children laid the foundation of a new life and a quite different happiness, and that life and happiness have lasted up to the present time." Whereas the climax of the first part found its symbol in the serenity of the cloudless sky of her wedding day, the climax of the second part and of the whole story, which coincides with this moment of understanding and self-revelation, is intimated by a sudden rain, or by the purifying tears of nature itself.

VI

Only in the second part is there a story, and this is why it is easier to sum up that part and to quote from it. If little or nothing can be quoted from the opening section, it is because one should quote almost everything. Every one of its phrases is full of poetry, beauty, and charm: every one of its moments is not an event but an *état d'âme*. Reversing Amiel's famous aphorism, one could say that each one of such *états d'âme* turns into a different *paysage*, since it reflects itself within the changing moods of the day, the varying backgrounds of the landscape, the passing phases of nature's cycle. As we have already said, the first part of *Domestic Happiness* is not only a pastoral of love but also an outdoor idyll, wholly dominated by the pathetic fallacy, since all of nature's objects and images seem to reecho or to mirror Masha's every emotion and feeling, even the dimmest and vaguest of them. In the whole of Western literature there is perhaps only one other work evoking with equal bewitchment the experience of sentimental love as rehearsed by a youthful heart, as projected by a self feeling in communion with God's world. This work is Rousseau's *Nouvelle Héloïse*, which Tolstoy certainly took as a model, especially (and this is less strange than it seems) in the letters that describe the idyll of Julie and Saint-Preux as it unfolds not before, but after Julie's marriage to Wolmar.

If not the whole second part, at least its end, which closes the whole diptych, could at first sight be interpreted, like the first half of the tale, in idyllic terms. Its final scene seems indeed to bring about a restoration of the pastoral of innocence after the pastoral of happiness has failed to succeed. If this were really true, *Domestic Happiness* could be viewed as an anticipation of *War and Peace*, a historical novel or prose epos that at least one critic did indeed read as a "heroic idyll." [16] Even so, one should not fail to point out an outstanding difference between this minor, and that major, masterpiece: that the peace regained at the end of *Domestic Happiness* is the peace of the spirit, and that the crisis which for a while threatens that peace is but a war of hearts. Yet their message coincides at least in this: that in both stories it is the selfsame institution, the family, that triumphs over the powers of disorder, over the chaos of either passion or war. Yet even the admission of such coincidence should be qualified by remarking that *Domestic Happiness* views that institution in intimate and private terms, reducing it to its minimum common denominator, which is the tie between husband and wife, whereas *War and Peace* expands the family into the dimension of a clan, extending, so to speak, in space and time, including within itself the representatives of three generations, embracing within its fold serfs and retainers, as well as kindred of other branches. But the most fundamental distinction is that in Tolstoy's later novel the family meets primarily challenges that threaten its existence from without, whereas in the earlier tale it faces challenges that endanger its stability from within. The external factor determining this challenge in *Domestic Happiness* is not the greater world of history but the lesser one of "high life," what the French call simply *le monde* and pastoral poetry embodies in society, the city, the court.

All this notwithstanding, the general curve of *War and Peace* seems to coincide with the idyllic pattern more fully than *Domestic Happiness* does. The reason for this is that in the former the heart's desire of the characters agrees with the demands of life, whereas in the latter, at least in Masha's case, it is at odds with them. Unlike *War and Peace, Domestic Happiness* is a fable with a moral. The moral is that life chastises those who think that life is a dream. It is a sign of Tolstoy's artistic stature that despite the personal motivations that dictated the writing of this story, he chose to have Masha chastened by life rather than by her husband, in whom he had portrayed himself. There is no doubt that the lesson of life has something to teach even the older, stronger, and more experienced partner, and this is why, after writing the first part as a temporary victory of woman, Tolstoy refrained from writing the second as man's final revanche. In Freudian terms one could say that the first panel of this diptych evokes the passing triumph of the pleasure principle, whereas the second celebrates the lasting triumph of the reality principle. Since Tolstoy knew Schopenhauer and loved him well, one could convey the peculiar quality and meaning of the first half by saying that it is ruled by the cosmic will, which deludes us into believing that we freely want what a blind and impersonal instinct seeks through us and beyond us, who are but its passive, or voluntary, victims. The second half, on the contrary, is ruled by the active, self-controlling power of the ethical will, which restrains all inner urgings imperiling the safety of our being and the integrity of our soul.

Hence the moral adorning this tale is moral in the highest sense of this epithet and turns the fable into a feminine equivalent of the

evangelical parable of the prodigal son. Masha, this prodigal daugh-
ter-wife, takes again the place that belongs to her within the family
order, without undue festivities, but also without unseemly recrim-
inations. The woman-child has grown into a real woman, and what
she has gained from the lesson of life is not a sentimental education
but its very opposite, which is ethical growth. Masha has finally dis-
educated herself from all "sentimental sense," from the fancies of
pastoral and romantic love. She now knows that that kind of love
is but a make-believe that deludes us into thinking that falling in love
and loving are one and the same thing. Now she has learned that
love may become stronger and truer by surviving the short-lived
honeymoons of the spirit and the flesh. Now she knows with her
husband that "each time of life has its kind of love": so there is happiness after all, a happiness suited to the present time of their lives,
and to the kind of love that corresponds to it. Thus the youthful,
transitory, and deceitful dream of romantic love vanishes forever
and will never return, since normally it should appear only once
in a lifetime, like one of those pastoral oases that dissolve like mirages
just when they seem within reach.

Masha once thought that it was feeling that should guide life;
now she discovers that it is life that should guide feeling. At this
point the bucolic ends, to be replaced by the georgic, or by a life
close to nature in the moral rather than in the sentimental sense.
From now on she will accept not only "the days," but also "the
works," becoming a full partner of her husband, sharing with him
not only the joys of life but also its responsibilities and hardships.
So the story, which had begun as a pastoral and unfolded as a romance, closes with the conventional ending of a bourgeois novel,
with the implication that Masha and Sergey Mikhaylych lived happily ever after. Masha simply says that she and her husband have
lived happily "up to the present time," or up to the very day or hour
she has been telling her story. Yet, even if the narrator of the story
had been the writer, rather than the heroine, the thought that they
lived happily therafter might have still been left unsaid. It seems
indeed that the reader of *Domestic Happiness* should not need the
help of anyone else, even the author, to realize that after the end
of the story Masha and Sergey Mikhaylych were destined to live as

happily as a married couple possibly can—neither more nor less. The story ends on such a note, and its double, paradoxical message is that passion is deemed limitless only as long as man and woman remain within the sphere of pastoral and romantic love, which is but an enchanted circle. But as soon as two lovers go beyond the boundaries of pastoral fantasy and romantic fancies they discover that love can last, and grow stronger and truer, only if and when it is circumscribed.

14
"L'Heure du Berger": Mallarmé's Grand Eclogue

I

We disregard too often the obvious. Almost no critic of Mallarmé has paid due attention to two clues contained in the title and subtitle of *L'Après-midi d'un faune*. The first of these clues is "après," and at the proper moment it will be shown how important for the poem's interpretation it is to realize that its real action takes place not at the culmination of the day ("midi"), but in the aftermath of the panic hour ("après"). The second clue is the single word that forms the subtitle of the poem ("églogue"). There is no similar subtitle in all the other poetic works of Mallarmé, who, except in this case, never deigned (at least publicly) to assign any piece of his own making to the literary genre to which it officially is supposed to belong.

The uniqueness of the circumstance emphasizes the exceptional significance of an allusion so explicit as to violate those strict standards of literary discretion that are Mallarmé's intransigent norm. This consideration should entitle and even enjoin the critic to take that rare label as seriously as it deserves. Thus, instead of being content with a few vague remarks about the affinities tying *L'Après-midi* to the bucolic tradition, remarks that most of its critics forget as soon as they set them forth, we shall pursue an interpretation of the poem that finds its bearings within the frame of reference that its rubric has up to now provided without appreciable effect.

Before doing so, however, we must remember that at the time it first appeared in print, in the famous "plaquette de luxe" of 1876, "intérieurement décorée par Manet," which consoled the author for the rejection of that piece one year earlier by the editors of the third issue of *Le Parnasse contemporain,* the poem had existed for about a decade in a manuscript version entitled "Monologue d'un faune." That version, which may be read in Mallarmé's *Oeuvres complètes,*[1] was never supplied with the subtitle of which we make so much. The absence at that stage of the label "églogue" is no less significant than its presence later on; this is but one of the considerations that will compel us to return once in a while to the text of the early draft in our attempt to reinterpret the poem. The same necessity justifies at this point a brief digression to establish the connections existing between the handwritten and the published version, which we shall distinguish with the respective designations *monologue* and *églogue.*

As we know from a letter he wrote to Henri Cazalis from Tournon, probably in June 1865, Mallarmé started working on the poem which in the long run was to become *L'Après-midi d'un faune* during a pause in the composition of *Hérodiade,* which, unlike *L'Après-midi,* preserved in all its fragments and versions its original dramatic intent. "Cette oeuvre solitaire m'avait stérilisé," wrote the poet in that letter, "et, dans l'intervalle, je rime un intermède héroïque, dont le héros est un Faune."[2] In the rest of the letter that strange expression, "intermède héroïque," appears to mean a short dramatic piece, entailing only a few scenes, and at the end the writer states his intention to present it for performance by the Théâtre français. After a brief lapse of time the piece, ultimately limited to a single scene, was finished, and the poet submitted it to Théodore de Banville and Constant Coquelin. In the late summer of the same year the poet reported the negative outcome of that step in a letter to Théodore Aubanel: "Les vers de mon *Faune* ont plu infiniment, mais de Banville et Coquelin n'y ont pas rencontré l'anecdote nécessaire que demande le public. . . ."[3]

Despite one or two vague references in the letters of those years, Mallarmé's correspondence is devoid of any hint as to why, how, and when, during the intervening decade, the poet turned that early version into *L'Après-midi d'un faune*. What we may guess, however, is that the metamorphosis took place as soon as the author realized that the dramatic structure was not genuine to the inspiration of the poem, when he saw that the *monologue* was in reality an *églogue* in form as well as in content. Such a realization must have determined both the change of the title and the addition of the subtitle, as well as the omission of the stage directions, which were no longer proper or apt. Yet the transformation was not as radical as it may seem; in a sense it was merely changing from unfitting clothes to more appropriate ones. After all, Mallarmé initially adopted the dramatic form only in order to dress his work after the pattern of his immediate model, Banville's two-acter in verse *Diane au bois*, staged in 1864. While borrowing a theatrical mask, Mallarmé had from the very beginning composed a piece preeminently lyrical, as Banville and Coquelin sensed as soon as they read it. The composition's lyrical temper was evident also in the reduction of the would-be play to the single and subjective monologue of the lonely protagonist. Yet the title "Monologue" was still equivocal, and this explains why the poet was bound to discard it many years later, as he had almost immediately discarded the earliest of all the poem's headings, the transparent and yet misleading "Improvisation d'un faune."

The idea that Mallarmé took from *Diane au bois* was something more important and permanent than the ephemeral dramatic dress which a superficial imitative impulse led him to impose on his *improvisation* or *monologue*. That idea coincides with the moral archetype of the faun as well as with the psychological situation he is confronted with. What we mean is that Banville's little dramatic poem presents to its spectators or readers the rather novel figure of the youthful satyr Gryphon, so comic and mischievous as to make us think of Cherubino in *Le Mariage de Figaro*. We might even define Gryphon as a "faunet," through an anachronistic analogy with Lolita, Nabokov's "nymphet." What matters is that Banville's "faunet," even if in a different manner and for different reasons, hesitates like Mallarmé's young faun between two nymphs equally attractive and evenly matched.

Albert Thibaudet was the first and remained one of the few critics of the poet to claim that Mallarmé may have found inspiration if not for the type of the faun at least for the situation he faces in another model: a Boucher painting he may have seen in the National Gallery in 1862 or 1863 during his stay in London. While agreeing with Henri Mondor that *Diane au bois* is the only certain source of *L'Après-midi*, we must admit that the situation that the painting suggests recalls the "anecdote" of the poem; even there a faunlike figure surprises among reedlike plants two lying or recumbent nymphs. Only the title of the painting tells us that the faunlike figure is the god Pan; that he pursues only one of the two nymphs; and that one is Syrinx. If the poet saw that painting, he must have at first been far more impressed by the actual situation it seems to convey than by the stated subject of Boucher's rococo idyll; yet at a later stage of his reworking of the poem his imagination may well have been directly affected by its title or by the fable it suggests. At any rate the fable itself seems to have determined the reelaboration of the poem in at least one significant detail, as, at the proper time, we shall try to prove.

As for the traits that Mallarmé obviously took from Banville's playlet, there is no doubt that they determined the main features of the poem. Yet, despite its erotic innuendo, *Diane au bois*, as hinted at by the very name of the goddess mentioned in its title, remains a "cold pastoral," or a pastoral of innocence. Mallarmé's poem moves instead within the broader confines of the pastoral of happiness, even though, like many love idylls, it turns into a lover's complaint, into that kind of elegy that springs from "hedonism disappointed." [4] Yet, while ending in failure, the passion of Mallarmé's faun is no mere whim or caprice, since it partakes of that panic urge or cosmic will which rules life and the organic universe. The Wagnerian or Schopenhauerian dimensions of Mallarmé's creation dwarf Banville's Parnassian and adolescent "faunet" to the size of an elegant and frivolous statuette. From this viewpoint Mallarmé's poem is more directly comparable with Hugo's *Le Satyre*, from which he must have borrowed his own faun's blasphemous wish to conquer Venus, the very goddess of love.

II

To understand the novelty of the character of the young faun as conceived by Mallarmé we must do what we have promised to do: to relate the poet's invention to the bucolic invention, and read the poem, as it should be read, as an eclogue. We shall begin this task by reminding the reader that the normal protagonist of the pastoral of love is the male shepherd and that if he is often in love with a nymph, rather than with a shepherdess, it is because the former stands even better than the latter for the eternal feminine. In such a context, the word "nymph" is but a synonym of "female," while the image is but a trope for woman as a sexual object. The nymph of the pastoral is not a siren, in the figurative as well as in the literal sense: she simply reflects the masculine erotic ideal of a yielding beauty, of a freshness without prudery, of a youth without coyness. In brief, she represents more fully than the shepherdess the dream of free love, which she embodies in the passive terms of feminine consent.

Yet the sentimental vision of the pastoral always refuses to reduce the behavior of its nymphs to that sexual frenzy which is the characteristic attribute of their sisters within the realm of legend and myth. When confronted with the pastoral nymph, the bucolic shepherd, even if he is or looks young, represents the middle-aged lover, *l'homme moyen sensuel,* still full of desire, but restricted and restrained by the prohibitions and inhibitions that social taboos or moral scruples impose on the gratification of the erotic impulse. The idyllic shepherd is, then, like the bucolic nymph, an all too human mask, and there is no doubt that the pastoral poet not only humanizes the standard figures he borrows from the traditions and conventions of the genre; he also transforms into psychological types most of the godlike creatures or fabulous beings he takes from mythological lore. This is what he does for instance with such a monster as Polyphemus: since Theocritus the one-eyed giant too fond of the charming nymph Galatea has been made to play the stock role of the uncouth and unshapely swain, whom nature has made at once loving and unlovely, and thus unable to kindle in the object of his passion a fire like the one burning in his heart. The Cyclops has thus been turned into a special or, at most, extreme variation of the type of the tenderhearted but ugly shepherd destined to know all the pangs but none of the joys of love.

Pastoral poetry, however, has been unable to tame with equal effectiveness the type of the faun. The latter stands at the opposite pole of poor Polyphemus, since he represents sexual fulfillment of an abnormal or superhuman degree. He cannot then typify the average love situation as experienced by the average male. The bucolic imagination reflects life in the mirror of fancy, yet it refrains from disregarding life's common values and standard norms. Often pathetic and naive, it may take too seriously the casuistry of passion but can never accept the heroic exaggeration of all genuine myths. Thus, while mythology celebrates the satyr as a demigod of fertility, the eclogue at most treats him as a figuration of sexual freedom, embodying the dream of free love in the active terms of masculine potency.

In brief, the pastoral faun, even more than the nymph, is but a fantasy, in the psychological meaning of the term, a wishful projection of the frustrated instinct. This is the same as saying that he is a symbol in the Freudian sense, and as such a morbid and subdolous image. The behavior of this figure remains perilously near, even if only in the realm of wish, to that deviation or excess which sexual pathology quite properly designates with the clinical term "satyriasis." Pastoral poetry avoids a similar danger in the case of his feminine counterpart: there is no nymphomania in the bucolic nymph, who is willing to yield to love while avoiding the pitfalls of promiscuity, and who, as we have already said, is but a normal young woman, at least as seen by man, in mythical disguise. Since they cannot reduce their fauns to the same kind of passivity they reduce their nymphs, pastoral poets tend to keep the former in the background. The bucolic is able to bring the satyr into the foreground only when he has become a superannuated Silenus or, in other words, a caricature of himself, humanized by the very decrepitude that makes him impotent, by the weakness that induces him to find solace in Bacchus now that Venus is out of reach. A minor character in D. H. Lawrence's *St. Mawr* claims that the average man shows all too visibly "the old satyr . . . the fallen Pan" in himself—a spiritual or moral reality that Silenus reveals more simply and directly through a physiological mask.

All these observations tend to show how novel and daring Mallarmé's idea was to make of his faun not one of the many extras but the leading man or, rather, the single actor of his eclogue. The originality of the conception looms even greater when we realize that while the satyr of the fable, as proved by his wiry beard and fleecy hair, is an ageless or, rather, perennial impersonation of physiological and sexual maturity, Mallarmé's faun is instead an immature youth. The paradox is an interesting one: one could say that after breaking the pastoral pattern by making a faun the hero of his idyll, Mallarmé restores that pattern by turning him into a shepherd who looks like a faun, or, if we wish, into a faun who behaves like a shepherd. While doing so, the faun still tries to play his normal or natural role, which is that of the *surmâle*, as shown by the feat, or rather the attempt, of making love with two nymphs at the same time.

Yet the double seduction ends in double failure, and while outbidding pastoral man in the realm of desire, the faun fares as badly in the realm of actuality. A loving shepherd acts too often like a *faune manqué*; but here the satyr himself behaves like a timid, self-conscious, and awkward human male, thus becoming, so to speak, a *faune raté*. At the end of the poem the faun looks forward to finding consolation for his frustration in drink, thus imitating the behavior of old Silenus, at least in thought. But Silenus drinks to forget the natural blight of senility, whereas the faun's failure is but the effect of inexperience and immaturity. This seems to have been the view of the poet, as belatedly implied in the apostrophe, "Satyre aux baisers inexperts," by which he opened one of the many quatrains he inscribed on the presentation copies of the poem. We may make too much of this apostrophe, written some time afterward. The line itself belongs to one of the four *offrandes* to Victor Margueritte: and what makes it worth quoting in full is that there the poet gives for the failure of the faun a reason contrary to that suggested in the text. Whereas in the poem the faun's "crime" seems to have been the preference he had suddenly shown for one nymph over the other, this *offrande* clearly implies that he had erred by making love to both of them:

> Satyre aux baisers inexperts
> Qui pourchasses outre la brune
> La fauve nymphe, tu les perds
> Il n'est d'extase qu'avec une.

Whether the faun strove for too little or for too much, we know that he failed, and we believe that the failure was due to an immaturity and inexperience he shared with the nymphs. This is one of the many paradoxes of this eclogue. There is no doubt in our mind that the failure of the sexual encounter which the poem reevokes must be explained, at least on the literal plane, by the virginity of the three partners. If this is true, then one might say that whereas the theme of *Hérodiade* is "l'horreur d'être vierge," the theme of *L'Après-midi* is "la frayeur secrète de la chair." It is evident that we must prove this unheard-of virginity of the nymphs, as well as the even more extraordinary virginity of the faun. It is from the closing line of the *monologue* that we learn that the two nymphs were virgin before the encounter: "Adieu, femmes; duo de vierges quand je vins," and it is from the same line, as rewritten for the *églogue*, with its significant omission of the word "femmes," that we may infer that they remained such even after the encounter had taken place: "Couple, adieu; je vais voir l'ombre que tu devins." The two nymphs are about to turn into a shadowy dream precisely because the faun never knew (in the biblical sense) either one.

As for the masculine protagonist, it may suffice to remark that in the *églogue* he speaks of his breast as being "vierge de preuves," by which he strictly means that that part of his body shows none of the marks that might have been left by the nymphs' lips or teeth. But those words clearly imply more than this: the figure is a synecdoche, and its real meaning is that the whole body of the faun is unsullied by any previous contact. This finds confirmation in that passage of the *monologue* in which the "désire torride" still affecting the faun deludes him into believing that the encounter may not have been a failure after all, so that he wonders aloud whether or not he has lost his virginity: "Serai-je pur?" All these testimonials, which are the more persuasive for being offered by two texts, prove without a shadow of a doubt not only that the outcome of that strange love match which is the central story of the poem is a negative one, but that the story itself is but that of a reciprocal sexual initiation *manqué*. A further demonstration of this point may be found in the lines by which the faun dreams of a future sexual revanche, which paradoxically he describes in terms of a violent feminine initiative to which he will submit as a passive and even unwilling partner:

> Tant pis! vers le bonheur d'autres m'entraîneront
> Par leur tresse nouée aux cornes de mon front.

These lines read almost like a parody, since they envisage a situation inverting the satyr's normal role, which is to drag into the woods one or more reluctant nymphs, in brief, to act as the agent of a rape, not as its victim.

We have thus reached a purely sexual interpretation of the poem's "anecdote" (which exists, despite Banville's and Coquelin's opinion to the contrary) by bringing to their extreme consequences the implications of the literary genre to which it belongs. We have read the poem in the key in which it was written, and we have found that it makes sense only within the frame of reference of the pastoral. Within the same frame of reference we have recognized and understood also the poem's non-sense: like all masterpieces, Mallarmé's creation reacts against the very convention on which it feeds. We have also not forgotten (and we shall keep this constantly in mind) that *L'Après-midi* is quite a modern eclogue. A faun doubting the reality of his nymphs is utterly modern, says the German critic Franz Rauhut. We agree, but we would locate the modernity of this work primarily in the ambiguity of its literary structure and only secondarily in the psychological complexity of the protagonist. This poem is a modern pastoral precisely because at many points it finds itself in a state of tension toward the bucolic mode and the idyllic mood.

III

There is another minor literary problem to solve before proceeding further with the poem's analysis. It is the question whether *L'Après-midi* must be taken, like many other eclogues, as a "pastoral song." The fact that its earliest title was "Improvisation d'un faune" seems to imply that it should indeed be read as a pastoral song, if so it would be irrelevant that this time the improvising singer is a faun in lieu of a shepherd. We feel, however, that hypothesis is wrong—we are even inclined to surmise that the replacement of "Improvisation" with "Monologue" as the poem's heading was motivated by Mallarmé's desire to prevent the future reader from mistaking the composition for a pastoral song rather than by the need to reemphasize its dramatic intent. By that new term Mallarmé probably wanted to hint that the faun's statement, whether dramatic or not, was not a chant but a discourse. The faun does not sing: he merely speaks in verse, a medium that the character, not the author, uses as if it were prose. The most glaring misunderstandings to be met in the poem's critical history are indeed due to the tendency on the part of even some of its keenest interpreters to view *L'Après-midi* as the poem of a poem, as a faun's song resung by Mallarmé.

We must repeat that despite its early dramatic disguise, which the *églogue* was to discard, *L'Après-midi* is a lyrical work par excellence; but we must add that its stance, as well as its *melos*, is that of a *méditation*. This term was coined by Lamartine to designate one of the most typical creations of Romantic lyricism, the reflective or contemplative poem, by which the poet avows his feelings and thoughts not so much to his readers as to nature and himself, in a mood of elegiac melancholy, quiet if not serene. *L'Après-midi*, however, is a *méditation* of the kind that could be conceived by a poet used to the very different literary atmosphere of *Parnasse* and symbolism: a *méditation* that the poet makes objective and deprives of all personal pathos by attributing it to what Yeats would have called a mask, which in this case is the faun himself. (If we wish to look for a romantic precedent, we may find it in such a work as Guerin's *Centaure*, which also employs a mythological mask and which, significantly, is a poem in prose.) Mallarmé may have become aware that the quality of his poem was that of a *méditation* just when he decided to throw aside its dramatic shell; when, while dropping the *monologue*'s stage directions, which were no longer useful or proper, he still kept the single caption "LE FAUNE" at the head of the *églogue*. This was the more necessary since as long as it was part of the title the word *monologue* could suggest by itself that the poem consists of the utterance of a single character, speaking in the first person, and thinking aloud. Yet the caption's significance would remain equivocal were we unable to reinterpret its function and meaning through the word now missing from the poem's heading. The knowledge that the *églogue* was once a *monologue* may serve as a reminder that the poem is not the song of a song, but a song of thought, that the words and sounds the faun utters are a reflective soliloquy, not a musical solo.

This implies that it is also a mistake to take for granted, as most critics do, that the faun stands for the figure of the artist, and that in the poem he acts as such. It is true that Mallarmé attributes to him the artistic or, more precisely, the musical calling, following also in this the tradition of the pastoral, which both conceals and reveals the type of the poet under a shepherd's garb. By doing so, the pastoral, however, aims at portraying the poet as man, and primarily as a man of feeling. Mallarmé pursues a similar course, since, even if he sees in his faun the emblem of the artist, he depicts him in other moments than those of creation. The poem, except for a few fleeting moments, most of which do not belong to the present, being projections and evocations of time future or of time past, shows the faun playing what Valéry would call "l'appareil de la raison," or no other instrument but that of thought. What he does is something taking place in his mind and soul: he reflects and wonders, muses and broods. In brief, the poem's actual hero is a thoughtful introvert, who may well represent the artist, but only as a being who thinks. By taking literally one of the expressions by which the faun conveys the mental operation he is now performing ("les femmes dont tu gloses"), one could even say that the faun behaves here more like a critic than like an artist. One of the *monologue*'s stage directions, "le front dans les mains," freezes him for a while in the same pose as Rodin's *Penseur*.

Now we realize what such a deliberate artist as Mallarmé could mean by the word *improvisation* before he dropped it: not a spontaneous creation bursting out in song but a free flow of feelings and thoughts, the unrehearsed utterance of an emotional and intellectual experience to which not the character, but only the author, can give order and form.

We are led to the same truth by what we have called the first clue, which is the "après" of the final title. It indicates that the real action of the poem, which is the faun's meditation, takes place "after noon," when the panic hour is over, as a rethinking of the experience that has just failed to fulfill itself. While rethinking that experience, the faun reenacts it, and this is the real meaning of the opening words: "Ces nymphes, je les veux perpétuer." The perpetuation at which he aims is not to be reached through sex (the perpetuation of the species) or art (the immortality of the aesthetic object as postulated by the Parnassian creed), since it is merely the perpetuation of experience, as resurrected by, and relived through, the faculty of memory. Recollection will then merge with meditation: and this will contribute to the chronological and structural complexity of the poem. Hence its perplexing confusion, which the poet tried to clarify once for all with the typography he adopted since the original edition. *L'Après-midi* contains four passages in italics and between quotation marks, alternating with four longer passages in normal type. The former, as hinted at by the capitalized words which announce and anticipate the first two of them ("CONTEZ" and "SOUVENIRS") seem to indicate that the flow of meditation is suddenly broken by the wave of recollection: that from the *après* we now go back to the *midi*, to the event which then happened, or failed to occur. It is in the quoted and italicized passages that the *églogue* goes backward in time and the faun replaces introspection with remembrance of things past. In them, and even more in the passages in normal type, the faun sometimes projects his longings forward, as well as backward: so that the real dimension of the poem, even more than the limbo between the *midi* and the *après*, is the no-man's-land between life and conscience, between senses and thought. Hence the problematic character of the protagonist or, rather, single actor, who, despite his faunesque shape, plays the role of a Hamlet of both the mind and the will.

All this is quite novel and strange, precisely because the *après* of the title is not merely a chronological determination but a dramatic and psychological one. *Midi,* or the panic hour, is in the context of the poem but another name for that all too human experience which a clever and lovely French idiom calls *l'heure du berger*. The moment or occasion so defined is that fleeting and crucial *Erlebnis* when a human being, or rather a human male, suddenly feels that the fulfillment of love, or simply the gratification of desire, is at last within reach. *L'heure du berger* is the moment of seduction, or the hour of Cupid, and it is filled with the certainty that the erotic climax is imminent, that the hour of Venus is at hand. There is a moment in the poem when that hour is projected in a blasphemous and distant daydream, as a conquest by the faun of the very goddess of love—but the poem itself or, rather, its "anecdote," is concerned only with *l'heure du berger*.

The shepherd of this lovely idiom must not be taken for the shepherd of pastoral poetry, who is never sure that his wishes may be readily fulfilled. Yet our faun, just like the latter, fails to seize the opportunity offered by a "shepherd's hour" which in his case occurs not at dusk, as the idiom normally implies, but at noon. After that failure the faun reflects about it not as a literary shepherd but as a human being would. In one of the poem's *offrandes* Mallarmé defined the faunlike Pan as a "tronc qui s'achève en homme," and one could say that the faun ends by embodying, in the *après* of the "anecdote," *homo sapiens* at his best. The same creature who, as we shall see, will throw away his pipe, hoping that it will turn back into a reed, turns himself at the same time into a *roseau pensant*. In the poem he reevokes his own *vis-à-vis* with the nymphs; he even fancies that he will win his *corps-à-corps* with them in a retrial which is but a redream—yet all this, and many other similar things, happen only in a *tête-à-tête* with himself. When the critic abandons the sphere of abstraction and generality to undertake a close analysis of the text, he may well lose himself in the poem's labyrinth unless he holds in his hand this guiding thread: the simple certainty that the time and the tempo of the poem is but that of a long and complex "afterthought." It is with the help of such a certainty that we shall try, in the following commentary, to reconstruct the varying phases, and the changing moods, of this afternoon conversation between faun and self.

The noon is just over, and the day is still heavy with slumber ("assoupi de sommeils touffus"); yet a trace of the rosy radiance of the nymphs' skins ("leur incarnat léger") seems still to flutter in the air. The faun would like to preserve that trace, thus renewing and even fixing forever the vision he had beheld: "Ces nymphes, je les veux perpétuer." The wish of doing so is the stronger since he is wondering whether that vision had been a real fact or a mere dream ("Aimai-je un rêve?"). The faun is seized by a doubt which, for being an utter denial of the bright certainty of timeless noon, is conveyed as if it were the obscure mass of a night of old ("amas de nuit ancienne"), or a heart of darkness. Fully aware of the etymological meaning of the word "doute," which suggests the forking out of a road, or the branching out of a twig, the poet embodies the faun's doubt in an external object which is but a reflection of the image of the inner night: in the surrounding bush, which seems to break and divide its own wholeness into numberless little branches ("en maint rameau subtil"). Those branches stand for the ramification and proliferation of doubt, which is born in perplexity, but grows into a maze of negative certainties. This is what the faun means when he says that, by transforming its unity into multiplicity, the doubt-bush

> . . . prouve, hélas! que bien seul je m'offrais
> Pour triomphe la faute idéale de roses.

What the doubt-bush testifies to is not that the nymphs never existed, but simply that they did not leave the faintest sign of their presence. This is the sense of the faun's allusion to roses that are not real but figurative flowers, acting as the traditional symbol of feminine beauty, of the fresh complexion of young and lovely women. What the faun means to say is that the impression that the nymph's short-lived appearance had left behind a shadowy reflection of the rosiness of their skin was but illusion and self-deceit. It was to find some consolation or compensation ("triomphe") for their absence that the faun had for a while nursed the delusion that the halo of their complexion was still hovering about or falling down around him. In reality that hovering or falling down had been but an ideal mistake ("faute idéale") taking place within his mind or, as the text suggests by a pun based on the semantic ambiguities of the word "faute," it had been a fault or default which might even indicate the unreality of the two nymphs.

Confronted with this negative hypothesis, the faun has no alternative but to put it to the test of thought. Doubt may be dualistic, but thought is dialectical, and it is with an august self-command, "Réfléchissons," that the faun ushers in the inner dialogue of his intellect. Hence the transition from wondering to self-questioning, with the grammatical shift from the first person plural to the second singular. Tell me, the faun enjoins himself, whether the women you are still thinking about were but a wishful projection of the prodigious senses of the mythical creature you are:

> Réfléchissons . . .
> ou si les femmes dont tu gloses
> Figurent un souhait de tes sens fabuleux!

It is to find an answer to this question that, while still speaking of himself in the second person, the faun rehearses within the dimension of memory (hence reusing the present tense) the vision once perceived by his physical senses. He does so by conjuring up in recollection the now vague figures of the two nymphs. The first one seems to have been blond, and certainly blue-eyed. The faun now realizes that he had perceived her primarily through the sense of sight, to the point of noticing that there were tears on her eyelids. This is why he represents her in terms of water, through the image of a spring:

> Faune, l'illusion s'échappe des yeux bleus
> Et froids, comme une source en pleurs, de la plus chaste.

As for the other, he now knows that she was undoubtedly dark-haired and dark-skinned, and that he had perceived her primarily through other senses than sight. He had approached her so blindly and nearly as to hear her soft sighs, touch her flesh, and feel the warmth of her body against his own. For this reason he represents her fire in terms of an ardent breath, through the metaphor of a hot wind:

> Mais, l'autre tout soupirs, dis-tu qu'elle contraste
> Comme brise du jour chaude dans ta toison!

At this point the faun picks up his pipe to see whether the wonder of art may help to make the images of recollected reality truer, or more vivid. But art destroys the charms of both memory and senses, and this is why the waterlike nymph melts into the fluidity of sound and the windlike one dissolves into the airiness of music. By simply touching his pipe, the faun has broken the spell of remembrance: but almost at the same time he breaks also the spell of music, since what concerns him now is not the enchantment of creation, but the disenchantment of experience. In brief, he stops playing almost as soon as he starts—hence the wonderful image of the sudden escape and the homeward ascent of that inspiration which had barely visited him. Inspiration, as the very word says, is the "breathing in" of the spirit; but what we witness here is its "exhaling," its return, in the shape of a wind clearly outlined against the purity of the sky, to its celestial abode. The only wind ("le seul vent") that now seems to blow, says the faun,

> C'est, à l'horizon pas remué d'une ride,
> Le visible et serein souffle artificiel
> De l'inspiration, qui regagne le ciel.

These lines have often been misunderstood because of the preconception that here and elsewhere the faun plays the role of a performing artist. Yet even here he makes hardly more than a musical gesture: he goes through the motion of playing only to give up immediately his halfhearted attempt. On any other occasion he fails to do even as little as that, as we may see by examining the next section of the poem. This section proceeds backward in time, being a reconstruction, in its phases and circumstance, of the actual incident.

It naturally begins with the account of what the faun was doing just before it. He was then busying himself with the tools of his craft or rather with the materials out of which they are made. In brief, he was cutting reeds; and once in a while he would test for sound this or that reed. At that moment he was thus performing but an artisan's task. To provide more convincing evidence as to the truth of this, the faun asks for supporting testimony from the external world: from the marshland that on that day, as on many others, his vanity as a would-be artist had despoiled of its reeds, thus laying it waste with no less cruelty than the sun's. This is the sense of the lovely apostrophe:

> O bords siciliens d'un calme marécage
> Qu'à l'envi des soleils ma vanité saccage,
> Tacite sous les fleurs d'étincelles, CONTEZ.

Yet the faun reports in the first person what the marshland, or rather its shores, were supposed to relate on his behalf:

> *Que je coupais ici les creux roseaux domptés*
> *Par le talent. . . .*

From the faun's direct account we also learn that he saw the two white beings which he took at first for swans just when he was testing two joint reeds for sound. This is hinted at by the description of that moment as the "prélude lent où naissent les pipeaux"; a phrase whose meaning is made fully clear by the corresponding line in the *monologue:* "Et qu'au bruit de ma flûte où j'ajuste un pipeau." With the help of this line we may clarify another little detail, which remains vague in the final version of the faun's account: that it was the very noise he had just made (it had scarcely been a musical sound) that frightened the creatures whom he recognized as being two nymphs only in the act of their flight.

At this point the faun abandons for a while the reconstruction of the incident to ponder about their second and final disappearance, which was to occur after he overtook and almost overwhelmed them. The mental digression filling the interruption deals with the faun's failure to seize the opportunity that chance had offered him. The "shepherd's hour" had for him coincided, if only for a brief time, with the panic hour ("l'heure fauve"). He had been unable to avail himself of an occasion that had lasted but a fleeting instant; and after that instant high noon had seemed to stand still in the brutal indifference of nature, in the dumb fullness of matter, in the blinding brightness of the sun at the zenith. In that indifference, fullness, and brightness no trace had been left, no hint could be found, by which he might explain to himself how and why the two objects of his lust had vanished together from his arms already embracing them:

> Inerte, tout brûle dans l'heure fauve
> Sans marquer par quel art ensemble détala
> Trop d'hymen souhaité de qui cherche le *la*.

As we see, the faun has now replaced the second person with the third, while still using the present tense. These grammatical devices emphasize the detachment and the objectivity by which he tries to judge an experience which now is a thing of the past. It is in order to do so that he describes himself as he might have appeared, just before the incident, to an onlooker. An onlooker would have noticed that at the moment he was tuning his instrument: a situation concisely conveyed by the Faun's self-definition as "the one seeking the A." This is clear, but the mental vision suggested by the lines that follow is not. These lines, as a matter of fact, are the most obscure of the whole poem. As usual, they are marked by new grammatical shifts, by the replacing of the third person with the first, and of the historical present with the future tense. Yet this time the reader is unprepared for such shifts, since the poet has suppressed all syntactical links between the passage in question and the preceding one. The interpreter should try to reestablish the transition omitted, a task that one could not even try without first explaining the implication contained in the temporal adverb introducing these three lines:

> Alors m'éveillerai-je à la ferveur première,
> Droit et seul, sous un flot antique de lumière,
> Lys! et l'un de vous tous pour l'ingénuité.

As used here, "alors" should be accompanied by its twin, which is "quand." Only by determining the sense of the absent "when" may we interpret a "then" otherwise meaningless. The missing link must be an unexpressed sentence, ideally located in the dividing pause. A chasm may well be also a bridge, uniting the opposite sides. Let us then juxtapose the phrases facing each other beyond the pause. The closing phrase of the first passage defines the faun as someone who seeks, and we know, with the French proverb, that *qui cherche trouve*. It is on no other knowledge than this that we surmise that the missing sentence must be understood as meaning: when I find the keynote I once sought. This may be paraphrased into the statement: when I am ready again for musical performance. If this is the sense of the subordinate clause that Mallarmé omitted in his daring ellipse, it is not too hard to understand aright the mysterious clause beginning with "alors." What the faun means to say in the three lines opened by that adverb is then as follows: (When I find the A note, and play again my pipe,) then I shall no longer lie down, as I did at noon, in the heavy slumber of sense; nor sit down, as I am doing this afternoon, in the drowsy mist of my thoughts: but I shall instead awake in the luminous clarity of early morning; I shall stand up, as a noble creature, straight and erect like you, lilies of these bogs; and (by playing my flute) I shall become as pure and innocent as you are.

What all this amounts to is but an affirmation on the part of the faun that some time in the near future he will become again the artist he was born to be. The validity of this interpretation is confirmed by internal and external evidence. The first is supplied by an earlier passage, the one in which the faun had unwillingly exorcised the reality of his vision by merely touching his flute. By telling us that he had then turned to his flute too late, when noon had just overwhelmed the lingering morn (*"le matin frais s'il lutte"*), the faun had already suggested that the creative moment coincides with the early hours of the day. The external evidence is provided by a later poem, the *Prose (pour des Esseintes)*. We may recall that in the *Prose* Mallarmé selects as the fitting emblem of the poetic creation flowers of a species very similar to the lilies appearing in this passage of *L'Après-midi*, and belonging like them to "la famille des iridées." At the end of the same poem Mallarmé also symbolizes poetic glory in a "trop grand flaieul." No doubt is now left about the significance of the three lines in question, which have been regularly, if variously, misunderstood since Juysmans commented on them in a famous page of *Arebours*. The author of that page, showing at once bad judgment and bad taste, mistook for a phallic symbol those lilies that the mystical tradition had always treated as an allegory of chastity and spiritual purity, and which in this passage of *L'Après-midi* stand for the catharsis of poetry and the sublimation of art.

V

This catharsis or sublimation, which the poet here recommends incidentally, is supposed to take place only without or beyond the limits of the poem, its convention being, as we know, that of a meditation, not of a song. This finds confirmation in the next section, in which the faun turns his attention from the external world to his own physical being, to see whether his body preserves any sign of its contact with the two nymphs. Aside from the sweet nothing of a kiss so light as to have been more a brush than of a touch—"Autre que ce doux rien par leur lèvre ébruité, / Le baiser"—no sign, says the faun, has been left on my untouched breast, except the mysterious bites of a sacred tooth:

> Mon sein, vierge de preuve, atteste une morsure
> Mystérieuse, due à quelque auguste dent.

Only a misreading of this passage would lead one to believe that this tooth mark is a physical and visible sign made by either of the two nymphs. Mythologically speaking, nymphs are divine beings, even if lesser ones: but neither the pastoral nor the faun treats them seriously as such, even when calling them goddesses, as the faun does in another passage of the poem. Hence that mark must have been invisibly branded by a higher agency: it must be the "bite of the serpent," or the "wound" of Apollo's "bow."

That the mark or sign stands for the divine calling of art or poetry is made evident in the lines that follow, in which the poet, or the faun, makes use of the rhetorical device called preterition. This device involves on one hand the stated promise, on the part of the character or the author, to leave something unsaid; and, on the other, the violation of that promise by the very statement within which it is made. While alluding to the awful secret hidden in that invisible sign, the faun feels he has already said too much. Enough! says he: such a mystery cannot be spoken by human lips nor heard by human ears; it is only to art that it can be avowed, it is only by art that it can be voiced:

> Mais, bast! arcane tel élut pour confident
> Le jonc vaste et jumeau dont sous l'azur on joue.

After stating that the only instrument by which that mystery may be revealed is the hollow and twin reed on which at that moment he does not care to lay his hand, the faun bares the mystery itself by describing the operations of that instrument, or the wonder he may himself work out when playing again his flute.

While evoking the charm of music and the prodigy of art the faun speaks again in the present: yet what he projects is but a vision of the future. He knows that when he plays again a solo song he will feel free from pain and sorrow, as if the instrument would waylay toward itself the player's tears ("detournant à soi le trouble de la joue"); he also knows that then he may contemplate again the images of illusion and memory by transfiguring them into the images of art. Precisely for being no longer clouded by the veils of passion and feeling, the figures of the two nymphs will then appear to him not in the complexity of nature and life, but in the sublime simplicity of form, or as a composition reduced to the musical and symmetrical purity of a single-colored outline: "Une sonore, vaine et monotone ligne." Most critics recognize that this alexandrine reechoes Baudelaire's no less famous alexandrine: "Je hais le mouvement qui déplace les lignes," in which Mallarmé's master had proclaimed, in terms which sound already Parnassian, the creed of aesthetic impassibility.

Mallarmé restates the same creed in a line which, belonging to a poem far from Parnassian (we would rather consider L'Après-midi as a verbal anticipation of impressionist painting as well as a foreshadowing of poésie pure), ends by recommending a style that is of neither the past nor the present but of the future: the style of abstract art. This suggestion is quite proper in view of the fact that when anticipating the moment he will re-create and revive his experience in aesthetic terms, the faun chooses to portray himself not in a musician's attitude but in the pose of a painter, looking at his ideal or real model with a vague and fixed gaze ("avec mes regards clos"), to be better able to translate a too sensual vision in the purity of art and the symmetry of form; to reshape that vision into a mental composition that will be, in the faun's words, "sonore," or harmonic; "vaine," or insubstantial and fleshless; "monotone," or perfectly simple.

The line concluding this passage is the more significant for conveying an aesthetic ideal diametrically opposed to the physical image it is supposed to represent. What the faun says in the passage closed by that line is that the artist must reduce to an abstract contour a vision as grossly concrete as that of a nymph seen "de dos ou de flanc." This is the first time we realize that just before the seduction attempt the faun had approached the two nymphs while one of them was lying on her side, with her back turned to him. This means that for a moment he had caught that nymph in the same perspective and position in which Boucher fixed forever one of her sisters in his painting *Pan et Syrinx*.

This may well suggest that Mallarmé had indeed seen that painting, as maintained by Thibaudet—a circumstance that may help to explain the next section of the poem, where the poet mentions the name Syrinx, even though he employs it as a common rather than as a proper noun. The very fact that the poet does so may suggest that he was familiar not only with Boucher's painting but also with the fable it represents. These two hypotheses must be proved: hence the necessity of a brief digression from our running commentary of the poem. This digression will find a higher justification in our conviction that at a given stage of the poem's elaboration Mallarmé repatterned a significant detail after the fable of Pan and Syrinx.

This fable, as told by Ovid and retold numberless times after him, is a late myth, relating the simple story or legend of the god Pan, who loved a water nymph called Syrinx, and pursued her. When the god was about to overtake her, Syrinx cried for help from her sister nymphs, and was suddenly transformed into a tuft of reeds. Then, to make her his all the same, Pan turned into the first shepherd's pipe the plant she had become. According to tradition, the very meaning of the nymph's name was "pipe," and this explains Ovid's concluding statement (*Met.* i.711–712):

> Atque ita disparibus calamis conpagine cerae
> inter se iunctis nomen tenuisse puellae.

And so the pipes, made of unequal reeds fitted together by a joining of wax, took and kept the name of the maiden.[5]

If Thibaudet is right in claiming that Mallarmé saw the original of Boucher's painting (he could have done so during his single stay in London, which took place two or three years before he first conceived of this poem), then that fable must have haunted the poet's imagination since the composition of the earliest draft, even though it failed to affect, in any recognizable way, the *monologue*. It is only in the *églogue* that we find visible allusion to the fable, vague and dim as it is. It is only there that the word "syrinx" appears, to designate, however, not a person but an object. What we may guess is that during the ten years that divided the *églogue* from the *monologue,* probably just before rewriting the latter into the former, Mallarmé suddenly turned the passive reminiscence of the Ovidian fable into an active one. Perhaps it was by mere chance that the poet rethought creatively about that fable at the proper time; a clue to this chance may perhaps be found in *Les Dieux antiques.* Mallarmé published that translation or adaptation of an English handbook of mythology as late as 1880, but he had been working at it since the early seventies, and had announced its publication as imminent in 1877. Part of its manuscript must then have been ready at the time he wrote the final draft of the poem. It is quite possible that the word "syrinx" appeared on that draft only after appearing first in the manuscript of *Les Dieux antiques.* In the latter there is a section devoted to Pan, where we can still read this laconic summing up of the fable: "Syrinx, la nymphe aimée de Dieu, nom de flûte, est elle même le vent dans les roseaux."

The quote is significant precisely because Syrinx reappears in the poem only as "nom de flûte." Yet there is more than a verbal tie between the myth and the poem, as Laforgue seems to have guessed when he wrote his *Pan et Syrinx,* which is an intentional parody of Mallarmé's masterpiece. The connection, however, consists of a reversal of the legend itself. In the fable, Pan pursues the nymph he loves, and since the nymph escapes him by changing into a plant, the god turns the plant into the pipe that will take the name of the nymph. Marvell paradoxically telescoped the whole story in the famous lines of *The Garden:*

> And Pan did after Syrinx speed
> Not as a nymph, but for a reed.

The process is both inverted and cut short in Mallarmé's *églogue:* when the faun decides to lay his pipe aside, he states the wish, conveyed in command form, that his syrinx be changed back not into a nymph but merely into a reed. What the poet suggests then is an inverted metamorphosis, stopping short of its last phase, which would have restored the syrinx to its original, feminine essence.

What all this means is simply that the faun decides to reject for the time being, which may well be the rest of the day, the consolation or compensation of art. If he calls his pipe "maligne," it is because he considers it an "instrument des fuites", and now he does not care or, better, refuses to be seduced by the allurements of renunication and escape. Now he is not concerned with expression and creation but with self-expression and experience. If he now wants his pipe to remain mute, it is because he wants to give vent to the noisy tumult of his feelings ("moi, de ma rumeur fier"). It is in order to avoid any further temptation that he wants to see restored to its natural state the pipe he has just laid aside:

> Tâche donc, instrument des fuites, ô maligne
> Syrinx, de refleurir aux lacs où tu m'attends!

At this point, to use an antinomy which Mallarmé was to use in the prose poem *Bucolique,* the syrinx ceases being part of "la musique," to become again part of "La premiere en date, la nature."

VI

The rest of the poem, far less obscure in itself, is easier to understand now that we know that the poet will make no further confu-

sion between "la beauté d'alentour" and "notre chant crédule." Now
that he has cast aside his pipe and rejected the sublimation of art,
the faun can fully abandon himself to the self-indulgence of wishful
thought. In brief, he will transform the figures of recollection into
the fantasies of wish fulfillment. By a blasphemous imagination, says
the faun, I shall more and more denude the two feminine bodies still
reflected within my mind; and by doing so I shall act as when unable
to satisfy my craving for wine I must content myself with sucking
the juice of the grape, and with looking at the sky through the empty
skins of the despoiled cluster:

> Moi, de ma rumeur fier, je vais parler longtemps
> Des déesses; et par d'idolâtres peintures,
> A leur ombre enlever encore des ceintures:
> Ainsi, quand des raisins j'ai sucé la clarté,
> Pour bannir un regret par ma feinte écarté,
> Rieur, j'élève au ciel d'été la grappe vide
> Et, soufflant dans ses peaux lumineuses, avide
> D'ivresse, jusqu'au soir je regarde au travers.

That Mallarmé is dealing here with one of those operations of the
soul that only depth psychology has revealed to us in all their be-
wildering complexity is made evident by the line "Pour bannir un
regret de ma feinte écarté." By this line the poet seems to give us,
along with the motivation of the faun's daydreaming, a perfect definition of repression, or of the Freudian notion which the French language later rendered with the term *refoulement*. Such an awareness
of the inner workings of our psyche should not surprise us: Freud
himself stated more than once that he was but the theorist of the unconscious, since the poets had discovered it before him. The pastoral
is, of all the poetic forms or literary genres, the most obviously determined by the fears and desires of the heart, and, if this is true,
then it is neither far-fetched nor anachronistic to use the hindsight
of psychoanalysis to clarify the psychological insight that marks this
eclogue. It is such an insight that dictates not only the line just
quoted, or the particular situation conveyed therein, but the outlook
of the whole poem. We have already stated that the poem's incident

has an objective reality, and that the failure of the encounter is but a case of sexual initiation *manqué*. Yet most of the poem's first part seems to hinge on the question of whether the encounter had indeed occurred, nay whether the two nymphs had ever existed. If so, the doubt of the faun must be seen as produced by the unconscious will to disbelieve, out of a sense of sexual self-respect, the reality of that encounter; or, if we prefer, by an equally unconscious will to believe that the love which has seemingly escaped him was but a dream of love ("Aimai-je un rêve?").

At this point, however, according to that law of contradiction that rules the world of the psyche, the faun is doing just the reverse: instead of dreaming his failure away, he tries to redream and redeem that failure through the fantasy of success. While doing so he attempts to fill up the empty grapeskins of self-delusion with the real, although ghostly, figures of memory; and he even urges the two absent nymphs to do the same on their own account, as if it were possible to compare such recollections, and reconstruct the episode from a plural perspective: "O nymphes, regonflons des SOUVENIRS divers." The faun now remembers the incident in all its detail: and since from now on he will give utterance only to the remembrance of things past, his discourse loses all obscurity and ambiguity. The emotion attending to that remembrance is recollected in passion rather than in tranquillity, and it really seems that the light of the second part is but a product of its heat. Yet that light is so constant and clear that we need no other guide but a brief summary to explore the rest of the poem.

Most of what is left is simply a straightforward narrative of the incident. The faun retells how he had spied from afar the two nymphs bathing; how he had found them lying, embracing each other, in a shadowy grove; how he had taken them jointly ("sans les désenlacer") in his arms, to bring them to a rosebush exposed without cover to the glowing and burning rays of the vertical sun. It was in order to make the fulfillment of sexual desire coincide with the fullness of nature and the culmination of noonday that he had carried them to a place, as he says, "Où notre ébat au jour consumé soit pareil." While carrying his prey the faun had joyfully felt their maidenly wrath ("courroux des vierges"); had tasted the wild delight ("délice farouche") of approaching pleasure; had perceived the fear and trembling of the two bodies ("la frayeur secrète de la chair") seeking to avoid his lips. Then, having laid down the sacred burden of their nudity ("sacré fardeau nu") on the bare and sunny earth, he had separated the two nymphs, and hidden his face ("rire ardent") in what Diderot would have called "les bijoux indiscrets" of the dark maiden, while still holding by a single finger the fair one. By this fault ("crime") he had made it possible for his double prey to escape all too early from his weary and languished arms.

Here the narrative ends, and the faun yearns for a while after a sexual revanche, which he projects first in the vision of another bevy of nymphs, who will yield to him, or rather, to whom he will yield; and then in the sacrilegious fantasy of conquering Venus herself, not in the splendor of noon but in the evening dusk, which is the proper time for *l'heure du berger*. The faun, however, is well aware of the vanity of all such fictions or figments of his imagination; and he soon tires of them. He now realizes that his body is benumbed ("alourdi"); and that his soul is emptied of all articulate thought ("de paroles vacante"). Now, like Silenus, he is left with no other consolation or release than that provided by drink. He thus lies down with a sigh:

> Sans plus il faut dormir en l'oubli du blasphème,
> Sur le sable altéré gisant et comme j'aime
> Ouvrir ma bouche à l'astre efficace des vins!

At this point the faun does not need any more the active images of memory and desire, because the time has come for the oblivion of intoxication, for the passive or automatic images haunting a brain no longer lucid or awake. He thus says farewell to the nymphs, to dismiss their presence, still lingering in the perception of his senses, or in the reflection of that perception within his feelings and thoughts. All perceptions and reflections disappear, to be replaced by the shadowy imaginations of the psyche when our brain and senses are asleep. The daydream is over: what is now at hand is the real dream, the dream of sleep, which may be either a nightmare or the sweet fancy of a self-fulfilling wish. The faun knows all this, and this is all he means to say in the closing line of the poem: "Couple, adieu; je vais voir l'ombre que tu devins."

VII

It was toward no other reading than the one just given that, with a keen literary and artistic intuition, the author of the *Prélude à l'après-midi d'un faune* tended. In a brief "composer's note" Claude Debussy conveyed simply and concisely his own insight into the meaning of the text he had chosen to reinterpret in musical terms: "The music of this *Prélude* is a very free illustration of Mallarmé's lovely poem. It doesn't aim at being a synthesis. It rather deals with the successive backgrounds through which there shifts the wishes and dreams of the faun. Finally, wearied of pursuing the frightened nymphs, he yields to an intoxicating sleep, *rich with fulfilled dreams, and with the full possession of universal nature.*" As suggested by the italicized words in this note, the *Prélude* itself seems, however, more naively sensual and panic than Mallarmé's *églogue*, and this makes it paradoxically nearer to the *monologue*, which Debussy never read, than to the text he knew and rewrote. It is only by comparing the two drafts that we are now able to realize that the long elaboration of the poem consisted in a steady and gradual spiritualization of its essential erotic motive. If Debussy's faun seems far less psychologically complicated than his model, perhaps it is only because the musician had to simplify and clarify the complex and obscure structure of the literary text. Mallarmé seems to have foreseen this, if we must take for more than a vague compliment the charming quatrain he wrote for the exemplar of the poem inscribed to the composer:

> Silvain d'haleine première
> Si ta flûte a réussi
> Ouïs toute la lumière
> Qu'y sofflera Debussy.

Yet, even though the *Prélude* is more suggestive and less problematic than *L'Après-midi*, it is difficult to accept in full the interpretation of it that Thomas Mann gave in a brilliant page of his most famous novel. Sometime during his long stay on "the magic mountain" Hans

Castorp becomes the unofficial keeper of the sanitarium's collection of musical records: hence the long section of the novel giving a detailed account of the hero's impressions and emotions as a music lover. Castorp listens to Debussy's *Prélude* just after listening to Verdi's *Aida,* and particularly to the famous injunction, "O Radames, discòlpati," by which the Italian composer dramatized in that opera the eternal conflict between ethos and pathos, passion and will. This is how the protagonist and the author of *The Magic Mountain* feel and judge about Debussy's *Prélude:* "The youthful faun was very happy on his flowery meadow. Here there was no 'justify yourself!' [*discòlpati*], no responsibility . . . Here reigned oblivion itself, the blissful arrest of very motion, the innocence of timelessness. It was licentiousness in quiet conscience, the daydreamlike apotheosis of each and every denial of the Western imperative of action."

Such an interpretation, of dubious validity for Debussy's faun, becomes utterly false if extended to Mallarmé's. The latter is certainly an amoral, or unethical, figure, but he is also a far more self-conscious and self-critical creature than the passage just quoted suggests. Although a product of the poetic imagination, Mallarmé's poem is a portrayal of the psychological imagination, of its workings as well as of its works, and its very obscurity is due to the fact that it deals with two realities at once related and unrelated, sex and self. What is indeed faunesque in the poem is the junction, within a single representation, of the spiritual and the natural, of the human and the bestial, of the instinctive and the self-conscious. In mythological terms, one could say that Mallarmé's poem is a rehearsal of the musical contest between Marsyas and Apollo. Here the victor is again the god of music and art, or rather the poet working on his behalf—and what makes his triumph even more exciting is the wildness of the sounds he turned into melodious song.

Bibliographical Note

Notes

Index

Bibliographical Note

The revival of scholarly interest in the pastoral really began in the late 1950s. Before that, the interested reader had to depend on the much older, though still useful works by E. K. Chambers and W. W. Greg; two studies published just before the Second World War, William Empson's *Some Versions of Pastoral* (Chatto & Windus, 1935) and T. P. Harrison's anthology *The Pastoral Elegy* (University of Texas, 1939); and three studies published in 1952: a chapter in Hallett Smith's *Elizabethan Poetry* (Harvard University Press), J. C. Congleton's *Theories of Pastoral Poetry in England: 1684–1789* (Florida University Press), and Frank Kermode's fine introduction to and selection of *English Pastoral Poetry: From the Beginnings to Marvell* (Barnes & Noble). Save for specialized essays and occasional introductions, notable among them Kermode's to the Arden edition of *The Tempest* (Harvard University Press, 1954), these were the major sources in English for information about and criticism on the pastoral tradition.

In 1957 Northrop Frye published his *Anatomy of Criticism* (Princeton University Press). This provocative and wide-ranging book effectively rehabilitated the modes of pastoral and romance. Yet Frye's work was not alone responsible for the subsequent surge of writing on pastoral. Also in 1957, in the *Harvard Library Bulletin*, Renato Poggioli published "The Oaten Flute," and he followed this essay with four others: "The Pastoral of the Self," *Daedalus* (1959): "Dante 'Poco Tempo Silvano': A 'Pastoral

Oasis' in the Commedia," *Eightieth Annual Report of the Dante Society* (1962); "Naboth's Vineyard: The Pastoral View of the Social Order," *Journal of the History of Ideas* (1963); and "Gogol's *Old-fashioned Landowners:* An Inverted Eclogue," *Indiana Slavic Studies* (1963). These penetrating and original essays, included in this book, played a crucial role, here and abroad, in stimulating thinking and writing on the pastoral.

As for recent work on the pastoral, there is a useful collection of critical essays in *Pastoral and Romance: Modern Essays in Criticism,* edited by Eleanor Terry Lincoln (Prentice-Hall, 1969), and a very good overview of the pastoral and helpful bibliography in the volume in The Critical Idiom series by Peter Marinelli, *Pastoral* (Methuen, 1971). To Marinelli's bibliography one might add the following items: Richard Cody's *The Landscape of the Mind* (Clarendon Press, 1969), Harold Toliver's *Pastoral Forms and Attitudes* (University of California Press, 1971), David Young's *The Heart's Forest* (Yale University Press, 1972) and Michael J. K. O'Loughlin's "Woods Worthy of a Consul: Pastoral and the Sense of History," in *Literary Studies: Essays in Memory of Francis A. Drumm,* edited by John H. Dorenkamp (Holy Cross College Press, 1973).

A. B. G.

Notes

1   The Oaten Flute

1. E. R. Curtius, *European Literature and the Latin Middle Ages*, trans. Willard R. Trask (Princeton: Princeton University Press, 1953) chap. x.

2. George Santayana, *Three Philosophical Poets: Lucretius, Dante, and Goethe* (Cambridge: Harvard University Press, 1910; reprint ed., New York: Doubleday, Anchor Books, 1953).

3. Erwin Panofsky, *Meaning and the Visual Arts* (New York: Doubleday, 1955), chap. vii.

4. William Empson, *Some Versions of Pastoral* (London: Chatto & Windus, 1935; reprint ed., New York: New Directions, 1950).

5. Ibid.

2   Pastoral Love

1. For this chorus we prefer to quote from the most recent (and yet already old-fashioned) translation of Tasso's pastoral drama: *Amyntas: A Sylvan Fable by Torquato Tasso, Now first rendered into English by Frederic Whitmore* (Springfield, Mass., 1900). Besides being warned that the title-page claim is false (the piece was translated into English several times, from the seventeenth century on), the reader must also be warned that the translator chose to replace with the word and idea of *Shame* the *Onore* of the original.

2. *On Love* (New York: Boni & Liveright, 1927), fragment lxvii.

3. George Santayana, *Three Philosophical Poets: Lucretius, Dante, and Goethe* (Cambridge: Harvard University Press, 1910; reprint ed., New York: Doubleday, Anchor Books, 1953).

4. Maxim Gorki, *The Reminiscences of Leo Nikolaevich Tolstoy*, trans. S. S. Koteliansky and Leonard Woolf (New York: B. W. Huebsch, 1920), p. 17.

5. For a full discussion of the pastoral of solitude, see chapter 8, "The Pastoral of the Self."

3 The Funeral Elegy

1. "Discorso sopra Mosco" (1815–16), in *Tutte le opere di Giocomo Leopardi*, ed. Francesco Flora (Milan, 1945), I, 571.

2. That Moschus knew Theocritus' *Thyrsis* is shown by the fact that in the *Lament* the poet takes upon himself the task of delivering into the hands of Pan the pipe of his master and friend.

3. These two lines open a famous apostrophe in the eighteenth stanza of Paul Valéry's poem "Le Cimitière marin."

4. This is the standpoint which pastoral poetry normally takes toward the rewards that fame promises to the shepherd endowed with the gift of the poetic or musical song. Such a standpoint implies a high estimation of the poetic or artistic faculty, even though the pastoral chooses to view aesthetic creation as a fruit of leisure, or as a labor of love. In spite or rather because of this, the pastoral attitude toward art implies at the same time an utter indifference for the prize of glory as well as contempt and distrust for its price. The only important pastoral poem that deviates from this norm is *Lycidas*, the highest of all Christian funeral elegies. Milton brings in there the theme of the deliberate and meritorius pursuit of literary glory, which may vanquish death, even if only to be vanquished in its turn by heavenly glory. (See chapter 4, "Milton's *Lycidas*.")

5. This clarifies the meaning of the lovely lines in which, after promising to turn the pipe of his friend into Pan's hands, Moschus suggests (and this is the only compliment he pays to Bion's prestige as a poet) that not even the god will dare to touch that pipe with his lips.

6. The Greek bucolic tradition has preserved up to our times, besides Bion's *Lament for Adonis*, Theocritus' mime *The Women at the Adonis Festival* (*Id.* xv), which celebrates at once, with a wedding song and a dirge, Aphrodite's love and Adonis' death.

7. For the significance of this motif, see the analysis of Vergil's Fourth Eclogue in chapter 5, "The Christian Pastoral."

8. One of two panegyrics are to be found in Theocritus' canon, even though unrelated to death: see particularly *The Panegyric of Ptolemy* (*Id.* xvii).

9. Theocritus himself had cultivated this genre: *The Hymn to the Dioscuri* (*Id.* xxii) is certainly written in the key of the Homeric Hymns.

10. Gallus later rose very high under Augustus, but his character and destiny made him fall into disgrace. He ended his stormy life by his own hand, just twelve years after the probable composition date of the Tenth Eclogue.

11. What renders such a metamorphosis particularly fitting is that the most famous of Gallus' poems were love elegies, and they are Gallus' only works referred to in this eclogue.

12. Within the frame of reference of Gallus' biography the utterance of such regret appears to be an early manifestation of one of the most typical pastoral motifs: that of the highly placed friend or patron of a pastoral poet expressing through the poetry of the latter his own longing for a retreat from the world which his office and duty either hinder or prevent.

13. Perhaps more in Roman than in Greek terms.

14. There are two paintings by Poussin with the same title: one in the Devonshire Collection at Chatsworth, the other at the Louvre. The latter, which is the more famous, is the one we refer to.

15. Now in the Corsini Gallery in Rome.

16. Erwin Panofsky, *Meaning and the Visual Arts* (New York: Doubleday, 1955), chap. vii.

17. This prelate was Cardinal Giulio Rospigliosi, who later became Pope Clement IX.

18. Poussin's mourners might be simply passersby, paying their tribute not to a fellow shepherd but simply to a fellow man, of whose death they learn only by chance, by suddenly encountering his tomb on their path. This might be the case, but I doubt it.

19. For all we know, the unnamed dead of Poussin's *Et in Arcadia ego* might be imagined as a woman. Yet this is highly improbable: shepherdesses are almost as frequent as shepherds in the pastoral groves of Renaissance poetry, but hardly so in those of pastoral painting. Nor must we forget that in both versions of the picture there is a single female among the mourners, as if to suggest that their grief transcends the boundaries of sex and love.

4 Milton's *Lycidas*

1. This is the entire statement: "In this Monody the Author bewails a learned Friend, unfortunately drowned in his passage from Chester on the Irish Seas, 1637; and, by occasion, foretells the ruin of our corrupted Clergy, then in their height."

2. This impression of immediacy and wholeness fails to be dispelled by the closing strophe or, rather, stanza, since it is an ottava in the Italian style. The final stanza is as incongruous with the metrical pattern of the

song as its content is inconsistent with the stance of the poem. It is indeed only from this unexpected coda that we learn that what had sounded for so long like a direct song has been but a quoted one. See below in this chapter for a probable explanation of this coda, as well as for other comment upon the singleness of the poem.

3. They belong to his garden, and Corydon thinks of gathering them into a bouquet he wishes to offer the youth Alexis, whom he loves without hope of return. In brief, Vergil's line is to be read within the context of the pastoral of love or, rather, of its elegy, which deals only with love's disappointments or failures. In such a context it matters little that the passion which Corydon cannot satisfy is not for a woman but for a boy. For the role that homosexual eroticism plays in bucolic poetry, see chapter 2, "Pastoral Love."

4. None in fact did refuse. *Lycidas* appeared in *Obsequies to the Memory of Mr. Edward King*, a memorial volume published by his former Cambridge friends.

5. The repeated "once more" probably refers to the previous composition of *L'Allegro* and *Il Penseroso*.

6. Such a denial is not only theoretical, because it finds practical confirmation in the fact that most of the bucolic poems Milton wrote are pastorals either of solitude or of friendship. In Milton's canon the pastoral of love appears only once, in his earliest work, and even there only in passing, since *Comus* tends to reaffirm the platonic ideal as Spenser had interpreted it before him.

7. Hence the definition of Edward King as "a learned Friend" in the prose statement preceding the poem.

8. It is not unlikely that in this closing line Milton imitates in reverse the opening of Vergil's Fourth Eclogue: "Sicelides Musae, paulo maiora canamus" (Sicilian Muses, let us sing a somewhat loftier strain). If this is true, then the intention of Milton's apostrophe to the Muses of Mantua and Syracuse is to say the very opposite of Vergil's line: that is, "let us sing of lesser things."

9. This "sanguine flower" is the one that grew from the blood of Hyacinth, the youth Apollo had slain by mistake. Its presence here is due to a reminiscence from the Ovidian episode relating Hyacinth's transformation into the flower that was to bear his name, and to wear on its petals the letters of the Greek word for "alas." Or in Ovid's words: "AI AI flos habet inscriptum" (AI AI is inscribed in the flower; *Met.* x.215–216).

10. Milton's is but one of the longest and richest of all the similar catalogues in Renaissance and baroque pastoral poetry. Their most common use is in the funeral elegy: hence the prevalent choice of mournful flowers, as being more proper for a funeral tribute. One of the most immediate models for Milton's catalogue may indeed have been a similar floral list in

Clément Marot's *Complainte de Madame Loyse de Savage*. But the motif of nature's floral tribute, with a varying selection in order to befit different occasions or intents, appears, though less frequently, in the bucolic panegyric or in the courtly idyll; see for instance the April piece, or Fourth Eclogue, in Spenser's *Shepherd's Calendar*, which is a pastoral homage to Queen Elizabeth.

11. That this passage implies a parallel between the poet Arion and the poet Lycidas is made evident by the previous passage relating Lycidas to Orpheus.

12. See chapter 6, "Dante 'Poco Tempo Silvano.' "

13. The meter of Ergasto's song is that of the so-called canzone libera, which rejects all strophic pattern, being divided not into identical stanzas but into uneven verse series. Each one of such series mixes freely a varying number of eleven- and seven-syllable lines, many of which are left unrhymed. This is also the meter of *Lycidas*, and this is why in the text I have labeled each of its units, which are more syntactical than metrical phrases, with the term "section"—which may be vague, but not as misleading as the term "strophe." The main difference in the use of this meter by the Italian and by the English poet is that whereas in the far shorter units of Sannazaro's poem the frequency of the *endecasillabo* is far greater than that of the *settenario*, in Milton's the very opposite happens: there the iambic pentameter prevails overwhelmingly over the versicle. I do not claim that Sannazaro's Fifth Eclogue was the direct metrical model of *Lycidas*; Milton may have found that model in *Aminta*, where Tasso developed that meter in larger and less regular units, in keeping with the new function it was then made to serve, which was to act as a vehicle of dramatic dialogue. If the metrical identity of *Lycidas* and of Sannazaro's Fifth Eclogue cannot be left unnoticed, it is simply because of an even greater coincidence: the fact that both of them are funeral elegies. These two coincidences are made more meaningful by Milton's borrowing of the passage discussed in the text.

14. This is how St. Peter's speech should be defined in rhetorical terms.

15. See especially the famous lines (*L'Art poétique*, iii): "De la foi d'un chrétien les mystères terribles/D'ornemens égayés ne sont point susceptibles."

16. That there is some imbalance in the poem may be proved by a count of the variations in line number between the verse units of the poem, which are ten, since we must exclude from their list the coda, which has a strophic structure. The four units forming the first part are the shortest, varying in length from ten to fifteen lines. The four units of the central part go from a minimum of fourteen to a maximum of twenty-nine, the last being the unit that contains St. Peter's speech. Of the two units of the last part, the first, which begins with the apostrophe to Alpheus, unfolds with the flower

catalogue, and ends with the appeal to St. Michael, is thirty-three lines, while the last, which coincides with the apotheosis, is only twenty-one.

17. The ambiguity of this passage makes meaningful the fact that, unlike Sannazaro, Marot, and many other of his predecessors, Milton never wrote a funeral elegy about a person of the fairer sex, nor could he have ever done otherwise. The poet who writes a complaint over the death of a lovely woman, even if she could never have been a love object (as when the pastoral mask disguises a lady of high degree), tends to yield to the temptation of transforming the funeral elegy into an elegy of love, since the lament over the beauty of her dead body may hardly be turned into the apotheosis of her eternal soul.

18. The Greek bucolic tradition always calls its own song "Doric"; yet there is no funeral elegy in which the term is so frequently repeated as in Moschus' *Lament for Bion*, as part of its very refrain. Milton's use of the formula "Doric lay" may well prove his familiarity with Moschus' poem.

5   The Christian Pastoral

1. *Beyond Good and Evil*, trans. Helen Zimmern (London: T. N. Foulis, 1907; reprint ed., New York: Modern Library, n.d.).

2. This and the following quotations are from Virgil, *The Pastoral Poems*, trans. E. V. Rieu (Baltimore: Penguin Books, 1949).

6   Dante "Poco Tempo Silvano"

1. For the notion of pastoral oasis, by which I mean a bucolic episode or idyllic interlude within a fictional narrative in verse or prose, such as the epic, the chivalric poem, the romance, and, as *Don Quixote* shows, even the novel, see chapter 1, "The Oaten Flute."

2. A pastoral oasis is indeed almost always introduced by a *locus amoenus*, or by the exalted description of a lovely landscape. For the topos itself, see R. Curtius, *European Literature and the Latin Middle Ages*, trans. Willard R. Trask (Princeton: Princeton University Press, 1953), chap. x.

3. This, and the quotes that follow, are given as rendered by John D. Sinclair in his translation of *The Divine Comedy* (London: Oxford University Press, 1948).

4. This critic is the outstanding American Dante scholar, Charles S. Singleton. See his *Dante Studies 2: Journey to Beatrice* (Cambridge: Harvard University Press, 1958), pp. 212–213. All of part 2 of that volume, "Return to Eden," is necessary reading for students of this section of the *Purgatorio*.

5. *Pastorela* is the Provençal as well as the Spanish term. The Italian is *pastorella*; the French, *pastourelle*.

6. She is for instance a guardian of cows ("vaquera") in a late Spanish *pastorela* by the Marquis de Santillana, one of his most charming poems.

7. Dante knows that the Golden Age represents also the simple bounty

of Mother Nature, satisfying the hunger of its children, including primitive man, with her humblest gifts, such as the fruit of the oak. See the
words uttered by the mysterious voice teaching the lesson of frugality to
the souls expiating the sin of gluttony (*Purg.* xxii): "Lo secol primo, quant'
oro fu bello,/fé savorose con fame le ghiande,/e nettare con sete ogne ru-
scello" (The first age was beautiful as gold; it made acorns savoury with
hunger and with thirst made nectar of every brook).

8. Matelda and Dante seem to recommend here to man the same contemplative task which, in a different and very modern vein, Goethe and
Eleonora d'Este recommend in a famous passage of *Tasso* (II.i). The heroine denies any validity to the vision of the Golden Age as dreamed by the
Italian poet in his *Aminta*; yet, she says, kindred spirits may still meet
and share together "the joy of the lovely universe."

9. This interpreter is Edward Williamson; see "Beatitudo hujus vitae,"
Seventy-sixth Annual Report of the Dante Society, 1958, pp. 15–16.

10. The founders of the American commonwealth based man's right to
the "pursuit of happiness" more on Rousseau's pastoral dream than on any
Christian utopia, yet it is indeed symbolic that the United States Depart-
ment of the Treasury chose to rephrase the most famous hemistich of
Vergil's Fourth Eclogue ("saeclorum nascitur ordo") as a motto ("novus
ordo seclorum") engraved beneath the emblem on the back of the one-dol-
lar bill.

11. The pastoral oasis of the *Gerusalemme liberata* (Erminia's stay
among the shepherds; vii) is on the contrary a pastoral of innocence.

12. Singleton, *Dante Studies 2*, pp. 190–201.

13. This and the quotations that follow are given as translated by Frank
Justus Miller, *Metamorphoses*, Loeb Classical Library (Cambridge: Harvard
University Press, 1960).

14. Thélème obviously means "of the will."

15. If Cato "censors" Casella for indulging in song (*Purg.* ii), it is only
because what Casella does is improper in the Ante-Purgatory, as it would
be in any purging place of the sacred mountain. Yet the same musical performance would have been fitting and seemly in the Earthly Paradise.

16. The formula is that of the late G. A. Borgese, as part of his conversation if not of his writings.

17. While admitting the pastoral of simplicity, Dante never admits the
pastoral of the natural or of the primitive, as shown by his positive reply
to the question from Charles Martel (*Par.* viii): "Sarebbe il peggio/per
l'omo in terra, se non fosse cive?" (Would it be worse for man on earth
if he were not a citizen?).

18. Such a pastoral oasis is to be seen in Book Eight, particularly in
Aeneas' visit to Evander, king of the shepherds, living in the place in which
Rome will be built.

19. Given as rendered by E. V. Rieu in Virgil, *The Pastoral Poems* (Baltimore: Penguin Books, 1949).

20. The original meaning of the word "paradise" is "enclosed garden."

7 The Poetics of the Pastoral

1. The translation used in this chapter is by Soame, as given in Albert S. Cook, ed., *The Art of Poetry: The Poetical Treatises of Horace, Vida, and Boileau* (New York: G. E. Stechert, 1926).

2. To understand this point better we must remember that Boileau's, like all classical ages, knew what "realism" is, although it failed to appreciate it as much as we do. After all, the literary ideals conveyed by that term are taken into account in every epoch, even if they are given different labels, being suggested preferably by such epithets as sincere, popular, natural, and the like. That the norms and values designated by those adjectives were not ignored in Boileau's time may be shown by the famous episode in Molière's *Misanthrope* (I.ii), when Alceste compares unfavorably the artificial sonnet of Oronte (so similar to the sonnets written by the *précieux*, unless it was one of them), with an old song where, the protagonist says, "passion speaks in all its purity." While probably sharing Molière's distaste for Oronte's sonnet, Boileau would perhaps not have partaken of Molière's enthusiasm for such a quaint piece of folklore as the *chanson du roi Henri*. Yet we must not forget that even Molière states his preference for a more popular and natural type of poetry only indirectly and ambiguously, attributing it to the character playing the eccentric and asocial role of the misanthrope, and who by doing so deviates from the canons of the behavior that characterizes the type of the *honnête homme*. This means in brief that "realism" is good for Alceste but not, at least in the same measure, for Molière, and we know that it is even less good for Boileau. This is particularly true of Boileau as a critic of the pastoral, although Molière's position toward this genre does not greatly differ. It is in one of his most famous plays, *Le Bourgeois Gentilhomme*, that he gives in the words of the dancing master a classical justification of the pastoral, paradoxically defined as a form, so to speak, naturally artificial. The validity of the statement is not decreased by its being made by a minor character (Monsieur Jourdain's dancing master); nor by its being limited to the pastoral in music: "Lorsqu'on a des personnes à faire parler en musique, il faut bien que, pour la vraisemblance, on donne dans la bergerie. Le chant a été de tout temps affecté aux bergers; et il n'est guère naturel en dialogue que des princes ou des bourgeois chantent leur passions." (When characters must speak in music, they are required by verisimilitude to fall into the pastoral. Singing has been from all time the shepherd's prerogative; and in dialogue it would hardly be natural for princes or burghers to sing their passions.) This digression about realism in the age of both

Molière and Boileau is meant as a reminder that classical or neoclassical art also claims to mirror reality.

3. Molière himself sometimes does precisely this. See, for instance, the peasant episode in *Dom Juan*. We must however not overrate the importance of this example; that play, which looks very much like a Spanish *comedia*, is exceptional, nay unique, in Molière's canon. Moreover, even here, the dialect spoken by the peasant characters is highly stylized and is used mainly to produce a comic effect.

4. The *Coloquio de los perros* is introduced in the *Novelas ejemplares* as a supplement to *El Casamiento engañoso*. It is the protagonist of the latter who reports, in the *Coloquio*, a conversation between two dogs, which he claims to have overheard while he was staying in a hospital.

5. This and the following quotations are from "The Dogs' Colloquy," in *The Deceitful Marriage and Other Exemplary Novels*, trans. Walter Starkie (New York: New American Library, Signet Classic, 1963).

6. For the terms *locus amoenus* and "pastoral oasis," see chapter 1, "The Oaten Flute."

7. This quotation is from J. M. Cohen's translation of *Don Quixote* (Baltimore, Penguin Books, 1950).

8   The Pastoral of the Self

1. This and the following quotations are from J. M. Cohen's translation of *Don Quixote* (Baltimore: Penguin Books, 1950).

9   Pastoral and *Soledad*

1. Karl Vossler, *La Soledad en la poesía española* (Madrid, 1941), p. 94.

2. A form that Fray Luis's predecessor Garcilaso had taken from an obscure Italian model and turned into one of the classical meters of Spanish lyrical verse.

3. This title, *Vida retirada*, which is missing from the earliest editions, is based on the authority of a few manuscripts and must be considered as more genuine and suitable than *Canción de la vida solitaria* and all the other titles preferred by many modern editors.

4. Fray Luis's emphatic repetition of the detail in question is the more significant since in his youthful translation of Vergil's First Eclogue he had twice avoided reproducing Tityrus in his characteristic indolent pose. In his all too free and redundant version Tityrus is described, in Meliboeus' words, as "a la sombra descansando—desta tendida haza" (resting in the shade of this stretched hedge), where the participle *tendida*, which corresponds to Vergil's *recubans*, and means "lying down" or "stretched," is transferred from a living being to an inanimate object that does not even exist in the original text. Further down the translation fails completely to give an equivalent to *lentus in umbra*, even though he expands consider-

ably the sentence of which that phrase is a part: "Tu, sin pena,/Cantas de tu pastora, alegre, ocioso,/y tu pastora el valle y monte suena (You sing of your shepherdess without worry, idle and mirthful, and hill and dale resound with her name). Except for the omission of this amorous note, one may certainly claim that Fray Luis is a far better translator of this passage in *Vida retirada* than in his avowed version of Vergil's poem.

5. The one entitled *A Francisco Salinas*, addressed, as well as dedicated, to the great composer, who was a friend of the author.

6. See *La Soledad*, the section "El Quietismo," pp. 145–147.

7. Which, in one of his many translations of Horace, Fray Luis quite faithfully rendered as: "Dichoso el que de pleitos alejado."

8. Strangely enough, in such Italian meters as the ottava and the terza rima.

9. Nobody doubts that Fray Luis composed the translation in ottava rima which follows his *Exposición al Cantar de los Cantares*, and there is good reason to believe that he composed also the version in liras reported in a manuscript recently discovered. Fray Luis's pastoral obsession is evident also in his translations of the Psalms, as well as in that famous chapter of *Los Nombres de Dios* dealing with the bucolic symbolism of Jesus and his mission.

10. For this aspect of Vergil's First Eclogue, as well as for a full analysis of the poem, see chapter 10, "Naboth's Vineyard: The Pastoral View of the Social Order."

10 Naboth's Vineyard

1. For an explanation of the term "pastoral oasis," as well as of the antithetical notions of the pastoral of innocence and the pastoral of happiness, see chapter 1, "The Oaten Flute."

2. This and the quotations that follow are from Virgil, *The Pastoral Poems*, trans. E. V. Rieu (Baltimore: Penguin Books, 1949).

3. At least through the words of his hero, who is his mouthpiece. See *Don Quixote* (I.xxxviii), "que trata del curioso discurso que hizo Don Quijote de las armas y las letras" (dealing with the strange speech that Don Quixote made about the arms and the letters).

4. This and the quotations that follow are from J. M. Cohen's translation of *Don Quixote* (Baltimore: Penguin Books, 1950).

5. For *Aminta's* first chorus, see chapter 2, "Pastoral Love."

6. That chivalry, if it ever existed, was finally destroyed by the invention of firearms, is Ariosto's view. See the episode about Cimosco's harquebus, which Orlando throws into the sea in order to prevent that engine from weakening the brave and emboldening the cowardly (*Orlando furioso*, ix. 88–91).

7. This is why *Don Quixote* is full of pastoral oases. For the treatment

of one of them, the Marcela and Grisóstomo episode, see chapter 8, "The Pastoral of the Self." The reader will also remember that the library of the knight included many pastoral romances, which his niece wanted to see burned along with the books of chivalry, fearing that her uncle might sometime be affected by the pastoral craze as he had been affected by the chivalric one. That her fears were founded is proved at the end of the novel, when Don Quixote is forced to lay down his arms and thinks of enacting the pastoral dream since he is no longer allowed to enact the chivalric one.

8. This and the quotations that follow are from the old translation of *Faust* by Bayard Taylor, reprinted by the Modern Library (New York, 1950).

9. To be more exact, the guest had lost his life not by fire but by the sword. Whereas Philemon and Baucis had withstood only passively the violence done to them, their visitor had chosen to resist weapon in hand and had been killed in the attempt.

10. For an analysis of the original, Ovidian version of the fable, see chapter 2, "Pastoral Love."

11. For more on the Arcadian episode, see chapter 11, " 'Arkadisch Frei Sei Unser Glück!': Goethe and the Pastoral."

12. As I have tried to prove in all my writings on bucolic poetry and the idyllic ideal, most of these pastoral interludes, which I call pastoral oases and which appear in many epic and fictional narratives, especially those of the Renaissance, tend to begin with the neoclassical topos of the *locus amoenus*, or the exalted description of a beautiful natural landscape. The absence of such a "commonplace" from Goethe's version of the tale of Philemon and Baucis (as well as from the oldest version, Ovid's) is indicative of the poet's realization that the commonness of their habitat would further emphasize the exemplary humility and the ideal simplicity of their way of life. A pastoral oasis may more easily do without a *locus amoenus* if it is a pastoral of innocence rather than of happiness. The *Faust* Arcadia episode is a pastoral of happiness par excellence; hence Goethe's decision to introduce it with the most luscious *locus amoenus* that the pastoral imagination ever envisaged.

13. It was perhaps this Goethean remaking that suggested to Gogol that he write a modern and realistic version of the same tale. But whereas Goethe accepted as a point of departure the bucolic idealization of the Ovidian couple and had them destroyed along with the pastoral ideal for which they stand by an external agency, Gogol deliberately deprived his modern, Russian equivalents of that ancient pair of any inner life and made their Arcadia crumble into the dust of its own nothingness. Thus, instead of producing a modern version of the pastoral of innocence, the Russian writer gave us a pseudopastoral or, rather, an anti-idyll, mirroring

not innocence and simplicity but triviality and commonness. See chapter 12, "Gogol's *Old-fashioned Landowners:* An Inverted Eclogue."

14. This immortal quip is from the pen of George Orwell, from his celebrated political satire in the form of a fable, *Animal Farm.*

15. Dostoevski used this vision, sometimes almost with the same words, in the "Confession of Stavrogin," a chapter that his publisher forced him to omit from *The Possessed;* in one of Versilov's conversations in *A Raw Youth;* and in a late tale, *The Dream of a Ridiculous Man.*

16. The story of Naboth has been interpreted in many ways—in one case as suggesting the "unnatural" foundation of private property. See the discussion of St. Ambrose's commentary *De Nabuthe* (M.P.L., xiv, 778) in Arthur O. Lovejoy, "The Communism of St. Ambrose," *Journal of the History of Ideas,* III (1942), 458–468.

11 "Arkadisch Frei Sei Unser Glück!"

1. As any reader of *La Nouvelle Héloïse* and *Les Confessions* well knows, three Italian poets strongly affected Rousseau's imagination, and especially his views about love. They are, in this order, Tasso, Metastasio, and Petrarch.

2. For an analysis of this chorus see chapter 2, "Pastoral Love."

3. "The fierce youth" may be Hercules, and the faun's chastisement one of that hero's early deeds.

4. For an explanation of the term *locus amoenus,* and the related term "pastoral oasis," see chapter 1, "The Oaten Flute."

5. An analysis of this episode, which forms the pastoral oasis of Tasso's epic, may be found in chapter 1, "The Oaten Flute."

6. In one of the *Gespräche* (May 6, 1827), Goethe confirmed Eckermann's guess that Faust's monologue in "Anmutige Gegend," written at a much earlier date than the rest of the scene, had been inspired by the impressions of his own youthful visit to Switzerland.

7. The terms "great" and "little world" belong to Goethe. The last critic to use them in the sense in which they are reused here was Stuart Atkins, in his excellent book, *Goethe's Faust: A Literary Analysis* (Cambridge: Harvard University Press, 1958), p. 105.

8. As to what kind of experience, it may perhaps by explained by a fuller and closer reading of the scene, by a clarification of the symbolic meaning of the apparition of the sun (from which Faust turns away) and the rainbow, and, finally, by a reinterpretation of the closing line of the scene, when Faust concludes (4727): "Am farbigen Ablanz haben wir das Leben" (Let's now have life in its colored reflection).

9. For a fuller treatment of the Philemon and Baucis episode, see chapter 10, "Naboth's Vineyard."

10. See chapter 2, "Pastoral Love."

11. Or, in the author's full phrase: "A nymphet, by Pan!"

12. It is obvious that by this Goethe wishes to suggest a reconciliation of the Germanic and the Hellenic spirit—or, as others (but not he) would say, of the "romantic" and the "classical" mind.

13. This and the quotations that follow are from the old translation of *Faust* by Bayard Taylor (New York: Modern Library, 1950). Taylor's renderings are very often quite successful. Unfortunately that is not the case with this passage. "Who shares the joy" would be a far better equivalent of *"war mitgeniesst"* than "who shares the glow," a poor solution forced on the translator by the tyranny of the rhyme scheme.

14. Needless to say, the terms *amour-passion* and *amour-vanité* come from Stendhal's *De l'amour*.

15. The phrase appears in the second of his *Two Songs from a Play*.

16. This is why Homunculus breaks his glass bottle and destroys himself against Galathea's chariot, to merge with the sea's "life moisture," and to start his existence at the lowest stage of the biological process.

17. These words ("Die and become") are part of the closing verse of *Selige Sehnsucht*.

18. Atkins, *Goethe's Faust*, p. 105.

19. This aphorism is one of the "fragments" that Novalis collected and published in his lifetime under the title of *Blütenstaub* (Pollen).

20. The meaning of this colorful expression is obvious; yet the comments that Stendhal made on this clever Italian idiom may still be read with profit in *La Chartreuse de Parme*.

21. The formula belongs to W. B. Yeats.

22. It is in order to deny the pastoral spirit that Giordano Bruno introduces in the third dialogue of *Lo Spraccio della bestia trionfante* a contest between Ocio and Sollesitudino. (This passage has been brought to our attention by Lienhard Bergel.) It may be worth remembering that Care is the last of the apparitions to haunt Faust before his death.

23. The subtitle is *Eine Tragödie*.

24. This critic is Erich Heller. See his essay, "Goethe and the Avoidance of Tragedy," in *The Disinherited Mind* (Cambridge: Bowes & Bowes, 1952).

12 Gogol's *Old-fashioned Landowners*

1. This is the translation of Herbert E. Bowman, *Vissarion Belinski, 1811–1848: A Study in the Origins of Social Criticism in Russia* (Cambridge: Harvard University Press, 1954), p. 75. The other quotations of Belinski's relatively early essay (written in 1835), *O russkoj povesti i o povestjax g. Gogolja* [On Russian storytelling and on Mr. Gogol's tales], are my translations, based on the text of a Soviet edition of Belinski's complete works, *Sobranie Sochinenij* (Moscow, 1946), vol. I.

2. D. S. Mirsky, *A History of Russian Literature* (New York: Knopf, 1946), p. 152.

13 Tolstoy's *Domestic Happiness*

1. For the diaries and letters dealing with this episode see the Jubilee Edition of Tolstoy's complete works, *Polnoe sobranie sochinenii* (Moscow and Leningrad, 1928), vols. XLVII, LX. A full account of the episode may be read in the authoritative English biography of the Russian master, Ernest J. Simmons, *Leo Tolstoy* (Boston: Little, Brown, 1946), pp. 139–146.

2. The Russian title is *Semeynoe schastie*. The tale appeared in two installments, in the first and second April issues of the journal *Russki vestnik* [Russian Messenger]. I have followed the text of the Jubilee Edition, vol. VII. For my quotations I have used the translation of Aylmer Maude, *Family Happiness*, in *The Short Novels of Tolstoy*, ed. Philip Rahv (New York: Dial Press, 1949).

3. The Franco-Swiss writer stated this opinion in his *Vie de Tolstoï* (Paris, 1911). One could say that in Tolstoy's canon *Domestic Happiness* plays the same role that *Bérénice* plays in Racine's and that the relation between *Domestic Happiness* and *Anna Karenina* is not too different from that between *Bérénice* and *Phèdre*.

4. In the essay "Tolstoy as Man and Artist," *Oxford Slavonic Papers*, X (1962), 25–37, reprinted in *The Spirit of the Letter* (Cambridge: Harvard University Press, 1965), we have already stated that many of Tolstoy's works, including *War and Peace*, are diptychs at least in a figurative sense. *Domestic Happiness*, however, is also literally so. This is made evident by its division into two antithetical and yet symmetrical parts. In a real diptych, neither of the two panels can stand alone, and it was perhaps to emphasize the fundamental singleness of his dual creation that Tolstoy numbered the subdivisions in a single series. The first part is made of five sections, and the second of four, but the latter are numbered from six to nine, as if to indicate that the two parts are linked together and that there is no dissolution of continuity between them.

5. All of George Sand's "rustic idylls" had been published toward the end of the preceding decade: *La Mare au diable* in 1846, *François le Champi* in 1848, *La Petite Fadette* in 1869.

6. In a talk with Gorki, reported by the latter in his *Reminiscences of Leo Nikolaevich Tolstoy*, trans. S. S. Koteliansky and Leonard Woolf (New York: B. W. Huebsch, 1920), p. 17.

7. These two prototypes might be viewed also as archetypes in the Jungian sense of the term; if so, Masha would stand for the *anima*, and Sergey Mikhaylych for its opposite, the *animus*.

8. Kitty loved Vronsky before marrying Levin. As for Natasha, she was the fiancée of Prince Andrey before marrying Pierre Bezukhov, and during

her betrothal to the former she almost eloped with the rake Anatole Kuragin.

9. The splendid isolation of Masha would suffice to prove how wrong Romain Rolland was in surmising that he saw a portrait of Tolstoy's future wife, Sonia Bers. Sonia Bers was one of many sisters, and Tolstoy avowed that at first he had fallen in love with all of them. The writer attributed the same attitude to Konstantin Levin, who, as Tolstoy says, "was in love with the Shcherbatsky household," especially "with its feminine half," at least as much as with Kitty herself (*Anna Karenina*, I.vii).

10. The validity of this parallel may be qualified, but not denied, by the consideration that Nikolay Rostov is more of a portrait than of a self-portrait: his real or main model is Tolstoy's father.

11. Masha is a familiar and intimate form of Mariya. Only once in the story are we told that her full name is Mariya Aleksandrovna.

12. For this code, see chapter 2, "Pastoral Love."

13. The return to the innocent nudity of the Golden Age is one of the most extreme demands of the pastoral code of free love.

14. For the connections between the pastorals of love and solitude, see chapter 7, "The Pastoral of the Self."

15. Masha is a gentlewoman, yet in the episode she finds herself in the stock situation, and plays the stock role, of the rural lassie about to be seduced by a city slicker. Such a situation is one of the standard episodes in the legend of Don Juan. See the scenes dealing with the peasant Charlotte in Molière's version of the legend, *Dom Juan ou le festin de Pierre*.

16. This critic is D. S. Mirsky. The pertinent passage is worth quoting in full: "The general tone [of *War and Peace*] may be properly described as idyllic. The inclination toward the idyllic was from first to last an ever present possibility in Tolstoy. It is the opposite pole to his increasing uneasiness. Before the time of *War and Peace* it pervades *Childhood*. Its roots are in a sense of unity with his class, with the happy and prosperous *byt* of the Russian nobility. And it is, after all, no exaggeration to say that, all said and done, *War and Peace* is a tremendous 'heroic idyll' of the Russian nobility" (*A History of Russian Literature* [New York: Knopf, 1946], p. 268).

14   "L'Heure du Berger"

1. "Notes et variantes," in *Oeuvres complètes*, ed. Henri Mondor and G. Jean-Aubry (Paris, 1945).

2. *Correspondance, 1862–1871*, ed. Henri Mondor (Paris, 1959), p. 166.

3. Ibid., p. 174.

4. This phrase is used by George Orwell in his essay *Inside the Whale* to describe Housman's poetry.

5. *Metamorphoses*, trans. Frank Justus Miller, Loeb Classical Library (Cambridge: Harvard University Press, 1960).

Index